# Workbook to Accompany

Mike Holt's Illustrated Guide to

# Understanding the NATIONAL ELECTRICAL CODE®

**Volume 1** • Articles 90 - 480

Based on the 2014 NEC®

**Mike Holt Enterprises, Inc.**
888.NEC.CODE (632.2633) • www.MikeHolt.com

## NOTICE TO THE READER

The publisher does not warrant or guarantee any of the products described herein or perform any independent analysis in connection with any of the product information contained herein. The publisher does not assume, and expressly disclaims, any obligation to obtain and include information other than that provided to it by the manufacturer.

The reader is expressly warned to consider and adopt all safety precautions that might be indicated by the activities herein and to avoid all potential hazards. By following the instructions contained herein, the reader willingly assumes all risks in connection with such instructions.

The publisher makes no representation or warranties of any kind, including but not limited to, the warranties of fitness for particular purpose or merchantability, nor are any such representations implied with respect to the material set forth herein, and the publisher takes no responsibility with respect to such material. The publisher shall not be liable for any special, consequential, or exemplary damages resulting, in whole or part, from the reader's use of, or reliance upon, this material.

*Workbook to Accompany Mike Holt's Illustrated Guide to Understanding the National Electrical Code®, Volume 1
Based on the 2014 NEC®*

*First Printing: March 2014*

Author: Mike Holt
Technical Illustrator: Mike Culbreath
Cover Design: Madalina Iordache-Levay
Layout Design and Typesetting: Cathleen Kwas

COPYRIGHT © 2014 Charles Michael Holt
ISBN 978-1-932685-75-6

Produced and Printed in the USA

For more information, call 888.NEC.CODE (632.2633), or e-mail Info@MikeHolt.com.

All rights reserved. No part of this work covered by the copyright hereon may be reproduced or used in any form or by any means graphic, electronic, or mechanical, including photocopying, recording, taping, or information storage and retrieval systems without the written permission of the publisher. You can request permission to use material from this text by either calling 888.632.2633, e-mailing Info@MikeHolt.com, or visiting www.MikeHolt.com.

*NEC®*, NFPA 70®, NFPA 70E® and *National Electrical Code®* are registered trademarks of the National Fire Protection Association.

 This logo is a registered trademark of Mike Holt Enterprises, Inc.

---

**If you are an instructor and would like to request an examination copy of this or other Mike Holt Publications:**

Call: 888.NEC.CODE (632.2633) • Fax: 352.360.0983
E-mail: Info@MikeHolt.com • Visit: www.MikeHolt.com

You can download a sample PDF of all our publications by visiting www.MikeHolt.com

*I dedicate this book to the
Lord Jesus Christ, my mentor and teacher*

# Our Commitment

We are committed to serving the electrical industry with integrity and respect by always searching for the most accurate interpretation of the *NEC*® and creating the highest quality instructional material that makes learning easy.

We are invested in the idea of changing lives, and build our products with the goal of not only helping you meet your licensing requirements, but also with the goal that this knowledge will improve your expertise in the field and help you throughout your career.

We are committed to building a life-long relationship with you, and to helping you in each stage of your electrical career. Whether you are an apprentice just getting started in the industry, or an electrician preparing to take an exam, we are here to help you. When you need Continuing Education credits to renew your license, we will do everything we can to get our online courses and seminars approved in your state. Or if you are a contractor looking to train your team, we have a solution for you. And if you have advanced to the point where you are now teaching others, we are here to help you build your program and provide tools to make that task easier.

We genuinely care about providing quality electrical training that will help you take your skills to the next level.

Thanks for choosing Mike Holt Enterprises for your electrical training needs. We are here to help you every step of the way and encourage you to contact us so we can be a part of your success.

God bless,

# TABLE OF CONTENTS

About This Workbook .................................................. vii

About the *National Electrical Code* ........................... ix

About the Author .......................................................... xiii

About the Illustrator .................................................... xiv

Article 90—Introduction to the *National Electrical Code* ............................................................................. 1

## CHAPTER 1—GENERAL ........................................ 5

Article 100—Definitions ............................................... 7

Article 110—Requirements for Electrical Installations ............................................................... 19

## CHAPTER 2—WIRING AND PROTECTION ........ 25

Article 200—Use and Identification of Grounded [Neutral] Conductors .................................................. 27

Article 210—Branch Circuits ..................................... 31

Article 215—Feeders .................................................. 41

Article 220—Branch-Circuit, Feeder, and Service Calculations ................................................................ 43

Article 225—Outside Branch Circuits and Feeders ......................................................................... 47

Article 230—Services ................................................. 51

Article 240—Overcurrent Protection ........................ 59

Article 250—Grounding and Bonding ...................... 65

Article 285—Surge Protective Devices (SPDs) ...... 83

## CHAPTER 3—WIRING METHODS AND MATERIALS ................................................................ 85

Article 300—General Requirements for Wiring Methods and Materials ............................................... 89

Article 310—Conductors for General Wiring .......... 97

Article 312—Cabinet and Cutout Boxes ................ 101

Article 314—Outlet, Device, Pull, and Junction Boxes; Conduit Bodies; and Handhole Enclosures ............................................... 103

Article 320—Armored Cable (Type AC) ................ 109

Article 330—Metal-Clad Cable (Type MC) ........... 111

Article 334—Nonmetallic-Sheathed Cable (Types NM and NMC) ............................................... 113

Article 338—Service-Entrance Cable (Types SE and USE) ................................................. 115

Article 340—Underground Feeder and Branch-Circuit Cable (Type UF) ............................................ 117

Article 342—Intermediate Metal Conduit (Type IMC) ................................................................. 119

Article 344—Rigid Metal Conduit (Type RMC) ...... 121

Article 348—Flexible Metal Conduit (Type FMC) ................................................................ 123

Mike Holt Enterprises, Inc. • www.MikeHolt.com • 888.NEC.CODE (632.2633)

## Table of Contents

Article 350—Liquidtight Flexible Metal Conduit (Type LFMC) .................................................. 125

Article 352—Rigid Polyvinyl Chloride Conduit (Type PVC) .................................................... 127

Article 356—Liquidtight Flexible Nonmetallic Conduit (Type LFNC) ..................................... 129

Article 358—Electrical Metallic Tubing (Type EMT) .............................................................. 131

Article 362—Electrical Nonmetallic Tubing (Type ENT) ....................................................... 133

Article 376—Metal Wireways ..................................... 135

Article 380—Multioutlet Assemblies .......................... 137

Article 386—Surface Metal Raceways ....................... 139

Article 392—Cable Trays ............................................ 141

### CHAPTER 4—EQUIPMENT FOR GENERAL USE .................................................. 145

Article 400—Flexible Cords and Flexible Cables ..... 147

Article 402—Fixture Wires ......................................... 149

Article 404—Switches ................................................ 151

Article 406—Receptacles, Cord Connectors, and Attachment Plugs (Caps) ........................................ 155

Article 408—Switchboards, Switchgear, and Panelboards .............................................................. 159

Article 410—Luminaires, Lampholders, and Lamps ........................................................................ 161

Article 411—Lighting Systems Operating at 30V or Less and Lighting Equipment Connected to Class 2 Power Sources ......................................... 169

Article 422—Appliances ............................................. 171

Article 424—Fixed Electric Space-Heating Equipment ................................................................. 175

Article 430—Motors, Motor Circuits, and Controllers ................................................................. 177

Article 440—Air-Conditioning and Refrigeration Equipment ................................................................. 181

Article 445—Generators ............................................. 183

Article 450—Transformers ......................................... 185

Article 480—Storage Batteries .................................. 187

### FINAL EXAM A—FINAL EXAM QUESTIONS FOR CHAPTER 1–4 ..................................................... 189

### FINAL EXAM B—FINAL EXAM QUESTIONS FOR CHAPTER 1–4 ..................................................... 199

# ABOUT THIS WORKBOOK

## Workbook to Accompany Mike Holt's Illustrated Guide to Understanding the National Electrical Code®, Volume 1, Based on the 2014 NEC®

This *Workbook to Accompany Mike Holt's Illustrated Guide to Understanding the National Electrical Code®, Volume 1, Based on the 2014 NEC®* contains over 1,200 *NEC* practice questions that are in *Code* order. It also includes two final exams with 200 questions that are in random order. These questions are designed to test your knowledge and comprehension of the material covered in the textbook. Text and graphics referred to in this Workbook can be found in *Mike Holt's Illustrated Guide to Understanding the National Electrical Code®, Volume 1, Based on the 2014 NEC* textbook.

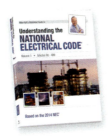

## How to Use This Workbook

All questions in this Workbook should be answered using the 2014 *National Electrical Code*. Be sure to have a copy handy.

## The Scope of This Workbook

This Workbook, being based on *Mike Holt's Illustrated Guide to Understanding the 2014 National Electrical Code, Volume 1*, covers the general installation requirements contained in Articles 90 through 480 (*NEC* Chapters 1 through 4), which was written with the following stipulations:

1. **Power Systems and Voltage.** All power-supply systems are assumed to be one of the following, unless identified otherwise:

   - 2-wire, single-phase, 120V
   - 3-wire, single-phase, 120/240V
   - 4-wire, three-phase, 120/240V Delta
   - 4-wire, three-phase, 120/208V or 277/480V Wye

2. **Electrical Calculations.** Unless the questions or examples specify three-phase, they're based on a single-phase power supply. In addition, all amperage calculations are rounded to the nearest ampere in accordance with Section 220.5(B).

3. **Conductor Material.** Conductors are assumed to be copper, unless aluminum is identified or specified.

4. **Conductor Sizing.** Conductors are sized based on a THHN/THWN-2 copper conductor terminating on a 75°C terminal in accordance with 110.14(C), unless the question or example indicates otherwise.

5. **Overcurrent Device.** The term "overcurrent device" refers to a molded-case circuit breaker, unless specified otherwise. Where a fuse is specified, it's a single-element type fuse, also known as a "one-time fuse," unless the text specifies otherwise.

## Workbook Corrections

We're committed to providing you the finest product with the fewest errors. We take great care in researching the *NEC* requirements to ensure our textbooks are correct, but we're realistic and know that there may be errors found and reported after this is printed. This can occur because the *NEC* is dramatically changed each *Code* cycle; new articles are added, some are deleted, some are relocated, and many are renumbered.

The last thing we want is for you to have problems finding, communicating, or accessing this information. Any errors found after printing are listed on our website, so if you find an error, first check to see if it's already been corrected by going to www.MikeHolt.com, click on "Books," and then click on "Corrections" (www.MikeHolt.com/bookcorrections.htm).

## About This Workbook

If you believe that there's an error of any kind (typographical, grammatical, technical, or anything else) in this textbook or in the Answer Key and it isn't already listed on the website, send an e-mail to Corrections@MikeHolt.com. Be sure to include the textbook title, page number, and any other pertinent information.

If you have adopted Mike Holt textbooks for use in your classroom you can register for Answer Keys that can be downloaded from our website. To register and receive a log-in password, go to our website www.MikeHolt.com, click on "Instructors" in the sidebar of links, and then click on "Answer Keys." On this same page you'll also find instructions for accessing and downloading these Answer Keys. Please note that this feature will only work after you've received a log-in password.

### Technical Questions

As you progress through this textbook, you might find that you don't understand every explanation, example, calculation, or comment. Don't become frustrated, and don't get down on yourself. Remember, this is the *National Electrical Code*, and sometimes the best attempt to explain a concept isn't enough to make it perfectly clear. If you're still confused, visit www.MikeHolt.com/forum, and post your question on our free Code Forum for help. The forum is a moderated community of electrical professionals where you can exchange ideas and post technical questions that will be answered by your peers.

### QR Codes

What's this symbol? It's a QR code and gives you the ability to use your smartphone to scan the image (using a barcode reader app) and be directed to a website. For example, the QR code to the right (when captured) will direct your smartphone to the Mike Holt Enterprises website. We include these in various places in our textbooks to make it easier for you to go directly to the website page referenced.

### Additional Products to Help You Learn

#### Detailed *Code* Library

When you really need to understand the *NEC*, there's no better way to learn it than with Mike's Detailed *Code* Library. It takes you step-by-step through the *NEC*, in *Code* order with detailed illustrations, great practice questions, and in-depth DVD analysis. This library is perfect for engineers, electricians, contractors, and electrical inspectors.

- *Understanding the National Electrical Code—Volume 1*
- *Understanding the National Electrical Code—Volume 2*
- *NEC Exam Practice Questions* workbook
- General Requirements DVD
- Wiring and Protection DVD
- Grounding versus Bonding DVDs (2)
- Wiring Methods and Materials DVDs (2)
- Equipment for General Use DVD
- Special Occupancies DVD
- Special Equipment DVD
- Limited Energy and Communications Systems DVD

Order Mike Holt's Detailed *Code* Library by calling 888.NEC.CODE (632.2633) or going to our website at www.MikeHolt.com/14DECO.

#### 2014 *Code* Book and Tabs

Whether you prefer the softbound, spiral bound, or the loose-leaf version, you should have an updated *Code* book for accurate reference. Placing tabs on *Code* articles, sections, and tables will make it easier for you to use the *NEC*. However, too many tabs will defeat the purpose. Mike's best-selling tabs make organizing your *Code* book easy.

To order your *Code* book and set of tabs visit www.MikeHolt.com/14code, or call 1.888.NEC.CODE (632.2633).

# ABOUT THE NATIONAL ELECTRICAL CODE

The *National Electrical Code* is written for persons who understand electrical terms, theory, safety procedures, and electrical trade practices. These individuals include electricians, electrical contractors, electrical inspectors, electrical engineers, designers, and other qualified persons. The *Code* isn't written to serve as an instructional or teaching manual for untrained individuals [90.1(A)].

Learning to use the *NEC* can be likened to learning the strategy needed to play the game of chess well; it's a great game if you enjoy mental warfare. When learning to play chess, you must first learn the names of the game pieces, how they're placed on the board, and how each one is moved.

Once you understand the fundamentals, you're ready to start playing the game. Unfortunately, at this point all you can do is make crude moves, because you really don't understand how all the information works together. To play chess well, you'll need to learn how to use your knowledge by working on subtle strategies before you can work your way up to the more intriguing and complicated moves.

The *Code* is updated every three years to accommodate new electrical products and materials, changing technologies, improved installation techniques, and to make editorial refinements to improve readability and application. While the uniform adoption of each new edition of the *NEC* is the best approach for all involved in the electrical industry, many inspection jurisdictions modify the *Code* when it's adopted. To further complicate this situation, the *NEC* allows the authority having jurisdiction, typically the "Electrical Inspector," the flexibility to waive specific *Code* requirements, and to permit alternative methods. This is only allowed when he or she is assured the completed electrical installation is equivalent in establishing and maintaining effective safety [90.4].

Keeping up with requirements of the *Code* should be the goal of everyone involved in the safety of electrical installations. This includes electrical installers, contractors, owners, inspectors, engineers, instructors, and others concerned with electrical installations.

## About the 2014 *NEC*

The actual process of changing the *Code* takes about two years, and it involves hundreds of individuals making an effort to have the *NEC* as current and accurate as possible. Let's review how this process worked for the 2014 *Code*:

**Step 1. Proposals—November, 2011.** Anybody can submit a proposal to change the *Code* before the proposal closing date. Thousands of proposals were submitted to modify the 2011 *NEC* and create the 2014 *Code*. Of these proposals, several hundred rules were revised that significantly affect the electrical industry. Some changes were editorial revisions, while others were more significant, such as new articles, sections, exceptions, and Informational Notes.

**Step 2. *Code*-Making Panel(s) Review Proposals—January, 2012.** All *Code* change proposals were reviewed by *Code*-Making Panels. There were 19 panels in the 2014 revision process who voted to accept, reject, or modify proposals.

**Step 3. Report on Proposals (ROP)—July, 2012.** The voting of the *Code*-Making Panels on the proposals was published for public review in a document called the "Report on Proposals," frequently referred to as the "ROP."

**Step 4. Public Comments—October, 2012.** Once the ROP was available, public comments were submitted asking the *Code*-Making Panel members to revise their earlier actions on change proposals, based on new information. The closing date for "Comments" was October, 2012.

**Step 5. Comments Reviewed by *Code* Panels—December, 2012.** The *Code*-Making Panels met again to review, discuss, and vote on public comments.

**Step 6. Report on Comments (ROC)—March, 2013.** The voting on the "Comments" was published for public review in a document called the "Report on Comments," frequently referred to as the "ROC."

**Step 7. Electrical Section—June, 2013.** The NFPA Electrical Section discussed and reviewed the work of the *Code*-Making Panels. The Electrical Section developed recommendations on last-minute motions to revise the proposed *NEC* draft that would be presented at the NFPA's annual meeting.

**Step 8. NFPA Annual Meeting—June, 2013.** The 2014 *NEC* was voted by the NFPA members to approve the action of the *Code*-Making Panels at the annual meeting, after a number of motions (often called "floor actions" or "NITMAMs") were voted on.

## About the *National Electrical Code*

**Step 9. Standards Council Review Appeals and Approves the 2014 *NEC*—July, 2013.** The NFPA Standards Council reviewed the record of the *Code*-making process and approved publication of the 2014 *NEC*.

**Step 10. 2014 *NEC* Published—September, 2013.** The 2014 *National Electrical Code* was published, following the NFPA Board of Directors review of appeals.

**Author's Comment:** Proposals and comments can be submitted online at the NFPA website (www.nfpa.org). From the homepage, click on "Codes and Standards", then find NFPA 70 (*National Electrical Code*). From there, follow the on screen instructions to download the proposal form. The deadline for proposals to create the 2017 *National Electrical Code* will be around November of 2014. If you would like to see something changed in the *Code*, you're encouraged to participate in the process.

## Not a Game

Electrical work isn't a game, and it must be taken very seriously. Learning the basics of electricity, important terms and concepts, as well as the basic layout of the *NEC* gives you just enough knowledge to be dangerous. There are thousands of specific and unique applications of electrical installations, and the *Code* doesn't cover every one of them. To safely apply the *NEC*, you must understand the purpose of a rule and how it affects the safety aspects of the installation.

## *NEC* Terms and Concepts

The *NEC* contains many technical terms, so it's crucial for *Code* users to understand their meanings and their applications. If you don't understand a term used in a *Code* rule, it will be impossible to properly apply the *NEC* requirement. Be sure you understand that Article 100 defines the terms that apply to two or more *Code* articles. For example, the term "Dwelling Unit" is found in many articles; if you don't know what a dwelling unit is, how can you apply the requirements for it?

In addition, many articles have terms unique for that specific article and definitions of those terms are only applicable for that given article. For example, Section 250.2 contains the definitions of terms that only apply to Article 250—Grounding and Bonding.

## Small Words, Grammar, and Punctuation

It's not only the technical words that require close attention, because even the simplest of words can make a big difference to the application of a rule. The word "or" can imply alternate choices for wiring methods, while "and" can mean an additional requirement. Let's not forget about grammar and punctuation. The location of a comma can dramatically change the requirement of a rule.

## Slang Terms or Technical Jargon

Electricians, engineers, and other trade-related professionals use slang terms or technical jargon that isn't shared by all. This makes it very difficult to communicate because not everybody understands the intent or application of those slang terms. So where possible, be sure you use the proper word, and don't use a word if you don't understand its definition and application. For example, lots of electricians use the term "pigtail" when describing the short conductor for the connection of a receptacle, switch, luminaire, or equipment. Although they may understand it, not everyone does.

## *NEC* Style and Layout

Before we get into the details of the *NEC*, we need to take a few moments to understand its style and layout. Understanding the structure and writing style of the *Code* is very important before it can be used and applied effectively. The *National Electrical Code* is organized into ten major components.

1. Table of Contents
2. Article 90 (Introduction to the *Code*)
3. Chapters 1 through 9 (major categories)
4. Articles 90 through 840 (individual subjects)
5. Parts (divisions of an article)
6. Sections and Tables (*NEC* requirements)
7. Exceptions (*Code* permissions)
8. Informational Notes (explanatory material)
9. Annexes (information)
10. Index

**1. Table of Contents.** The Table of Contents displays the layout of the chapters, articles, and parts as well as the page numbers. It's an excellent resource and should be referred to periodically to observe the interrelationship of the various *NEC* components. When attempting to locate the rules for a particular situation, knowledgeable *Code* users often go first to the Table of Contents to quickly find the specific *NEC* Part that applies.

**2. Introduction.** The *NEC* begins with Article 90, the introduction to the *Code*. It contains the purpose of the *NEC*, what's covered and what isn't covered along with how the *Code* is arranged. It also gives information on enforcement and how mandatory and permissive rules are written as well as how explanatory material is included. Article 90 also includes information on formal interpretations, examination of equipment for safety, wiring planning, and information about formatting units of measurement.

**3. Chapters.** There are nine chapters, each of which is divided into articles. The articles fall into one of four groupings: General Requirements (Chapters 1 through 4), Specific Requirements (Chapters 5 through 7), Communications Systems (Chapter 8), and Tables (Chapter 9).

- Chapter 1—General
- Chapter 2—Wiring and Protection
- Chapter 3—Wiring Methods and Materials
- Chapter 4—Equipment for General Use
- Chapter 5—Special Occupancies
- Chapter 6—Special Equipment
- Chapter 7—Special Conditions
- Chapter 8—Communications Systems (Telephone, Data, Satellite, Cable TV and Broadband)
- Chapter 9—Tables–Conductor and Raceway Specifications

**4. Articles.** The *NEC* contains approximately 140 articles, each of which covers a specific subject. For example:

- Article 110—General Requirements
- Article 250—Grounding and Bonding
- Article 300—General Requirements for Wiring Methods and Materials
- Article 430—Motors and Motor Controllers
- Article 500—Hazardous (Classified) Locations
- Article 680—Swimming Pools, Fountains, and Similar Installations
- Article 725—Remote-Control, Signaling, and Power-Limited Circuits
- Article 800—Communications Circuits

**5. Parts.** Larger articles are subdivided into parts. Because the parts of a *Code* article aren't included in the section numbers, we have a tendency to forget what "part" the *NEC* rule is relating to. For example, Table 110.34(A) contains working space clearances for electrical equipment. If we aren't careful, we might think this table applies to all electrical installations, but Table 110.34(A) is located in Part III, which only contains requirements for "Over 600 Volts, Nominal" installations. The rules for working clearances for electrical equipment for systems 600V, nominal, or less are contained in Table 110.26(A)(1), which is located in Part II—600 Volts, Nominal, or Less.

**6. Sections and Tables.**

**Sections.** Each *NEC* rule is called a "*Code* Section." A *Code* section may be broken down into subsections by letters in parentheses (A), (B), and so on. Numbers in parentheses (1), (2), and so forth, may further break down a subsection, and lowercase letters (a), (b), and so on, further break the rule down to the third level. For example, the rule requiring all receptacles in a dwelling unit bathroom to be GFCI protected is contained in Section 210.8(A)(1). Section 210.8(A)(1) is located in Chapter 2, Article 210, Section 8, Subsection (A), Sub-subsection (1).

Many in the industry incorrectly use the term "Article" when referring to a *Code* section. For example, they say "Article 210.8," when they should say "Section 210.8." Section numbers in this textbook are shown without the word "Section," unless they begin a sentence. For example, Section 210.8(A) is shown as simply 210.8(A).

**Tables.** Many *NEC* requirements are contained within tables, which are lists of *Code* rules placed in a systematic arrangement. The titles of the tables are extremely important; you must read them carefully in order to understand the contents, applications, limitations, and so forth, of each table in the *NEC*. Many times notes are provided in or below a table; be sure to read them as well since they're also part of the requirement. For example, Note 1 for Table 300.5 explains how to measure the cover when burying cables and raceways, and Note 5 explains what to do if solid rock is encountered.

**7. Exceptions.** Exceptions are *Code* requirements or permissions that provide an alternative method to a specific rule. There are two types of exceptions—mandatory and permissive. When a rule has several exceptions, those exceptions with mandatory requirements are listed before the permissive exceptions.

**Mandatory Exceptions.** A mandatory exception uses the words "shall" or "shall not." The word "shall" in an exception means that if you're using the exception, you're required to do it in a particular way. The phrase "shall not" means it isn't permitted.

**Permissive Exceptions.** A permissive exception uses words such as "shall be permitted," which means it's acceptable (but not mandatory) to do it in this way.

**8. Informational Notes.** An Informational Note contains explanatory material intended to clarify a rule or give assistance, but it isn't a *Code* requirement.

**9. Annexes.** Annexes aren't a part of the *NEC* requirements, and are included in the *Code* for informational purposes only.

Annex A. Product Safety Standards
Annex B. Application Information for Ampacity Calculation
Annex C. Raceway Fill Tables for Conductors and Fixture Wires of the Same Size
Annex D. Examples
Annex E. Types of Construction
Annex F. Critical Operations Power Systems (COPS)
Annex G. Supervisory Control and Data Acquisition (SCADA)
Annex H. Administration and Enforcement
Annex I. Recommended Tightening Torques
Annex J. ADA Standards for Accessible Design

**10. Index.** The Index at the back of the *Code* book is helpful in locating a specific rule.

Changes to the *NEC* since the previous edition(s), are identified by shading, but rules that have been relocated aren't identified as a change. A bullet symbol "•" is located on the margin to indicate the location of a rule that was deleted from a previous edition. New articles contain a vertical line in the margin of the page.

## Different Interpretations

Some electricians, contractors, instructors, inspectors, engineers, and others enjoy the challenge of discussing the *NEC* requirements, hopefully in a positive and productive manner. This give-and-take is important to the process of better understanding the *Code* requirements and application(s). However, if you're going to participate in an *NEC* discussion, please don't spout out what you think without having the actual *Code* book in your hand. The professional way of discussing an *NEC* requirement is by referring to a specific section, rather than talking in vague generalities.

## How to Locate a Specific Requirement

How to go about finding what you're looking for in the *Code* book depends, to some degree, on your experience with the *NEC*. *Code* experts typically know the requirements so well they just go to the correct rule without any outside assistance. The Table of Contents might be the only thing very experienced *NEC* users need to locate the requirement they're looking for. On the other hand, average *Code* users should use all of the tools at their disposal, including the Table of Contents and the Index.

**Table of Contents.** Let's work out a simple example: What *NEC* rule specifies the maximum number of disconnects permitted for a service? If you're an experienced *Code* user, you'll know Article 230 applies to "Services," and because this article is so large, it's divided up into multiple parts (actually eight parts). With this knowledge, you can quickly go to the Table of Contents and see it lists the Service Equipment Disconnecting Means requirements in Part VI.

**Author's Comment:** The number 70 precedes all page numbers because the *NEC* is NFPA Standard Number 70.

**Index.** If you use the Index, which lists subjects in alphabetical order, to look up the term "service disconnect," you'll see there's no listing. If you try "disconnecting means," then "services," you'll find that the Index indicates that the rule is located in Article 230, Part VI. Because the *NEC* doesn't give a page number in the Index, you'll need to use the Table of Contents to find it, or flip through the *Code* book to Article 230, then continue to flip through pages until you find Part VI.

Many people complain that the *NEC* only confuses them by taking them in circles. As you gain experience in using the *Code* and deepen your understanding of words, terms, principles, and practices, you'll find the *NEC* much easier to understand and use than you originally thought.

## Customizing Your *Code* Book

One way to increase your comfort level with the *Code* book is to customize it to meet your needs. You can do this by highlighting and underlining important *NEC* requirements, and by attaching tabs to important pages. Be aware that if you're using your *Code* book to take an exam, some exam centers don't allow markings of any type.

**Highlighting.** As you read through this textbook, be sure you highlight those requirements in the *Code* that are the most important or relevant to you. Use one color for general interest and a different one for important requirements you want to find quickly. Be sure to highlight terms in the Index and the Table of Contents as you use them.

**Underlining.** Underline or circle key words and phrases in the *NEC* with a red pen (not a lead pencil) and use a short ruler or other straightedge to keep lines straight and neat. This is a very handy way to make important requirements stand out. A short ruler or other straightedge also comes in handy for locating specific information in the many *Code* tables.

# ABOUT THE AUTHOR

### Mike Holt—Author

Founder and President
Mike Holt Enterprises
Groveland, FL
www.MikeHolt.com

**Mike Holt** worked his way up through the electrical trade. He began as an apprentice electrician and became one of the most recognized experts in the world as it relates to electrical power installations. He's worked as a journeyman electrician, master electrician, and electrical contractor. Mike's experience in the real world gives him a unique understanding of how the *NEC* relates to electrical installations from a practical standpoint. You'll find his writing style to be direct, nontechnical, and powerful.

Did you know Mike didn't finish high school? So if you struggled in high school or didn't finish at all, don't let it get you down. But, realizing that success depends on one's continuing pursuit of education, Mike immediately attained his GED, and ultimately attended the University of Miami's Graduate School for a Master's degree in Business Administration.

Mike resides in Central Florida, is the father of seven children, has five grandchildren, and enjoys many outside interests and activities. He's a nine-time National Barefoot Water-Ski Champion (1988, 1999, 2005–2009, 2012–2013). He's set many national records and continues to train year-round at a World competition level (www.barefootwaterskier.com).

What sets him apart from some is his commitment to living a balanced lifestyle; placing God first, family, career, then self.

**Special Acknowledgments**—First, I want to thank God for my godly wife who's always by my side and my children, Belynda, Melissa, Autumn, Steven, Michael, Meghan, and Brittney.

A special thank you must be sent to the staff at the National Fire Protection Association (NFPA), publishers of the *NEC*—in particular Jeff Sargent for his assistance in answering my many *Code* questions over the years. Jeff, you're a "first class" guy, and I admire your dedication and commitment to helping others understand the *NEC*. Other former NFPA staff members I would like to thank include John Caloggero, Joe Ross, and Dick Murray for their help in the past.

A personal thank you goes to Sarina, my long-time friend and office manager. It's been wonderful working side-by-side with you for over 25 years nurturing this company's growth from its small beginnings.

# ABOUT THE ILLUSTRATOR

## Mike Culbreath—Illustrator

Graphic Illustrator
Alden, MI
www.MikeHolt.com

**Mike Culbreath** devoted his career to the electrical industry and worked his way up from an apprentice electrician to master electrician. He started in the electrical field doing residential and light commercial construction. He later did service work and custom electrical installations. While working as a journeyman electrician, he suffered a serious on-the-job knee injury. As part of his rehabilitation, Mike completed courses at Mike Holt Enterprises, and then passed the exam to receive his Master Electrician's license. In 1986, with a keen interest in continuing education for electricians, he joined the staff to update material and began illustrating Mike Holt's textbooks and magazine articles.

He started with simple hand-drawn diagrams and cut-and-paste graphics. When frustrated by the limitations of that style of illustrating, he took a company computer home to learn how to operate some basic computer graphic software. Becoming aware that computer graphics offered a lot of flexibility for creating illustrations, Mike took every computer graphics class and seminar he could to help develop his computer graphic skills. He's now worked as an illustrator and editor with the company for over 25 years and, as Mike Holt has proudly acknowledged, has helped to transform his words and visions into lifelike graphics.

Originally from South Florida, Mike now lives in northern lower Michigan where he enjoys kayaking, photography, and cooking, but his real passion is his horses.

Mike loves spending time with his children Dawn and Mac and his grandchildren Jonah and Kieley.

**Special Acknowledgments**—I would like to thank Ryan Jackson, an outstanding and very knowledgeable *Code* guy, and Eric Stromberg, an electrical engineer and super geek (and I mean that in the most complimentary manner, this guy is brilliant), for helping me keep our graphics as technically correct as possible.

I also want to give a special thank you to Cathleen Kwas for making me look good with her outstanding layout design and typesetting skills and Toni Culbreath who proofreads all of my material. I would also like to acknowledge Belynda Holt Pinto, our Chief Operations Officer and the rest of the outstanding staff at Mike Holt Enterprises, for all the hard work they do to help produce and distribute these outstanding products.

And last but not least, I need to give a special thank you to Mike Holt for not firing me over 25 years ago when I "borrowed" one of his computers and took it home to begin the process of learning how to do computer illustrations. He gave me the opportunity and time needed to develop my computer graphic skills. He's been an amazing friend and mentor since I met him as a student many years ago. Thanks for believing in me and allowing me to be part of the Mike Holt Enterprises family.

# ARTICLE 90
# INTRODUCTION TO THE *NATIONAL ELECTRICAL CODE*

## Introduction to Article 90—Introduction to the *National Electrical Code*

Many *NEC* violations and misunderstandings wouldn't occur if people doing the work simply understood Article 90. For example, many people see *Code* requirements as performance standards. In fact, the *NEC* requirements are bare minimums for safety. This is exactly the stance electrical inspectors, insurance companies, and courts take when making a decision regarding electrical design or installation.

Article 90 opens by saying the *NEC* isn't intended as a design specification or instruction manual. The *National Electrical Code* has one purpose only, and that's the "practical safeguarding of persons and property from hazards arising from the use of electricity." The necessity of carefully studying the *NEC* rules can't be overemphasized, and the role of textbooks such as this one is to help in that undertaking. Understanding where to find the rules in the *Code* that apply to the installation is invaluable. Rules in several different articles often apply to even a simple installation.

Article 90 then describes the scope and arrangement of the *NEC*, and provides the reader with information essential to understanding the *Code* rules.

Typically, electrical work requires you to understand the first four chapters of the *NEC* which apply generally, plus have a working knowledge of the Chapter 9 tables. That understanding begins with Article 90. Chapters 5, 6, and 7 make up a large portion of the *Code*, but they apply to special occupancies, special equipment, or other special conditions. They build on, modify, or amend the rules in the first four chapters. Chapter 8 contains the requirements for communications systems, such as telephone systems, antenna wiring, CATV, and network-powered broadband systems. Communications systems aren't subject to the general requirements of Chapters 1 through 4, or the special requirements of Chapters 5 through 7, unless there's a specific reference in Chapter 8 to a rule in Chapters 1 through 7.

# Article 90 | Introduction to the National Electrical Code

**Please use the 2014 Code book to answer the following questions.**

1. The *NEC* is _____.

   (a) intended to be a design manual
   (b) meant to be used as an instruction guide for untrained persons
   (c) for the practical safeguarding of persons and property
   (d) published by the Bureau of Standards

2. The *Code* isn't intended as a design specification standard or instruction manual for untrained persons.

   (a) True
   (b) False

3. Compliance with the provisions of the *NEC* will result in _____.

   (a) good electrical service
   (b) an efficient electrical system
   (c) an electrical system essentially free from hazard
   (d) all of these

4. The *Code* contains provisions considered necessary for safety, which will not necessarily result in _____.

   (a) efficient use
   (b) convenience
   (c) good service or future expansion of electrical use
   (d) all of these

5. Hazards often occur because of _____.

   (a) overloading of wiring systems by methods or usage not in conformity with the *NEC*
   (b) initial wiring not providing for increases in the use of electricity
   (c) a and b
   (d) none of these

6. The following systems shall be installed in accordance with the *NEC* requirements:

   (a) signaling conductors, equipment, and raceways
   (b) communications conductors, equipment, and raceways
   (c) electrical conductors, equipment, and raceways
   (d) all of these

7. The *NEC* applies to the installation of _____.

   (a) electrical conductors and equipment within or on public and private buildings
   (b) outside conductors and equipment on the premises
   (c) optical fiber cables and raceways
   (d) all of these

8. This *Code* covers the installation of _____ for public and private premises, including buildings, structures, mobile homes, recreational vehicles, and floating buildings.

   (a) optical fiber cables
   (b) electrical equipment
   (c) raceways
   (d) all of these

9. The *NEC* does not cover electrical installations in ships, watercraft, railway rolling stock, aircraft, or automotive vehicles.

   (a) True
   (b) False

10. The *Code* covers underground mine installations and self-propelled mobile surface mining machinery and its attendant electrical trailing cable.

    (a) True
    (b) False

11. Installations of communications equipment that are under the exclusive control of communications utilities, and located outdoors or in building spaces used exclusively for such installations _____ covered by the NEC.

    (a) are
    (b) are sometimes
    (c) are not
    (d) may be

12. Electric utilities may include entities that install, operate, and maintain _____.

    (a) communications systems (telephone, CATV, Internet, satellite, or data services)
    (b) electric supply systems (generation, transmission, or distribution systems)
    (c) local area network wiring on the premises
    (d) a or b

13. Utilities may be subject to compliance with codes and standards covering their regulated activities as adopted under governmental law or regulation.

    (a) True
    (b) False

14. The NEC does not apply to electric utility-owned wiring and equipment _____.

    (a) installed by an electrical contractor
    (b) installed on public property
    (c) consisting of service drops or service laterals
    (d) in a utility office building

15. Utilities may include entities that are designated or recognized by governmental law or regulation by public service/utility commissions.

    (a) True
    (b) False

16. Communications wiring such as telephone, antenna, and CATV wiring within a building shall not be required to comply with the installation requirements of Chapters 1 through 7, except where specifically referenced in Chapter 8.

    (a) True
    (b) False

17. Chapters 1 through 4 of the NEC apply _____.

    (a) generally to all electrical installations
    (b) only to special occupancies and conditions
    (c) only to special equipment and material
    (d) all of these

18. The material located in the NEC Annexes are part of the requirements of the Code and shall be complied with.

    (a) True
    (b) False

19. The authority having jurisdiction shall not be allowed to enforce any requirements of Chapter 7 (Special Conditions) or Chapter 8 (Communications Systems).

    (a) True
    (b) False

20. The _____ has the responsibility for deciding on the approval of equipment and materials.

    (a) manufacturer
    (b) authority having jurisdiction
    (c) testing agency
    (d) none of these

21. By special permission, the authority having jurisdiction may waive specific requirements in this Code where it is assured that equivalent objectives can be achieved by establishing and maintaining effective safety.

    (a) True
    (b) False

22. The authority having jurisdiction has the responsibility for _____.

    (a) making interpretations of rules
    (b) deciding upon the approval of equipment and materials
    (c) waiving specific requirements in the Code and permitting alternate methods and material if safety is maintained
    (d) all of these

23. If the *NEC* requires new products that are not yet available at the time a new edition is adopted, the _____ may permit the use of the products that comply with the most recent previous edition of the *Code* adopted by that jurisdiction.

    (a) electrical engineer
    (b) master electrician
    (c) authority having jurisdiction
    (d) permit holder

24. In the *NEC*, the words "_____" indicate a mandatory requirement.

    (a) shall
    (b) shall not
    (c) shall be permitted
    (d) a or b

25. When the *Code* uses "_____," it means the identified actions are allowed but not required, and they may be options or alternative methods.

    (a) shall
    (b) shall not
    (c) shall be permitted
    (d) a or b

26. Explanatory material, such as references to other standards, references to related sections of the *NEC*, or information related to a *Code* rule, are included in the form of Informational Notes.

    (a) True
    (b) False

27. Nonmandatory Informative Annexes contained in the back of the *Code* book _____.

    (a) are for information only
    (b) aren't enforceable as a requirement of the *Code*
    (c) are enforceable as a requirement of the *Code*
    (d) a and b

28. Factory-installed _____ wiring of listed equipment need not be inspected at the time of installation of the equipment, except to detect alterations or damage.

    (a) external
    (b) associated
    (c) internal
    (d) all of these

29. Compliance with either the metric (SI) or the inch-pound unit of measurement system shall be permitted.

    (a) True
    (b) False

# CHAPTER 1
# GENERAL

## Introduction to Chapter 1—General

Before you can make sense of the *Code*, you must become familiar with a few basic rules, concepts, definitions, and requirements. As you study the *NEC*, you'll see that these are the foundation for a proper understanding of the *Code*.

Chapter 1 consists of two topics. Article 100 provides definitions so people can understand one another when trying to communicate about *Code*-related matters and Article 110 provides the general requirements needed to correctly apply the rest of the *NEC*.

Time spent learning this general material is a great investment. After understanding Chapter 1, some of the *Code* requirements that seem confusing to other people will become increasingly clear to you. The requirements will begin to make sense because you'll have the foundation from which to understand and apply them. When you read the *NEC* requirements in later chapters, you'll understand the principles upon which many of them are based, and not be surprised at all. You'll read them and feel like you already know them.

- **Article 100—Definitions.** Part I of Article 100 contains the definitions of terms used throughout the *Code* for systems that operate at 600V, nominal, or less. The definitions of terms in Part II apply to systems that operate at over 600V, nominal.

Definitions of standard terms, such as volt, voltage drop, ampere, impedance, and resistance, aren't listed in Article 100. If the *NEC* doesn't define a term, then a dictionary suitable to the authority having jurisdiction should be consulted. A building code glossary might provide better definitions than a dictionary found at your home or school.

Definitions located at the beginning of an article apply only to that specific article. For example, the definition of a swimming "Pool" is contained in 680.2, because this term applies only to the requirements contained in Article 680—Swimming Pools, Fountains, and Similar Installations. As soon as a defined term is used in two or more articles, its definition should be included in Article 100.

- **Article 110—Requirements for Electrical Installations.** This article contains general requirements for electrical installations for the following:
    - Part I. General
    - Part II. 600V, Nominal, Or Less

**Notes**

# ARTICLE 100 DEFINITIONS

## Introduction to Article 100—Definitions

Have you ever had a conversation with someone, only to discover that what you said and what he or she heard were completely different? This often happens when people in a conversation don't understand the definitions of the words being used, and that's why the definitions of key terms are located right at the beginning of the *NEC* (Article 100), or at the beginning of each article. If we can all agree on important definitions, then we speak the same language and avoid misunderstandings. Because the *Code* exists to protect people and property, it's very important to know the definitions presented in Article 100.

Here are a few tips for learning the many definitions in the *Code*:

- Break the task down. Study a few words at a time, rather than trying to learn them all at one sitting.
- Review the graphics in *Mike Holt's Illustrated Guide to Understanding the National Electrical Code, Volume 1, based on the 2014 NEC* textbook. These will help you see how a term is applied.
- Relate the definitions to your work. As you read a word, think about how it applies to the work you're doing. This'll provide a natural reinforcement to the learning process.

**Please use the 2014 *Code* book to answer the following questions.**

1. Admitting close approach not guarded by locked doors, elevation, or other effective means, is referred to as _____.

   (a) accessible (as applied to equipment)
   (b) accessible (as applied to wiring methods)
   (c) accessible, readily
   (d) all of these

2. Capable of being removed or exposed without damaging the building structure or finish, or not permanently closed in by the structure or finish of the building is known as _____.

   (a) accessible (as applied to equipment)
   (b) accessible (as applied to wiring methods)
   (c) accessible, readily
   (d) all of these

## Article 100 | Definitions

3. Capable of being reached quickly for operation, renewal, or inspections without resorting to portable ladders or the use of tools is known as _____.

    (a) accessible (as applied to equipment)
    (b) accessible (as applied to wiring methods)
    (c) accessible, readily
    (d) all of these

4. The maximum current, in amperes, that a conductor can carry continuously, where the temperature will not be raised in excess of the conductor's insulation temperature rating is called its "_____."

    (a) short-circuit rating
    (b) ground-fault rating
    (c) ampacity
    (d) all of these

5. "_____" means acceptable to the authority having jurisdiction.

    (a) Identified
    (b) Listed
    (c) Approved
    (d) Labeled

6. An arc-fault circuit interrupter is a device intended to de-energize the circuit when it recognizes characteristics unique to _____.

    (a) overcurrent
    (b) arcing
    (c) a ground fault
    (d) harmonic fundamental

7. A device that establishes a connection between the conductors of the attached flexible cord and the conductors connected to the receptacle is called a(n) "_____."

    (a) attachment plug
    (b) plug cap
    (c) plug
    (d) any of these

8. Where no statutory requirement exists, the authority having jurisdiction can be a property owner or his/her agent, such as an architect or engineer.

    (a) True
    (b) False

9. According to the *Code*, "automatic" is performing a function without the necessity of _____.

    (a) protection from damage
    (b) human intervention
    (c) mechanical linkage
    (d) all of these

10. A _____ is an area that includes a basin with a toilet, urinal, tub, shower, bidet, or similar plumbing fixtures.

    (a) bath area
    (b) bathroom
    (c) rest area
    (d) none of these

11. A battery system includes storage batteries and battery chargers, and can include inverters, converters, and associated electrical equipment.

    (a) True
    (b) False

12. "Bonded" can be described as _____ to establish electrical continuity and conductivity.

    (a) isolated
    (b) guarded
    (c) connected
    (d) separated

13. A reliable conductor that ensures electrical conductivity between metal parts of the electrical installation that are required to be electrically connected is called a(n) "_____."

    (a) grounding electrode
    (b) auxiliary ground
    (c) bonding conductor or jumper
    (d) tap conductor

14. The connection between the grounded circuit conductor and the equipment grounding conductor at the service is accomplished by installing a(n) _____ bonding jumper.

    (a) main
    (b) system
    (c) equipment
    (d) circuit

15. The connection between the grounded circuit conductor and the supply-side bonding jumper or equipment grounding conductor, or both, at a _____ is called a "system bonding jumper."

    (a) service disconnect
    (b) separately derived system
    (c) motor control center
    (d) separate building or structure disconnect

16. The circuit conductors between the final overcurrent device protecting the circuit and the outlet(s) are known as "_____ conductors."

    (a) feeder
    (b) branch-circuit
    (c) home run
    (d) none of these

17. For a circuit to be considered a multiwire branch circuit, it shall have _____.

    (a) two or more ungrounded conductors with a voltage potential between them
    (b) a grounded conductor having equal voltage potential between it and each ungrounded conductor of the circuit
    (c) a grounded conductor connected to the neutral or grounded terminal of the system
    (d) all of these

18. The *NEC* defines a(n) "_____" as a structure that stands alone or that is cut off from adjoining structures by fire walls or fire barriers, with all openings therein protected by approved fire doors.

    (a) unit
    (b) apartment
    (c) building
    (d) utility

19. An enclosure for either surface mounting or flush mounting provided with a frame in which a door can be hung is called a(n) "_____."

    (a) enclosure
    (b) outlet box
    (c) cutout box
    (d) cabinet

20. A cable routing assembly is composed of single or connected multiple channels as well as associated fittings, forming a structural system to _____ high densities of wires and cables, typically communications wires and cables, optical fiber and data (Class 2 and Class 3) cables.

    (a) support
    (b) route
    (c) protect
    (d) a and b

21. A circuit breaker is a device designed to _____ the circuit automatically on a predetermined overcurrent without damage to itself when properly applied within its rating.

    (a) energize
    (b) reset
    (c) connect
    (d) open

22. _____ is a term indicating that there is an intentional delay in the tripping action of the circuit breaker, which decreases as the magnitude of the current increases.

    (a) Adverse time
    (b) Inverse time
    (c) Time delay
    (d) Timed unit

23. A clothes closet is defined as a _____ room or space intended primarily for storage of garments and apparel.

    (a) habitable
    (b) non-habitable
    (c) conditioned
    (d) finished

24. Communications equipment includes equipment and conductors used for the transmission of _____.

    (a) audio
    (b) video
    (c) data
    (d) any of these

25. A communications raceway is an enclosed channel of nonmetallic materials designed for holding communications wires and cables in _____ applications.

    (a) plenum
    (b) riser
    (c) general-purpose
    (d) all of these

26. A separate portion of a raceway system that provides access through a removable cover(s) to the interior of the system, defines the term _____.

    (a) junction box
    (b) accessible raceway
    (c) conduit body
    (d) cutout box

27. A solderless pressure connector is a device that _____ between two or more conductors or between one or more conductors and a terminal by means of mechanical pressure and without the use of solder.

    (a) provides access
    (b) protects the wiring
    (c) is never needed
    (d) establishes a connection

28. A load is considered to be continuous if the maximum current is expected to continue for _____ or more.

    (a) one-half hour
    (b) 1 hour
    (c) 2 hours
    (d) 3 hours

29. A _____ is a device or group of devices that govern, in some predetermined manner, the electric power delivered to the apparatus to which it is connected.

    (a) relay
    (b) breaker
    (c) transformer
    (d) controller

30. The selection and installation of overcurrent devices so that an overcurrent condition will be localized and restrict outages to the circuit or equipment affected, is called "_____."

    (a) overcurrent protection
    (b) interrupting capacity
    (c) selective coordination
    (d) overload protection

31. The _____ of any system is the ratio of the maximum demand of a system, or part of a system, to the total connected load of a system.

    (a) load
    (b) demand factor
    (c) minimum load
    (d) calculated factor

32. A(n) _____ is a device, or group of devices, by which the conductors of a circuit can be disconnected from their source of supply.

    (a) feeder
    (b) enclosure
    (c) disconnecting means
    (d) conductor interrupter

33. An enclosure or piece of equipment constructed so that dust will not enter the enclosure under specified test conditions is known as "_____."

    (a) dusttight
    (b) dustproof
    (c) dust rated
    (d) all of these

34. "Continuous duty" is defined as _____.

   (a) when the load is expected to continue for five hours or more
   (b) operation at a substantially constant load for an indefinitely long time
   (c) operation at loads and for intervals of time, both of which may be subject to wide variations
   (d) operation at which the load may be subject to maximum current for six hours or more

35. "Varying duty" is defined as _____.

   (a) intermittent operation in which the load conditions are regularly recurrent
   (b) operation at a substantially constant load for an indefinite length of time
   (c) operation for alternate intervals of load and rest, or load, no load, and rest
   (d) operation at loads, and for intervals of time, both of which may be subject to wide variation

36. A _____ is a single unit that provides independent living facilities for one or more persons, including permanent provisions for living, sleeping, cooking, and sanitation.

   (a) one-family dwelling
   (b) two-family dwelling
   (c) dwelling unit
   (d) multifamily dwelling

37. A building that contains three or more dwelling units is called a "_____."

   (a) one-family dwelling
   (b) two-family dwelling
   (c) dwelling unit
   (d) multifamily dwelling

38. An effective ground-fault current path is an intentionally constructed, low-impedance electrically conductive path designed and intended to carry current under ground-fault conditions from the point of a ground fault on a wiring system to _____.

   (a) ground
   (b) earth
   (c) the electrical supply source
   (d) none of these

39. A fixed, stationary, or portable self-contained, electrically illuminated equipment with words or symbols designed to convey information or attract attention describes _____.

   (a) an electric sign
   (b) equipment
   (c) appliances
   (d) none of these

40. Surrounded by a case, housing, fence, or wall(s) that prevents persons from accidentally contacting energized parts is called "_____."

   (a) guarded
   (b) covered
   (c) protection
   (d) enclosed

41. As used in the NEC, equipment includes _____.

   (a) fittings
   (b) appliances
   (c) machinery
   (d) all of these

42. Equipment enclosed in a case that is capable of withstanding an explosion of a specified gas or vapor that may occur within it, and of preventing the ignition of a specified gas or vapor surrounding the enclosure by sparks, flashes, or explosion of the gas or vapor within, and that operates at such an external temperature that a surrounding flammable atmosphere will not be ignited thereby defines the phrase "_____."

   (a) overcurrent device
   (b) thermal apparatus
   (c) explosionproof equipment
   (d) bomb casing

43. When the term "exposed," as it applies to live parts, is used in the Code, it refers to _____.

   (a) being capable of being inadvertently touched or approached nearer than a safe distance by a person
   (b) parts that are not suitably guarded, isolated, or insulated
   (c) wiring on, or attached to, the surface or behind panels designed to allow access
   (d) a and b

## Article 100 | Definitions

44. For wiring methods, "on or attached to the surface, or behind access panels designed to allow access" is known as _____.

    (a) open
    (b) uncovered
    (c) exposed
    (d) bare

45. The NEC defines a "_____" as all circuit conductors between the service equipment, the source of a separately derived system, or other power supply source and the final branch-circuit overcurrent device.

    (a) service
    (b) feeder
    (c) branch circuit
    (d) all of these

46. An accessory, such as a locknut, intended to perform a mechanical function best describes _____.

    (a) a part
    (b) equipment
    (c) a device
    (d) a fitting

47. A "_____" is a building or portion of a building in which one or more self-propelled vehicles can be kept for use, sale, storage, rental, repair, exhibition, or demonstration purposes.

    (a) garage
    (b) residential garage
    (c) service garage
    (d) commercial garage

48. The word "Earth" best describes what NEC term?

    (a) Bonded
    (b) Ground
    (c) Effective ground-fault current path
    (d) Guarded

49. A(n) _____ is an unintentional, electrically conductive connection between an ungrounded conductor of an electrical circuit, and the normally noncurrent-carrying conductors, metallic enclosures, metallic raceways, metallic equipment, or earth.

    (a) grounded conductor
    (b) ground fault
    (c) equipment ground
    (d) bonding jumper

50. Connected to ground or to a conductive body that extends the ground connection is called "_____."

    (a) equipment grounding
    (b) bonded
    (c) grounded
    (d) all of these

51. A system or circuit conductor that is intentionally grounded is called a(n) "_____."

    (a) grounding conductor
    (b) unidentified conductor
    (c) grounded conductor
    (d) grounding electrode conductor

52. A device intended for the protection of personnel that functions to de-energize a circuit or portion thereof within an established period of time when a current to ground exceeds the values established for a Class A device, is a(n) "_____."

    (a) dual-element fuse
    (b) inverse time breaker
    (c) ground-fault circuit interrupter
    (d) safety switch

53. A Class A GFCI protection device is designed to trip when the current to ground is _____ or higher.

    (a) 4 mA
    (b) 5 mA
    (c) 6 mA
    (d) none of these

54. A system intended to provide protection of equipment from damaging line-to-ground fault currents by opening all ungrounded conductors of the faulted circuit at current levels less than the supply circuit overcurrent device defines the phrase "_____."

    (a) ground-fault protection of equipment
    (b) guarded
    (c) personal protection
    (d) automatic protection

55. The installed conductive path(s) that provide(s) a ground-fault current path and connects normally noncurrent-carrying metal parts of equipment together and to the system grounded conductor or to the grounding electrode conductor, or both, is known as a(n) _____.

    (a) grounding electrode conductor
    (b) grounding conductor
    (c) equipment grounding conductor
    (d) none of these

56. A conducting object through which a direct connection to earth is established is a "_____."

    (a) bonding conductor
    (b) grounding conductor
    (c) grounding electrode
    (d) grounded conductor

57. A conductor used to connect the system grounded conductor or the equipment to a grounding electrode or to a point on the grounding electrode system is called the "_____ conductor."

    (a) main grounding
    (b) common main
    (c) equipment grounding
    (d) grounding electrode

58. A "_____" is an accommodation that combines living, sleeping, sanitary, and storage facilities within a compartment.

    (a) guest room
    (b) guest suite
    (c) dwelling unit
    (d) single-family dwelling

59. A "_____" is an accommodation with two or more contiguous rooms comprising a compartment that provides living, sleeping, sanitary, and storage facilities.

    (a) guest room
    (b) guest suite
    (c) dwelling unit
    (d) single-family dwelling

60. A handhole enclosure is an enclosure for use in underground systems, provided with an open or closed bottom, and sized to allow personnel to _____.

    (a) enter and exit freely
    (b) reach into but not enter
    (c) have full working space
    (d) examine it visually

61. A hoistway is any _____ in which an elevator or dumbwaiter is designed to operate.

    (a) hatchway or well hole
    (b) vertical opening or space
    (c) shaftway
    (d) all of these

62. A hybrid system is comprised of multiple power sources, such as _____, but not the utility power system.

    (a) photovoltaic
    (b) wind
    (c) micro-hydro generators
    (d) all of these

63. A hybrid system includes the utility power system.

    (a) True
    (b) False

64. Recognized as suitable for the specific purpose, function, use, environment, and application is the definition of "_____."

    (a) labeled
    (b) identified (as applied to equipment)
    (c) listed
    (d) approved

## Article 100 | Definitions

65. Within sight means visible and not more than _____ ft distant from the equipment.

    (a) 10
    (b) 20
    (c) 25
    (d) 50

66. The highest current at rated voltage that a device is identified to interrupt under standard test conditions is the _____.

    (a) interrupting rating
    (b) manufacturer's rating
    (c) interrupting capacity
    (d) withstand rating

67. A device that provides a means to connect intersystem bonding conductors for _____ systems to the building grounding electrode system is an intersystem bonding termination.

    (a) limited energy
    (b) low-voltage
    (c) communications
    (d) power and lighting

68. "_____" means that an object is not readily accessible to persons unless special means for access are used.

    (a) Isolated
    (b) Secluded
    (c) Protected
    (d) Locked

69. A kitchen is defined as an area with a sink and _____ provisions for food preparation and cooking.

    (a) listed
    (b) labeled
    (c) temporary
    (d) permanent

70. Equipment or materials to which a label, symbol, or other identifying mark of a product evaluation organization that is acceptable to the authority having jurisdiction has been attached is known as "_____."

    (a) listed
    (b) labeled
    (c) approved
    (d) identified

71. An outlet intended for the direct connection of a lampholder or a luminaire is a(n) "_____."

    (a) outlet
    (b) receptacle outlet
    (c) lighting outlet
    (d) general-purpose outlet

72. Lighting track is a manufactured assembly and its length may not be altered by the addition or subtraction of sections of track.

    (a) True
    (b) False

73. Lighting track is a manufactured assembly designed to support and _____ luminaires that are capable of being readily repositioned on the track.

    (a) connect
    (b) protect
    (c) energize
    (d) all of these

74. Equipment or materials included in a list published by a testing laboratory acceptable to the authority having jurisdiction is said to be "_____."

    (a) book
    (b) digest
    (c) manifest
    (d) listed

75. A _____ location is protected from weather and not subject to saturation with water or other liquids.

    (a) dry
    (b) damp
    (c) wet
    (d) moist

76. A _____ location may be temporarily subject to dampness and wetness.

    (a) dry
    (b) damp
    (c) moist
    (d) wet

77. Conduit installed underground or encased in concrete slabs that are in direct contact with the earth is considered a _____ location.

    (a) dry
    (b) damp
    (c) wet
    (d) moist

78. The term "Luminaire" includes an individual lampholder.

    (a) True
    (b) False

79. A neutral conductor is the conductor connected to the _____ of a system, which is intended to carry neutral current under normal conditions.

    (a) grounding electrode
    (b) neutral point
    (c) intersystem bonding termination
    (d) none of these

80. The common point on a wye-connection in a polyphase system describes a neutral point.

    (a) True
    (b) False

81. "Nonautomatic" is defined as requiring _____ to perform a function.

    (a) protection from damage
    (b) human intervention
    (c) mechanical linkage
    (d) all of these

82. A(n) _____ is a point on the wiring system at which current is taken to supply utilization equipment.

    (a) box
    (b) receptacle
    (c) outlet
    (d) device

83. Outline lighting may include an arrangement of _____ to outline or call attention to the shape of a building.

    (a) incandescent lamps
    (b) electric-discharge lighting
    (c) electrically powered light sources
    (d) any of these

84. Any current in excess of the rated current of equipment or the ampacity of a conductor is called "_____."

    (a) trip current
    (b) fault current
    (c) overcurrent
    (d) a short circuit

85. A(n) _____ is intended to provide limited overcurrent protection for specific applications and utilization equipment such as luminaires and appliances. This limited protection is in addition to the protection provided by the required branch-circuit overcurrent protective device.

    (a) supplementary overcurrent device
    (b) surge protection device
    (c) arc-fault circuit interrupter
    (d) Class A GFCI

86. An overload is the same as a short circuit or ground fault.

    (a) True
    (b) False

87. A panel, including buses and automatic overcurrent devices, designed to be placed in a cabinet or cutout box and accessible only from the front is known as a "_____."

    (a) switchboard
    (b) disconnect
    (c) panelboard
    (d) switch

88. A _____ is the total components and subsystem that, in combination, convert solar energy into electric energy suitable for connection to a utilization load.

    (a) photovoltaic system
    (b) solar array
    (c) a and b
    (d) neither a nor b

## Article 100 | Definitions

89. The *NEC* defines a(n) "_____" as one who has skills and knowledge related to the construction and operation of the electrical equipment and installations and has received safety training to recognize and avoid the hazards involved.

    (a) inspector
    (b) master electrician
    (c) journeyman electrician
    (d) qualified person

90. NFPA 70E—Standard for Electrical Safety in the Workplace, provides information to help determine the electrical safety training requirements expected of a qualified person.

    (a) True
    (b) False

91. A raceway is an enclosure designed for the installation of wires, cables, or busbars.

    (a) True
    (b) False

92. Constructed, protected, or treated so as to prevent rain from interfering with the successful operation of the apparatus under specified test conditions defines the term "_____."

    (a) raintight
    (b) waterproof
    (c) weathertight
    (d) rainproof

93. A raintight enclosure is constructed or protected so that exposure to a beating rain will not result in the entrance of water under specified test conditions.

    (a) True
    (b) False

94. A contact device installed at an outlet for the connection of an attachment plug is known as a(n) "_____."

    (a) attachment point
    (b) tap
    (c) receptacle
    (d) wall plug

95. A single receptacle is a single contact device with no other contact device on the same _____.

    (a) circuit
    (b) yoke
    (c) run
    (d) equipment

96. An opening in an outlet box where one or more receptacles have been installed is called "_____."

    (a) a device
    (b) equipment
    (c) a receptacle
    (d) a receptacle outlet

97. When one electrical circuit controls another circuit through a relay, the first circuit is called a "_____."

    (a) primary circuit
    (b) remote-control circuit
    (c) signal circuit
    (d) controller

98. Equipment enclosed in a case or cabinet with a means of sealing or locking so that live parts cannot be made accessible without opening the enclosure is said to be "_____."

    (a) guarded
    (b) protected
    (c) sealable
    (d) lockable

99. A(n) _____ system is an electrical source, other than a service, having no direct connection(s) to circuit conductors of any other electrical source other than those established by grounding and bonding connections.

    (a) separately derived
    (b) classified
    (c) direct
    (d) emergency

100. The conductors and equipment from the electric utility that deliver electric energy to the wiring system of the premises is called a "_____."

    (a) branch circuit
    (b) feeder
    (c) service
    (d) none of these

101. Service conductors originate at the service point and terminate at the service disconnecting means.

    (a) True
    (b) False

102. Overhead service conductors are the conductors between the _____ and the first point of connection to the service-entrance conductors at the building or other structure.

    (a) service disconnect
    (b) service point
    (c) grounding electrode
    (d) equipment grounding conductor

103. Underground service conductors are the underground conductors between the service point and the first point of connection to the service-entrance conductors in a terminal box, meter, or other enclosure, _____ the building wall.

    (a) inside
    (b) outside
    (c) above
    (d) a or b

104. The service drop is defined as the overhead conductors between the utility electric supply system and the _____.

    (a) service equipment
    (b) service point
    (c) grounding electrode
    (d) equipment grounding conductor

105. The overhead system service-entrance conductors are the service conductors between the terminals of _____ and a point where they are joined by a tap or splice to the service drop or overhead service conductors.

    (a) service equipment
    (b) service point
    (c) grounding electrode
    (d) equipment grounding conductor

106. The underground system service-entrance conductors are the service conductors between the terminals of _____ and the point of connection to the service lateral or underground service conductors.

    (a) service equipment
    (b) service point
    (c) grounding electrode
    (d) equipment grounding conductor

107. The _____ is the necessary equipment, usually consisting of a circuit breaker(s) or switch(es) and fuse(s) and their accessories, connected to the load end of service conductors, and intended to constitute the main control and cutoff of the supply.

    (a) service equipment
    (b) service
    (c) service disconnect
    (d) service overcurrent device

108. The underground conductors between the utility electric supply system and the service point are known as the "_____."

    (a) utility service
    (b) service lateral
    (c) service drop
    (d) main service conductors

109. The _____ is the point of connection between the facilities of the serving utility and the premises wiring.

    (a) service entrance
    (b) service point
    (c) overcurrent protection
    (d) beginning of the wiring system

## Article 100 | Definitions

110. The prospective symmetrical fault current at a nominal voltage to which an apparatus or system is able to be connected without sustaining damage exceeding defined acceptance criteria is known as the "_____."

    (a) short-circuit current rating
    (b) arc flash rating
    (c) overcurrent rating
    (d) available fault current

111. A signaling circuit is any electrical circuit that energizes signaling equipment.

    (a) True
    (b) False

112. Special permission is the written consent from the _____.

    (a) testing laboratory
    (b) manufacturer
    (c) owner
    (d) authority having jurisdiction

113. A structure is that which is built or constructed.

    (a) True
    (b) False

114. A surge-protective device (SPD) intended for installation on the load side of the service disconnect overcurrent device, including SPDs located at the branch panel, is a _____ SPD.

    (a) Type 1
    (b) Type 2
    (c) Type 3
    (d) Type 4

115. A switch constructed so that it can be installed in device boxes or on box covers, or otherwise used in conjunction with wiring systems recognized by the NEC is called a "_____ switch."

    (a) transfer
    (b) motor-circuit
    (c) general-use snap
    (d) bypass isolation

116. "Ungrounded" means not connected to ground or to a conductive body that extends the ground connection.

    (a) True
    (b) False

117. Utilization equipment is equipment that utilizes electricity for _____ purposes.

    (a) electromechanical
    (b) heating
    (c) lighting
    (d) any of these

118. The voltage of a circuit is defined by the *Code* as the _____ root-mean-square (effective) difference of potential between any two conductors of the circuit concerned.

    (a) lowest
    (b) greatest
    (c) average
    (d) nominal

119. A value assigned to a circuit or system for the purpose of conveniently designating its voltage class, such as 120/240V, is called "_____ voltage."

    (a) root-mean-square
    (b) circuit
    (c) nominal
    (d) source

120. An enclosure constructed so that moisture will not enter the enclosure under specific test conditions is called "_____."

    (a) watertight
    (b) moistureproof
    (c) waterproof
    (d) rainproof

121. A(n) _____ enclosure is constructed or protected so that exposure to the weather will not interfere with successful operation.

    (a) weatherproof
    (b) weathertight
    (c) weather-resistant
    (d) all weather

# ARTICLE 110 — REQUIREMENTS FOR ELECTRICAL INSTALLATIONS

## Introduction to Article 110—Requirements for Electrical Installations

Article 110 sets the stage for how you'll implement the rest of the *NEC*. This article contains a few of the most important and yet neglected parts of the *Code*. For example:

- How should conductors be terminated?
- What kinds of warnings, markings, and identification does a given installation require?
- What's the right working clearance for a given installation?
- What do the temperature limitations at terminals mean?
- What are the *NEC* requirements for dealing with flash protection?

It's critical that you master Article 110—you're building your foundation for correctly applying the *NEC*. In fact, this article itself is a foundation for much of the *Code*. The purpose for the *National Electrical Code* is to provide a safe installation, but Article 110 is perhaps focused a little more on providing an installation that's safe for the installer and maintenance electrician.

Please use the 2014 *Code* book to answer the following questions.

1. In judging equipment for approval, considerations such as the following shall be evaluated:

   (a) mechanical strength
   (b) wire-bending space
   (c) arcing effects
   (d) all of these

2. Listed or labeled equipment shall be installed and used in accordance with any instructions included in the listing or labeling.

   (a) True
   (b) False

3. Conductors normally used to carry current shall be _____ unless otherwise provided in this *Code*.

   (a) bare
   (b) stranded
   (c) of copper
   (d) of aluminum

4. Conductor sizes are expressed in American Wire Gage (AWG) or in _____.

   (a) inches
   (b) circular mils
   (c) square inches
   (d) cubic inches

5. Wiring shall be installed so that the completed system will be free from _____, other than as required or permitted elsewhere in the *Code*.

   (a) short circuits
   (b) ground faults
   (c) connections to the earth
   (d) all of these

6. Only wiring methods recognized as _____ are included in this *Code*.

   (a) expensive
   (b) efficient
   (c) suitable
   (d) cost-effective

7. Equipment intended to interrupt current at fault levels shall have an interrupting rating at nominal circuit voltage sufficient for the current that is available at the line terminals of the equipment.

   (a) True
   (b) False

8. Unless identified for use in the operating environment, no conductors or equipment shall be _____ having a deteriorating effect on the conductors or equipment.

   (a) located in damp or wet locations
   (b) exposed to fumes, vapors, liquids, or gases
   (c) exposed to excessive temperatures
   (d) all of these

9. Some cleaning and lubricating compounds can cause severe deterioration of many plastic materials used for insulating and structural applications in equipment.

   (a) True
   (b) False

10. The *NEC* requires that electrical equipment be _____.

    (a) installed in a neat and workmanlike manner
    (b) installed under the supervision of a licensed person
    (c) completed before being inspected
    (d) all of these

11. Accepted industry workmanship practices are described in ANSI/NECA 1-2010, *Standard Practice of Good Workmanship in Electrical Construction*, and other ANSI-approved installation standards.

    (a) True
    (b) False

12. Unused openings other than those intended for the operation of equipment, intended for mounting purposes, or permitted as part of the design for listed equipment shall be _____.

    (a) filled with cable clamps or connectors only
    (b) taped over with electrical tape
    (c) repaired only by welding or brazing in a metal slug
    (d) closed to afford protection substantially equivalent to the wall of the equipment

13. Conductor terminal and splicing devices must be _____ for the conductor material and they must be properly installed and used.

    (a) listed
    (b) approved
    (c) identified
    (d) all of these

14. Connectors and terminals for conductors more finely stranded than Class B and Class C, as shown in Table 10 of Chapter 9, must be _____ for the specific conductor class or classes.

    (a) listed
    (b) approved
    (c) identified
    (d) all of these

15. Many terminations and equipment are either marked with _____, or have that information included in the product's installation instructions.

    (a) an etching tool
    (b) a removable label
    (c) a tightening torque
    (d) the manufacturer's initials

16. Connection of conductors to terminal parts shall ensure a thoroughly good connection without damaging the conductors and shall be made by means of _____.

    (a) solder lugs
    (b) pressure connectors
    (c) splices to flexible leads
    (d) any of these

17. The temperature rating associated with the ampacity of a _____ shall be selected and coordinated so as not to exceed the lowest temperature rating of any connected termination, conductor, or device.

    (a) terminal
    (b) conductor
    (c) device
    (d) all of these

18. Conductor ampacity shall be determined using the _____ column of Table 310.15(B)(16) for circuits rated 100A or less or marked for 14 AWG through 1 AWG conductors, unless the equipment terminals are listed for use with conductors that have higher temperature ratings.

    (a) 30°C
    (b) 60°C
    (c) 75°C
    (d) 90°C

19. For circuits rated 100A or less, when the equipment terminals are listed for use with 75°C conductors, the _____ column of Table 310.15(B)(16) shall be used to determine the ampacity of THHN conductors.

    (a) 30°C
    (b) 60°C
    (c) 75°C
    (d) 90°C

20. On a 4-wire, delta-connected system where the midpoint of one phase winding is grounded, the conductor having the higher phase voltage-to-ground shall be durably and permanently marked by an outer finish that is _____ in color.

    (a) black
    (b) red
    (c) blue
    (d) orange

21. Electrical equipment such as switchboards, switchgear, panelboards, industrial control panels, meter socket enclosures, and motor control centers, that are in other than dwelling units, and are likely to require _____ while energized, shall be field or factory marked to warn qualified persons of potential electric arc flash hazards.

    (a) examination
    (b) adjustment
    (c) servicing or maintenance
    (d) any of these

22. Where required by the *Code*, markings or labels on all electrical equipment shall contain voltage, current, wattage, or other ratings with sufficient durability to withstand _____.

    (a) the voltages encountered
    (b) painting and other finishes applied
    (c) the environment involved
    (d) any lack of planning by the installer

23. Each disconnecting means shall be legibly marked to indicate its purpose unless located and arranged so _____.

    (a) that it can be locked out and tagged
    (b) it is not readily accessible
    (c) the purpose is evident
    (d) that it operates at less than 300 volts-to-ground

24. The *NEC* requires tested series-rated installations of circuit breakers or fuses to be legibly marked in the field to indicate the equipment has been applied with a series combination rating.

    (a) True
    (b) False

25. _____ in other than dwelling units must be legibly field marked with the maximum available fault current, including the date the fault-current calculation was performed and be of sufficient durability to withstand the environment involved.

    (a) Service equipment
    (b) Sub panels
    (c) Motor control centers
    (d) all of these

26. When modifications to the electrical installation affect the maximum available fault current at the service, the maximum available fault current shall be verified or _____ as necessary to ensure the service equipment ratings are sufficient for the maximum available fault current at the line terminals of the equipment.

    (a) recalculated
    (b) increased
    (c) decreased
    (d) adjusted

27. Field markings of maximum available fault current at a service are not required in industrial installations where conditions of maintenance and supervision ensure that only qualified persons service the equipment.

    (a) True
    (b) False

28. Access and _____ shall be provided and maintained about all electrical equipment to permit ready and safe operation and maintenance of such equipment.

    (a) ventilation
    (b) cleanliness
    (c) circulation
    (d) working space

29. A minimum working space depth of _____ to live parts operating at 277 volts-to-ground is required where there are exposed live parts on one side and no live or grounded parts on the other side.

    (a) 2 ft
    (b) 3 ft
    (c) 4 ft
    (d) 6 ft

30. The minimum working space on a circuit that is 120 volts-to-ground, with exposed live parts on one side and no live or grounded parts on the other side of the working space, is _____.

    (a) 1 ft
    (b) 3 ft
    (c) 4 ft
    (d) 6 ft

31. Concrete, brick, or tile walls are considered _____, as applied to working space requirements.

    (a) inconsequential
    (b) in the way
    (c) grounded
    (d) none of these

32. The required working space for access to live parts operating at 300 volts-to-ground, where there are exposed live parts on one side and grounded parts on the other side, is _____.

    (a) 3 ft
    (b) 3½ ft
    (c) 4 ft
    (d) 4½ ft

33. The required working space for access to live parts operating at 300 volts-to-ground, where there are exposed live parts on both sides of the workspace is _____.

    (a) 3 ft
    (b) 3½ ft
    (c) 4 ft
    (d) 4½ ft

34. Working space distances for enclosed live parts shall be measured from the _____ of equipment or apparatus, if the live parts are enclosed.

    (a) enclosure
    (b) opening
    (c) a or b
    (d) none of these

35. The working space in front of the electric equipment shall not be less than _____ wide, or the width of the equipment, whichever is greater.

    (a) 15 in.
    (b) 30 in.
    (c) 40 in.
    (d) 60 in.

36. Equipment associated with the electrical installation can be located above or below other electrical equipment within their working space when the associated equipment does not extend more than _____ from the front of the electrical equipment.

    (a) 3 in.
    (b) 6 in.
    (c) 12 in.
    (d) 30 in.

37. The minimum height of working spaces about electrical equipment, switchboards, panelboards, or motor control centers operating at 600V, nominal, or less and likely to require examination, adjustment, servicing, or maintenance while energized shall be 6½ ft or the height of the equipment, whichever is greater, except for service equipment or panelboards in existing dwelling units that do not exceed 200A.

    (a) True
    (b) False

38. Working space shall not be used for _____.

    (a) storage
    (b) raceways
    (c) lighting
    (d) accessibility

39. When normally enclosed live parts are exposed for inspection or servicing, the working space, if in a passageway or general open space, shall be suitably _____.

    (a) accessible
    (b) guarded
    (c) open
    (d) enclosed

40. For equipment rated 1,200A or more and over 6 ft wide that contains overcurrent devices, switching devices, or control devices, there shall be one entrance to and egress from the required working space not less than 24 in. wide and _____ high at each end of the working space.

    (a) 5½ ft
    (b) 6 ft
    (c) 6½ ft
    (d) any of these

41. For equipment rated 800A or more that contains overcurrent devices, switching devices, or control devices; and where the entrance to the working space has a personnel door less than 25 ft from the working space, the door shall _____.

    (a) open either in or out with simple pressure and shall not have any lock
    (b) open in the direction of egress and be equipped with listed panic hardware
    (c) be equipped with a locking means
    (d) be equipped with an electronic opener

42. Illumination shall be provided for all working spaces about service equipment, switchboards, switchgear, panelboards, and motor control centers _____.

    (a) over 600V
    (b) located indoors
    (c) rated 1,200A or more
    (d) using automatic means of control

43. All switchboards, panelboards, and motor control centers shall be _____.

    (a) located in dedicated spaces
    (b) protected from damage
    (c) in weatherproof enclosures
    (d) a and b

44. The minimum height of dedicated equipment space for motor control centers installed indoors is _____ above the enclosure, or to the structural ceiling, whichever is lower.

    (a) 3 ft
    (b) 5 ft
    (c) 6 ft
    (d) 6½ ft

## Article 110 | Requirements for Electrical Installations

45. For indoor installations, heating, cooling, or ventilating equipment shall not be installed in the dedicated space above a panelboard or switchboard.

    (a) True
    (b) False

46. The dedicated equipment space for electrical equipment that is required for panelboards installed indoors is measured from the floor to a height of _____ above the equipment, or to the structural ceiling, whichever is lower.

    (a) 3 ft
    (b) 6 ft
    (c) 12 ft
    (d) 30 ft

47. The dedicated space above a panelboard extends to a dropped or suspended ceiling, which is considered a structural ceiling.

    (a) True
    (b) False

48. Electrical equipment rooms or enclosures housing electrical apparatus that are controlled by a lock(s) shall be considered _____ to qualified persons.

    (a) readily accessible
    (b) accessible
    (c) available
    (d) none of these

49. To guard live parts operating at 50V must be guarded by being _____.

    (a) located in a room accessible only to qualified persons
    (b) located on a balcony accessible only to qualified persons
    (c) elevated 8 ft or more above the floor or other working surface for 50V to 300V
    (d) any of these

50. Live parts of electrical equipment operating at _____ or more shall be guarded against accidental contact by approved enclosures or by suitable permanent, substantial partitions or screens arranged so that only qualified persons have access to the space within reach of the live parts.

    (a) 20V
    (b) 30V
    (c) 50V
    (d) 100V

51. In locations where electrical equipment is likely to be exposed to _____, enclosures or guards shall be so arranged and of such strength as to prevent such damage.

    (a) corrosion
    (b) physical damage
    (c) magnetic fields
    (d) weather

52. Entrances to rooms and other guarded locations containing exposed live parts shall be marked with conspicuous _____ forbidding unqualified persons to enter.

    (a) warning signs
    (b) alarms
    (c) a and b
    (d) neither a nor b

53. The term "rainproof" is typically used in conjunction with Enclosure-Type Number _____.

    (a) 3
    (b) 3R
    (c) 3RX
    (d) b and c

# CHAPTER 2
# WIRING AND PROTECTION

## Introduction to Chapter 2—Wiring and Protection

Chapter 2 provides general rules for wiring and for the protection of conductors. The rules in this chapter apply to all electrical installations covered by the *NEC*—except as modified in Chapters 5, 6, and 7 [90.3].

Communications systems (Chapter 8 systems) aren't subject to the general requirements of Chapters 1 through 4, or the special requirements of Chapters 5 through 7, unless there's a specific reference in Chapter 8 to a rule in Chapters 1 through 7 [90.3].

Chapter 2 is primarily concerned with correctly sizing and protecting circuits. Every article in this chapter deals with a different aspect of this purpose. This differs from the purpose of Chapter 3, which is to correctly install the conductors that make up those circuits.

Chapter 1 introduced you to the *NEC* and provided a solid foundation for understanding the *Code*. Chapters 2 (Wiring and Protection) and 3 (Wiring Methods and Materials) continue building the foundation for applying the *NEC*. Chapter 4 applies the preceding chapters to general equipment. It's beneficial to learn the first four chapters of the *Code* in a sequential manner because each of the first four chapters builds on the one before it. Once you've become familiar with the first four chapters, you can learn the next four in any order you wish.

- **Article 200—Use and Identification of Grounded [Neutral] Conductors.** This article contains the requirements for the use and identification of the grounded conductor and its terminals.

    **Author's Comment:**
    - Throughout this workbook and the corresponding textbook (*Mike Holt's Illustrated Guide to Understanding the National Electrical Code, Volume 1, based on the 2014 NEC*), we use the term "neutral" when referring to the grounded conductor when the application isn't related to PV systems or corner-grounded delta-connected systems.

- **Article 210—Branch Circuits.** Article 210 contains the requirements for branch circuits, such as conductor sizing, identification, and GFCI protection, as well as receptacle and lighting outlet requirements.
- **Article 215—Feeders.** This article covers the requirements for the installation and ampacity of feeders.

- **Article 220—Branch-Circuit, Feeder, and Service Calculations.** Article 220 provides the requirements for calculating the minimum size for branch circuits, feeders, and services. This article also aids in determining related factors such as the number of receptacles on a circuit in nondwelling installations, and the minimum number of branch circuits required.

- **Article 225—Outside Branch Circuits and Feeders.** This article covers the installation requirements for equipment, including branch circuits and feeders located outside (overhead and underground) that run on or between buildings, poles, and other structures on the premises.

- **Article 230—Services.** Article 230 covers the installation requirements for service conductors and equipment. It's very important to know where the service begins and ends when applying Article 230.

    **Author's Comment:**
    - Conductors from a battery, uninterruptible power supply, solar PV system, generator, or transformer aren't service conductors; they're feeder conductors.

- **Article 240—Overcurrent Protection.** This article provides the requirements for overcurrent protection and overcurrent devices. Overcurrent protection for conductors and equipment is provided to open the circuit if the current reaches a value that'll cause an excessive or dangerous temperature on the conductors or conductor insulation.

- **Article 250—Grounding and Bonding.** Article 250 covers the grounding requirements for providing a path to the earth to reduce overvoltage from lightning, and the bonding requirements for a low-impedance fault current path necessary to facilitate the operation of overcurrent devices in the event of a ground fault.

- **Article 285—Surge Protective Devices (SPDs).** This article covers the general, installation, and connection requirements for surge protective devices (SPDs) permanently installed on both the line side and load side of service equipment.

# ARTICLE 200 — USE AND IDENTIFICATION OF GROUNDED [NEUTRAL] CONDUCTORS

## Introduction to Article 200—Use and Identification of Grounded [Neutral] Conductors

This article contains the requirements for the identification of the grounded [neutral] conductor and its terminals. Article 100 contains definitions for both "Grounded Conductor" and "Neutral Conductor." In some cases, both of these terms apply to the same conductor. Figures 200–1 and 200–2

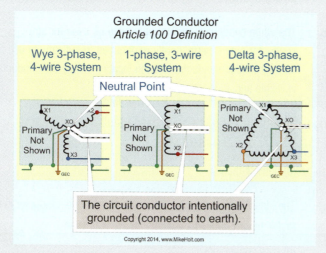

Figure 200–1

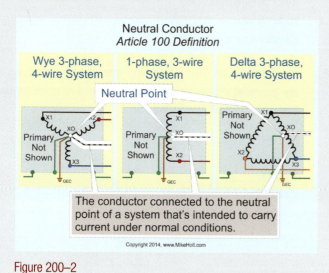

Figure 200–2

In a system that produces direct current, such as a PV system, the "grounded conductor" isn't a neutral conductor. Figure 200–3

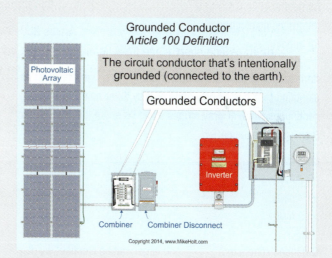

Figure 200–3

### Author's Comment:

- We use the term "neutral" when referring to the grounded conductor when the application isn't related to PV systems or corner-grounded delta-connected systems.

# Article 200 | Use and Identification of Grounded [Neutral] Conductors

**Please use the 2014 Code book to answer the following questions.**

1. The continuity of a grounded conductor shall not depend on a connection to a _____.

   (a) metallic enclosure
   (b) raceway
   (c) cable armor
   (d) all of these

2. _____ conductors shall not be used for more than one branch circuit, one multiwire branch circuit, or more than one set of ungrounded feeder conductors except as allowed elsewhere in the *Code*.

   (a) Equipment grounding
   (b) neutral
   (c) grounding electrode
   (d) bonding

3. An insulated grounded conductor of _____ or smaller shall be identified by a continuous white or gray outer finish, or by three continuous white or gray stripes along its entire length on other than green insulation.

   (a) 8 AWG
   (b) 6 AWG
   (c) 4 AWG
   (d) 3 AWG

4. Grounded conductors _____ and larger can be identified by distinctive white or gray markings at their terminations.

   (a) 10 AWG
   (b) 8 AWG
   (c) 6 AWG
   (d) 4 AWG

5. If grounded conductors of different voltage systems are installed in the same raceway, cable, or enclosure, each neutral conductor must be identified to distinguish the systems by _____.

   (a) a continuous white or gray outer finish for one system
   (b) a neutral conductor with a different continuous white or gray outer finish or white or gray with a stripe for one system
   (c) other identification allowed by 200.6(a) or (b) that distinguishes each system from other systems
   (d) any of these

6. The white conductor within a cable can be used for a(n) _____ conductor where permanently reidentified to indicate its use as an ungrounded conductor at each location where the conductor is visible and accessible.

   (a) grounded
   (b) ungrounded
   (c) a and b
   (d) none of these

7. The identification of _____ to which a grounded conductor is to be connected shall be substantially white in color.

   (a) wire connectors
   (b) circuit breakers
   (c) terminals
   (d) ground rods

8. Receptacles shall have the terminal intended for connection to the grounded conductor identified by a metal or metal coating that is substantially _____ in color.

   (a) green
   (b) white
   (c) gray
   (d) b or c

9. The screw shell of a luminaire or lampholder shall be connected to the _____.

   (a) grounded conductor
   (b) ungrounded conductor
   (c) equipment grounding conductor
   (d) forming shell terminal

10. No _____ shall be attached to any terminal or lead so as to reverse the designated polarity.

    (a) grounded conductor
    (b) grounding conductor
    (c) ungrounded conductor
    (d) grounding connector

## Notes

# ARTICLE 210
# BRANCH CIRCUITS

## Introduction to Article 210—Branch Circuits

This article contains the requirements for branch circuits, such as conductor sizing and identification, GFCI protection, and receptacle and lighting outlet requirements. It consists of three parts:

- **Part I. General Provisions**
- **Part II. Branch-Circuit Ratings**
- **Part III. Required Outlets**

Table 210.2 identifies specific-purpose branch circuits. The provisions for branch circuits that supply equipment listed in Table 210.2 amend or supplement the provisions given in Article 210 for branch circuits, so it's important to be aware of the contents of this table.

The following sections contain a few key items on which to spend extra time as you study Article 210:

- **210.4—Multiwire Branch Circuits.** The conductors of these circuits must originate from the same panel.

- **210.8—GFCI Protection.** Crawl spaces, unfinished basements, and boathouses are just some of the many locations that require GFCI protection.

- **210.11—Branch Circuits Required.** With three subheadings, 210.11 gives summarized requirements for the number of branch circuits in certain situations, states that a load calculated on a VA per area basis must be evenly proportioned, and covers some minimum branch circuit rules for dwelling units.

- **210.12—Arc-Fault Circuit-Interrupter Protection.** An arc-fault circuit interrupter (AFCI) is a device intended to de-energize a circuit when it detects the current waveform characteristics unique to an arcing fault. The purpose of an AFCI is to protect against a fire hazard, whereas the purpose of a GFCI is to protect people against electrocution.

- **210.19—Conductors—Minimum Ampacity and Size.** This section covers the basic rules for sizing branch-circuit conductors, including continuous and noncontinuous loads.

- **210.21—Outlet Devices.** Outlet devices must have an ampere rating at least as large as the load to be served, as well as following the other rules of this section.

- **210.22 and 210.23—Permissible Loads.** This is intended to prevent a circuit overload from occurring because of an improper design and planning of circuitry.

# Article 210 | Branch Circuits

- **210.52—Dwelling Unit Receptacle Outlets.** There are some specific receptacle spacing rules and branch-circuit requirements for dwelling units that don't apply to other occupancies.

Mastering the branch-circuit requirements in Article 210 will give you a jump-start toward completing installations that are free of *Code* violations.

**Please use the 2014 *Code* book to answer the following questions.**

1. The rating of a branch circuit shall be determined by the rating of the _____.

   (a) ampacity of the largest device connected to the circuit
   (b) average of the ampacity of all devices
   (c) branch-circuit overcurrent device
   (d) ampacity of the branch-circuit conductors according to Table 310.15(B)(16)

2. A three-phase, 4-wire, _____ power system used to supply power to nonlinear loads may necessitate that the power system design allow for the possibility of high harmonic currents on the neutral conductor.

   (a) wye-connected
   (b) delta-connected
   (c) wye/delta-connected
   (d) none of these

3. Each multiwire branch circuit shall be provided with a means that will simultaneously disconnect all _____ conductors at the point where the branch circuit originates.

   (a) circuit
   (b) grounded
   (c) grounding
   (d) ungrounded

4. Multiwire branch circuits shall _____.

   (a) supply only line-to-neutral loads
   (b) not be permitted in dwelling units
   (c) have their conductors originate from different panelboards
   (d) none of these

5. The ungrounded and grounded conductors of each _____ shall be grouped by wire ties or similar means at the panelboard or other point of origination.

   (a) branch circuit
   (b) multiwire branch circuit
   (c) feeder circuit
   (d) service-entrance conductor

6. Where more than one nominal voltage system supplies branch circuits in a building, each _____ conductor of a branch circuit shall be identified by phase and system at all termination, connection, and splice points.

   (a) grounded
   (b) ungrounded
   (c) grounding
   (d) all of these

7. In dwelling units, the voltage between conductors that supply the terminals of _____ shall not exceed 120V, nominal.

   (a) luminaires
   (b) cord-and-plug-connected loads of 1,440 VA or less
   (c) cord-and-plug-connected loads of more than ¼ hp
   (d) a and b

8. The GFCI protection required by 210.8(A), (B), (C), and (d) must be _____.

   (a) the circuit breaker type only
   (b) accessible
   (c) readily accessible
   (d) concealed

9. All 15A and 20A, 125V receptacles installed in bathrooms of _____ shall have ground-fault circuit-interrupter (GFCI) protection for personnel.

   (a) guest rooms in hotels/motels
   (b) dwelling units
   (c) office buildings
   (d) all of these

10. GFCI protection shall be provided for all 15A and 20A, 125V receptacles installed in a dwelling unit _____.

    (a) attic
    (b) garage
    (c) laundry room
    (d) all of these

11. GFCI protection shall be provided for all 15A and 20A, 125V receptacles in dwelling unit accessory buildings that have a floor located at or below grade level not intended as _____ and limited to storage areas, work areas, or similar use.

    (a) habitable rooms
    (b) finished space
    (c) a or b
    (d) none of these

12. All 15A and 20A, 125V receptacles located outdoors of dwelling units, including receptacles installed under the eaves of roofs, must be GFCI protected except for a receptacle that's supplied by a branch circuit dedicated to _____ if the receptacle isn't readily accessible and the equipment or receptacle has ground-fault protection of equipment (GFPE) [426.28 or 427.22].

    (a) electric snow-melting or deicing equipment
    (b) pipeline and vessel heating equipment
    (c) holiday decorative lighting
    (d) a or b

13. All 15A and 20A, 125V receptacles installed in crawl spaces at or below grade level of dwelling units shall have GFCI protection.

    (a) True
    (b) False

14. All 15A and 20A, 125V receptacles installed in _____ of dwelling units shall have GFCI protection.

    (a) unfinished attics
    (b) finished attics
    (c) unfinished basements and crawl spaces
    (d) finished basements

15. GFCI protection shall be provided for all 15A and 20A, 125V receptacles _____ in dwelling unit kitchens.

    (a) installed to serve the countertop surfaces
    (b) within 6 ft of the sink
    (c) for all receptacles
    (d) that are readily accessible

16. GFCI protection shall be provided for all 15A and 20A, 125V receptacles installed within 6 ft of all dwelling unit sinks located in _____.

    (a) laundry rooms
    (b) bathrooms
    (c) dens
    (d) all of these

17. All 15A and 20A, 125V receptacles installed in dwelling unit boathouses shall have GFCI protection.

    (a) True
    (b) False

18. All 15A and 20A, 125V receptacles _____ of commercial occupancies shall have GFCI protection.

    (a) in bathrooms
    (b) on rooftops
    (c) in kitchens
    (d) all of these

## Article 210 | Branch Circuits

19. In other than dwelling units, GFCI protection shall be provided for all outdoor 15A and 20A, 125V receptacles.

    (a) True
    (b) False

20. All 15A and 20A, 125V receptacles located outdoors or on rooftops in locations other than dwelling units must be GFCI protected except for a receptacle that's supplied by a branch circuit dedicated to _____ if the receptacle isn't readily accessible and the equipment or receptacle has ground-fault protection of equipment (GFPE) [426.28 and 427.22].

    (a) electric snow-melting or deicing equipment
    (b) pipeline and vessel heating equipment
    (c) holiday decorative lighting
    (d) a or b

21. In other than dwelling locations, GFCI protection is required in _____.

    (a) indoor wet locations
    (b) locker rooms with associated showering facilities
    (c) garages, service bays, and similar areas other than vehicle exhibition halls and showrooms
    (d) all of these

22. All 15A and 20A, 125V receptacles installed within 6 ft of the outside edge of a sink in locations other than dwelling units must be _____.

    (a) AFCI protected
    (b) GFCI protected
    (c) tamperproof
    (d) a and b

23. In industrial laboratories, 15A and 20A, 125V receptacles within 6 ft. of a sink used to supply equipment where removal of power would introduce a greater hazard aren't required to be GFCI protected.

    (a) True
    (b) False

24. 15A and 20A, 125V receptacles located in patient bed locations of general care or critical care areas of health care facilities, other than those covered by 210.8(B)(1), aren't required to be GFCI protected.

    (a) True
    (b) False

25. All 15A and 20A, 125V receptacles installed indoors, in other than dwelling units, in wet locations must be GFCI protected.

    (a) True
    (b) False

26. All 15A and 20A, 125V receptacles installed in locker rooms with associated showering facilities must be GFCI protected.

    (a) True
    (b) False

27. Ground-fault circuit-interrupter protection shall be provided for outlets not exceeding 240V that supply boat hoists installed in dwelling unit locations.

    (a) True
    (b) False

28. Two or more _____ small-appliance branch circuits shall be provided to supply power for receptacle outlets in the dwelling unit kitchen, dining room, breakfast room, pantry, or similar dining areas.

    (a) 15A
    (b) 20A
    (c) 30A
    (d) either 20A or 30A

29. There shall be a minimum of one _____ branch circuit for the laundry outlet(s) required by 210.52(F).

    (a) 15A
    (b) 20A
    (c) 30A
    (d) b and c

30. An individual 20A branch circuit can supply a single dwelling unit bathroom for receptacle outlet(s) and other equipment within the same bathroom.

    (a) True
    (b) False

31. All 15A or 20A, 120V branch circuits that supply outlets or devices in dwelling unit kitchens, family rooms, dining rooms, living rooms, parlors, libraries, dens, bedrooms, sunrooms, recreation rooms, closets, hallways, laundry areas, or similar rooms or areas shall be AFCI protected by a listed arc-fault circuit interrupter.

    (a) True
    (b) False

32. Where branch-circuit wiring in a dwelling unit is modified, replaced, or extended in any of the areas specified in 210.12(A), the branch circuit must be protected by a _____.

    (a) listed combination AFCI located at the origin of the branch circuit
    (b) listed outlet branch-circuit AFCI located at the first receptacle outlet of the existing branch circuit
    (c) GFCI circuit breaker or receptacle
    (d) a or b

33. The recommended maximum total voltage drop on branch-circuit conductors is _____ percent.

    (a) 2
    (b) 3
    (c) 4
    (d) 6

34. Where a branch circuit supplies continuous loads, or any combination of continuous and noncontinuous loads, the rating of the overcurrent device shall not be less than the noncontinuous load plus 125 percent of the continuous load.

    (a) True
    (b) False

35. A single receptacle installed on an individual branch circuit shall have an ampere rating not less than that of the branch circuit.

    (a) True
    (b) False

36. The total rating of utilization equipment fastened in place shall not exceed _____ percent of the branch-circuit ampere rating where lighting units and cord-and-plug-connected utilization equipment are supplied.

    (a) 50
    (b) 75
    (c) 100
    (d) 125

37. _____ in dwelling units shall supply only loads within that dwelling unit or loads associated only with that dwelling unit.

    (a) Service-entrance conductors
    (b) Ground-fault protection
    (c) Branch circuits
    (d) none of these

38. In multi-occupancy buildings, branch circuits for _____ shall not be supplied from equipment that supplies an individual dwelling unit or tenant space.

    (a) a central alarm
    (b) parking lot lighting
    (c) common area purposes
    (d) all of these

39. Receptacle outlets installed for a specific appliance in a dwelling unit, such as laundry equipment, shall be located within _____ of the intended location of the appliance.

    (a) sight
    (b) 3 ft
    (c) 6 ft
    (d) none of these

40. The *Code* provides rules for the minimum number of receptacle outlets required in a dwelling unit. The minimum required receptacle outlets shall be in addition to receptacle outlets that are _____.

    (a) part of a luminaire or appliance
    (b) controlled by a wall switch for use as required illumination
    (c) located more than 5½ ft above the floor
    (d) all of these

41. When applying the general provisions for receptacle spacing to the rooms of a dwelling unit which require receptacles in the wall space, no point along the floor line in any wall space of a dwelling unit may be more than _____ from an outlet.

    (a) 6 ft
    (b) 8 ft
    (c) 10 ft
    (d) 12 ft

42. In a dwelling unit, each wall space _____ or wider requires a receptacle.

    (a) 2 ft
    (b) 3 ft
    (c) 4 ft
    (d) 5 ft

43. In dwelling units, when determining the spacing of receptacle outlets, _____ on exterior walls shall not be considered wall space.

    (a) fixed panels
    (b) fixed glass
    (c) sliding panels
    (d) all of these

44. Receptacle outlets in or on floors shall not be counted as part of the required number of receptacle outlets for dwelling unit wall spaces, unless they are located within _____ in. of the wall.

    (a) 6
    (b) 12
    (c) 18
    (d) 24

45. Receptacles installed for countertop surfaces as required by 210.52(C) shall not be used to meet the receptacle requirements for wall space as required by 210.52(A).

    (a) True
    (b) False

46. In dwelling units, outdoor receptacles can be connected to one of the 20A small-appliance branch circuits.

    (a) True
    (b) False

47. A receptacle connected to one of the dwelling unit small-appliance branch circuits can be used to supply an electric clock.

    (a) True
    (b) False

48. A receptacle connected to a dwelling unit small-appliance circuit can supply gas-fired ranges, ovens, or counter-mounted cooking units.

    (a) True
    (b) False

49. A receptacle outlet shall be installed at each dwelling unit kitchen wall countertop space that is 12 in. or wider and receptacle outlets shall be installed so that no point along the wall line is more than _____ in., measured horizontally from a receptacle outlet in that space.

    (a) 10
    (b) 12
    (c) 16
    (d) 24

50. In dwelling units, at least one receptacle outlet shall be installed at each peninsular countertop having a long dimension of _____ in. or greater, and a short dimension of _____ in. or greater.

    (a) 12, 24
    (b) 24, 12
    (c) 24, 48
    (d) 48, 24

51. For the purpose of determining the placement of receptacles in a dwelling unit kitchen, a(n) _____ countertop is measured from the connecting edge.

    (a) island
    (b) usable
    (c) peninsular
    (d) cooking

52. When breaks occur in dwelling unit kitchen countertop spaces for rangetops, refrigerators or sinks, each countertop surface shall be considered a separate counter space for determining receptacle placement.

    (a) True
    (b) False

53. Kitchen and dining room countertop receptacle outlets in dwelling units shall be installed above the countertop surface, and not more than _____ in. above the countertop.

    (a) 12
    (b) 18
    (c) 20
    (d) 24

54. Receptacle outlets can be installed below the countertop surface in dwelling units when necessary for the physically impaired, or if there is no means available to mount a receptacle above an island or peninsular countertop.

    (a) True
    (b) False

55. In dwelling unit bathrooms, not less than one 15A or 20A, 125V receptacle outlet must be installed within _____ from the outside edge of each bathroom basin.

    (a) 20 in.
    (b) 3 ft
    (c) 4 ft
    (d) 6 ft

56. The receptacle outlet for a dwelling unit bathroom must be located on a _____ adjacent to the basin or basin counter surface, or on the side or face of the basin cabinet, and never more than 12 in. below the top of the basin.

    (a) wall
    (b) partition
    (c) light fixture
    (d) a or b

57. Receptacle outlet assemblies listed for the application can be installed in countertops of dwelling unit bathrooms.

    (a) True
    (b) False

58. In dwelling units, the required bathroom receptacle outlet can be installed on the side or face of the basin cabinet if no lower than _____ in. below the top of the basin.

    (a) 12
    (b) 18
    (c) 24
    (d) 36

59. There shall be a minimum of _____ receptacle(s) installed outdoors at a one-family or each unit of a two-family dwelling unit.

    (a) one
    (b) two
    (c) three
    (d) four

60. At least one receptacle outlet not more than _____ above a balcony, deck, or porch shall be installed at each balcony, deck, or porch that is attached to and accessible from a dwelling unit.

    (a) 3 ft
    (b) 6½ ft
    (c) 8 ft
    (d) 24 in.

61. A laundry receptacle outlet shall not be required in each dwelling unit of a multifamily building, if laundry facilities are provided on the premises for all building occupants.

    (a) True
    (b) False

62. For a one-family dwelling, at least one receptacle outlet shall be installed in each _____.

    (a) basement
    (b) attached garage
    (c) detached garage or accessory building with electric power
    (d) all of these

63. Where a portion of the dwelling unit basement is finished into one or more habitable rooms, each separate unfinished portion shall have a receptacle outlet installed.

    (a) True
    (b) False

Article 210 | Branch Circuits

64. Hallways in dwelling units that are _____ long or longer require a receptacle outlet.

    (a) 6 ft
    (b) 8 ft
    (c) 10 ft
    (d) 12 ft

65. Foyers with an area greater than _____ sq ft must have a receptacle located in each wall space 3 ft or more in width unbroken by doorways, windows next to doors that extend to the floor, and similar openings.

    (a) 40
    (b) 60
    (c) 80
    (d) 100

66. Guest rooms or guest suites provided with permanent provisions for _____ shall have receptacle outlets installed in accordance with all of the applicable requirements for a dwelling unit in accordance with 210.52.

    (a) whirlpool tubs
    (b) bathing
    (c) cooking
    (d) internet access

67. Receptacles installed behind a bed in the guest rooms in hotels and motels shall be located to prevent the bed from contacting an attachment plug, or the receptacle shall be provided with a suitable guard.

    (a) True
    (b) False

68. The number of receptacle outlets for guest rooms in hotels and motels shall not be less than that required for a dwelling unit. These receptacles can be located to be convenient for permanent furniture layout, but at least _____ receptacle outlet(s) shall be readily accessible.

    (a) one
    (b) two
    (c) three
    (d) four

69. At least one 125V, 15A or 20A receptacle outlet shall be installed within 18 in. of the top of a show window for each _____ linear ft, or major fraction thereof, of show-window area measured horizontally at its maximum width.

    (a) 10
    (b) 12
    (c) 18
    (d) 24

70. A 15A or 20A, 125V receptacle outlet shall be located within 25 ft of heating, air-conditioning, and refrigeration equipment for _____ occupancies.

    (a) dwelling
    (b) commercial
    (c) industrial
    (d) all of these

71. At least one wall switch-controlled lighting outlet must be installed in every habitable room and bathroom of a dwelling unit.

    (a) True
    (b) False

72. In rooms other than kitchens and bathrooms of dwelling units, one or more receptacles controlled by a wall switch shall be permitted in lieu of _____.

    (a) lighting outlets
    (b) luminaires
    (c) the receptacles required by 210.52(b) and (D)
    (d) all of these

73. In dwelling units, lighting outlets can be controlled by occupancy sensors where equipped with a _____ that will allow the sensor to function as a wall switch.

    (a) manual override
    (b) photo cell
    (c) sensor
    (d) none of these

74. In a dwelling unit, illumination from a lighting outlet shall be provided on the exterior side of each outdoor entrance or exit that has grade-level access.

    (a) True
    (b) False

75. Where a lighting outlet(s) is installed for interior stairways, there shall be a wall switch at each floor level and each landing level that includes an entryway where the stairway between floor levels has six risers or more unless remote, central, or automatic control is used.

    (a) True
    (b) False

76. In a dwelling unit, illumination for outdoor entrances that have grade-level access can be controlled by _____.

    (a) remote
    (b) central
    (c) automatic control
    (d) any of these

77. In a dwelling unit, at least one lighting outlet _____ shall be located at the point of entry to the attic, underfloor space, utility room, or basement where these spaces are used for storage or contain equipment requiring servicing.

    (a) that is unswitched
    (b) containing a switch
    (c) controlled by a wall switch
    (d) b or c

78. At least one wall switch-controlled lighting outlet shall be installed in every habitable room and bathroom of a guest room or guest suite of hotels, motels, and similar occupancies. A receptacle outlet controlled by a wall switch may be used to meet this requirement in other than _____.

    (a) bathrooms
    (b) kitchens
    (c) sleeping areas
    (d) a and b

79. For attics and underfloor spaces in other than dwelling units that contain heating, air-conditioning, and refrigeration equipment requiring servicing, at least one lighting outlet containing a switch or controlled by a wall switch shall be installed _____ the equipment requiring servicing.

    (a) at
    (b) near
    (c) a or b
    (d) none of these

Notes

# ARTICLE 215 — FEEDERS

## Introduction to Article 215—Feeders

Article 215 covers the rules for the installation and ampacity of feeders. The requirements for feeders have some similarities to those for branch circuits, but in some ways, feeders bear a resemblance to service conductors. It's important to understand the distinct differences between these three types of circuits in order to correctly apply the *Code* requirements.

Feeders are the conductors between the service equipment, the separately derived system, or other supply source, and the final branch-circuit overcurrent device. Conductors past the final overcurrent device protecting the circuit and the outlet are branch-circuit conductors and fall within the scope of Article 210 [Article 100 Definitions].

Service conductors are the conductors from the service point of the electric utility to the service disconnecting means [Article 100 Definition]. If there's no serving utility, and the electrical power is derived from a generator or other on-site power source, then the conductors from the supply source are defined as feeders and there are no service conductors.

It's easy to be confused between feeder, branch circuit, and service conductors, so it's important to evaluate each installation carefully using the Article 100 Definitions to be sure the correct *NEC* rules are followed.

Please use the 2014 *Code* book to answer the following questions.

1. The minimum feeder conductor ampacity must be no less than the noncontinuous load plus _____ percent of the continuous load, and not less than the maximum load after the application of adjustment and correction factors.

    (a) 80
    (b) 100
    (c) 125
    (d) 150

2. Feeder neutral conductors shall be permitted to be sized at _____ percent of the continuous and noncontinuous load.

    (a) 80
    (b) 100
    (c) 125
    (d) 150

3. When a feeder supplies _____ in which equipment grounding conductors are required, the feeder shall include or provide an equipment grounding conductor.

(a) an equipment disconnecting means
(b) electrical systems
(c) branch circuits
(d) electric-discharge lighting equipment

4. Ground-fault protection of equipment shall be required for a feeder disconnect if the disconnect is rated _____.

(a) 800A, 208V
(b) 800A, 480V
(c) 1,000A, 208V
(d) 1,000A, 480V

5. Ground-fault protection of equipment shall not be required at a feeder disconnect if ground-fault protection of equipment is provided on the _____ side of the feeder and on the load side of any transformer supplying the feeder.

(a) load
(b) supply
(c) service
(d) none of these

6. Where a premises wiring system contains feeders supplied from more than one nominal voltage system, each ungrounded conductor of a feeder shall be identified by phase or line and system by _____, or other approved means.

(a) color coding
(b) marking tape
(c) tagging
(d) any of these

# ARTICLE 220 — BRANCH-CIRCUIT, FEEDER, AND SERVICE CALCULATIONS

## Introduction to Article 220—Branch-Circuit, Feeder, and Service Calculations

This five-part article focuses on the requirements for calculating the minimum size of branch circuit, feeder, and service conductors.

Part I describes the layout of Article 220 and provides a table of where other types of load calculations can be found in the *NEC*. Part II provides requirements for branch-circuit calculations and for specific types of branch circuits. Part III covers the requirements for feeder and service calculations, using what's commonly called the "standard method of calculation." Part IV provides optional calculations that can be used in place of the standard calculations provided in Parts II and III—if your installation meets certain requirements. Farm Load Calculations are discussed in Part V of the article.

In many cases, either the standard method (Part III) or the optional method (Part IV) can be used; however, these two methods don't yield identical results. In fact, sometimes these two answers may be diverse enough to call for different service sizes. There's nothing to say that either answer is right or wrong. If taking an exam, read the instructions carefully to be sure which method the test wants you to use. As you work through Article 220, be sure to study the illustrations in *Mike Holt's Illustrated Guide to Understanding the National Electrical Code, Volume 1, based on the 2014 NEC* textbook to help you fully understand it. Also be sure to review the examples in Annex D of the *NEC* to provide more practice with these calculations.

Please use the 2014 *Code* book to answer the following questions.

1. When calculations in Article 220 result in a fraction of an ampere that is less than _____, such fractions can be dropped.

    (a) 0.49
    (b) 0.50
    (c) 0.51
    (d) 0.80

2. The 3 VA per-square-foot general lighting load for dwelling units does not include _____.

    (a) open porches
    (b) garages
    (c) unused or unfinished spaces not adaptable for future use
    (d) all of these

# Article 220 | Branch-Circuit, Feeder, and Service Calculations

3. Where fixed multioutlet assemblies are used in other than dwelling units or the guest rooms of hotels or motels, each _____ or fraction thereof of each separate and continuous length shall be considered as one outlet of not less than 180 VA where appliances are unlikely to be used simultaneously.

   (a) 5 ft
   (b) 5½ ft
   (c) 6 ft
   (d) 6½ ft

4. For other than dwelling occupancies, banks, or office buildings, each receptacle outlet shall be calculated at not less than _____ VA.

   (a) 90
   (b) 180
   (c) 270
   (d) 360

5. A device comprised of _____ or more receptacles shall be calculated at not less than 90 VA per receptacle.

   (a) one
   (b) two
   (c) three
   (d) four

6. The 3 VA per-square-foot general lighting load for dwelling units includes general-use receptacles and lighting outlets.

   (a) True
   (b) False

7. Branch circuits that supply lighting units that have ballasts, autotransformers, or LED drivers shall have the calculated load based on _____ of the units, not to the total wattage of the lamps.

   (a) 50 percent of the rating
   (b) 80 percent of the rating
   (c) the total ampere rating
   (d) 150 percent of the rating

8. The minimum feeder load for show-window lighting is _____ per linear foot.

   (a) 180 VA
   (b) 200 VA
   (c) 300 VA
   (d) 400 VA

9. For other than dwelling units or guest rooms of hotels or motels, the feeder and service calculation for track lighting shall be calculated at 150 VA for every _____ ft of lighting track or fraction thereof unless the track is supplied through a device that limits the current to the track.

   (a) 1
   (b) 2
   (c) 3
   (d) 4

10. Feeder and service loads for fixed electric space heating shall be calculated at _____ percent of the total connected load.

    (a) 80
    (b) 100
    (c) 125
    (d) 200

11. A dwelling unit containing three 120V small-appliance branch circuits has a calculated load of _____ VA for the small appliance circuits.

    (a) 1,500
    (b) 3,000
    (c) 4,500
    (d) 6,000

12. A dwelling unit containing two 120V laundry branch circuits has a calculated load of _____ VA for the laundry circuits.

    (a) 1,500
    (b) 3,000
    (c) 4,500
    (d) 6,000

13. When sizing a feeder for the fixed appliance loads in dwelling units, a demand factor of 75 percent of the total nameplate ratings can be applied if there are _____ or more appliances fastened in place on the same feeder.

    (a) two
    (b) three
    (c) four
    (d) five

14. The load for electric clothes dryers in a dwelling unit shall be _____ watts or the nameplate rating, whichever is larger, per dryer.

    (a) 1,500
    (b) 4,500
    (c) 5,000
    (d) 8,000

15. Using the standard load calculation method, the feeder demand factor for five household clothes dryers is _____ percent.

    (a) 50
    (b) 70
    (c) 85
    (d) 100

16. Table 220.56 may be applied to determine the load for thermostatically controlled or intermittently used _____ and other kitchen equipment in a commercial kitchen.

    (a) commercial electric cooking equipment
    (b) dishwasher booster heaters
    (c) water heaters
    (d) all of these

17. The demand factors of Table 220.56 apply to space heating, ventilating, or air-conditioning equipment.

    (a) True
    (b) False

18. When applying the demand factors of Table 220.56, the feeder or service demand load shall not be less than the sum of the _____.

    (a) total number of receptacles at 180 VA per receptacle outlet
    (b) VA rating of all of the small-appliance branch circuits combined
    (c) largest two kitchen equipment loads
    (d) kitchen heating and air-conditioning loads

19. Where it is unlikely that two or more noncoincident loads will be in use simultaneously, only the _____ the loads used at one time is required to be used in computing the total load to a feeder.

    (a) smaller of
    (b) largest of
    (c) difference between
    (d) none of these

20. The maximum unbalanced feeder load for household electric ranges, wall-mounted ovens, and counter-mounted cooking units shall be considered as _____ percent of the load on the ungrounded conductors.

    (a) 50
    (b) 70
    (c) 85
    (d) 115

21. There shall be no reduction in the size of the neutral or grounded conductor on _____ loads supplied from a 4-wire, wye-connected, three-phase system.

    (a) dwelling unit
    (b) hospital
    (c) nonlinear
    (d) motel

22. Under the optional method for calculating a single-family dwelling service, general loads beyond the initial 10 kVA are assessed at a _____ percent demand factor.

    (a) 40
    (b) 50
    (c) 60
    (d) 75

Notes

# ARTICLE 225 — OUTSIDE BRANCH CIRCUITS AND FEEDERS

## Introduction to Article 225—Outside Branch Circuits and Feeders

This article covers the installation requirements for equipment, including branch circuit and feeder conductors (overhead and underground), located outdoors on or between buildings, poles, and other structures on the premises. Conductors installed outdoors can serve many purposes such as area lighting, power for outdoor equipment, or providing power to a separate building or structure. It's important to remember that the power supply for buildings isn't always a service conductor, but in many cases may be feeders or branch-circuit conductors originating in another building. Be careful not to assume that the conductors supplying power to a building are service conductors until you've identified where the utility service point is and reviewed the Article 100 Definitions for feeders, branch circuits, and service conductors. If they're service conductors, use Article 230. For outside branch-circuit and feeder conductors, whatever they feed, use this article.

Table 225.3 shows other articles that may furnish additional requirements, then Part I of Article 225 goes on to address installation methods intended to provide a secure installation of outside conductors while providing sufficient conductor size, support, attachment means, and maintaining safe clearances.

Part II of this article limits the number of supplies (branch circuits or feeders) permitted to a building or structure and provides rules regarding disconnects for them. These rules include the disconnect rating, construction characteristics, labeling, and where to locate the disconnecting means and the grouping of multiple disconnects.

Outside branch circuits and feeders over 1,000V are the focus of Part III of Article 225.

Please use the 2014 *Code* book to answer the following questions.

1. Open individual conductors shall not be smaller than _____ AWG copper for spans up to 50 ft in length and _____ AWG copper for a longer span, unless supported by a messenger wire.

   (a) 10, 8
   (b) 8, 8
   (c) 6, 8
   (d) 6, 6

2. The point of attachment of overhead premises wiring to a building shall in no case be less than _____ above finished grade.

   (a) 8 ft
   (b) 10 ft
   (c) 12 ft
   (d) 15 ft

3. Where a mast is used for overhead branch-circuit or feeder conductor support, it shall be of adequate strength or be supported by braces or guy wire to withstand safely the strain imposed by the conductors.

   (a) True
   (b) False

4. Overhead feeder conductors shall have a minimum _____ vertical clearance over residential property and driveways, as well as those commercial areas not subject to truck traffic, where the voltage is limited to 300 volts-to-ground.

   (a) 10 ft
   (b) 12 ft
   (c) 15 ft
   (d) 18 ft

5. The minimum clearance for overhead feeder conductors not exceeding 1,000V that pass over commercial areas subject to truck traffic is _____.

   (a) 10 ft
   (b) 12 ft
   (c) 15 ft
   (d) 18 ft

6. The minimum clearance for overhead feeder conductors that pass over track rails of railroads is _____.

   (a) 10 ft
   (b) 12 ft
   (c) 24.50 ft
   (d) 30 ft

7. Overhead feeder conductors installed over roofs shall have a vertical clearance of _____ above the roof surface, unless permitted by an exception.

   (a) 3 ft
   (b) 8 ft
   (c) 12 ft
   (d) 15 ft

8. If a set of 120/240V overhead feeder conductors terminates at a through-the-roof raceway or approved support, with less than 6 ft of these conductors passing over the roof overhang, the minimum clearance above the roof for these conductors is _____.

   (a) 12 in.
   (b) 18 in.
   (c) 2 ft
   (d) 5 ft

9. The requirement for maintaining a 3-foot vertical clearance from the edge of the roof shall not apply to the final feeder conductor span where the conductors are attached to _____.

   (a) a building pole
   (b) the side of a building
   (c) an antenna
   (d) the base of a building

10. Overhead feeder conductors to a building shall have a vertical clearance of final spans above, or within _____ measured horizontally from platforms, projections, or surfaces from which they might be reached.

    (a) 3 ft
    (b) 6 ft
    (c) 8 ft
    (d) 10 ft

11. Outside wiring shall not be installed beneath openings through which materials may be moved, and shall not be installed where they will obstruct entrance to these buildings' openings.

    (a) True
    (b) False

12. Raceways on exterior surfaces of buildings or other structures shall be arranged to drain, and be suitable for use in _____ locations.

    (a) damp
    (b) wet
    (c) dry
    (d) all of these

13. Vegetation such as trees shall not be used for support of _____.

    (a) overhead conductor spans
    (b) surface wiring methods
    (c) luminaires
    (d) electric equipment

14. Underground raceways entering a _____ from an underground distribution system shall be sealed or plugged at either or both ends to prevent moisture from contacting energized live parts.

    (a) building
    (b) structure
    (c) highway right-of-way
    (d) a or b

15. A building or structure shall be supplied by a maximum of _____ feeder(s) or branch circuit(s), unless specifically permitted otherwise.

    (a) one
    (b) two
    (c) three
    (d) four

16. The disconnecting means for a building supplied by a feeder shall be installed at a(n) _____ location.

    (a) accessible
    (b) readily accessible
    (c) outdoor
    (d) indoor

17. Where documented safe switching procedures are established and maintained and the installation is monitored by _____ individuals, the disconnecting means for a building supplied by a feeder can be located elsewhere on the premises.

    (a) maintenance
    (b) management
    (c) service
    (d) qualified

18. There shall be no more than _____ switches or circuit breakers to serve as the disconnecting means for a building supplied by a feeder.

    (a) two
    (b) four
    (c) six
    (d) eight

19. The two to six disconnects for a disconnecting means for a building supplied by a feeder shall be _____.

    (a) the same size
    (b) grouped
    (c) in the same enclosure
    (d) none of these

20. In a multiple-occupancy building, each occupant shall have access to his or her own _____.

    (a) disconnecting means
    (b) building drops
    (c) building-entrance assembly
    (d) lateral conductors

21. When the disconnecting means for a building supplied by a feeder is a power-operable switch or circuit breaker, it shall be able to be opened by hand in the event of a _____.

    (a) ground fault
    (b) short circuit
    (c) power surge
    (d) power failure

22. The disconnecting means for a building supplied by a feeder shall plainly indicate whether it is in the _____ position.

    (a) open or closed
    (b) correct
    (c) up or down
    (d) none of these

## Article 225 | Outside Branch Circuits and Feeders

23. A building disconnecting means that supplies only limited loads of a single branch circuit shall have a rating of not less than _____.

    (a) 15A
    (b) 20A
    (c) 25A
    (d) 30A

24. For installations consisting of not more than two 2-wire branch circuits, the building disconnecting means shall have a rating of not less than _____.

    (a) 15A
    (b) 20A
    (c) 25A
    (d) 30A

# ARTICLE 230 SERVICES

## Introduction to Article 230—Services

This article covers the installation requirements for service conductors and service equipment. The requirements for service conductors differ from those for other conductors. For one thing, service conductors for one building can't pass through the interior of another building or structure [230.3], and you apply different rules depending on whether a service conductor is inside or outside a building. When are they "outside" as opposed to "inside?" The answer may seem obvious, but 230.6 should be consulted before making this decision.

Let's review the following definitions in Article 100 to understand when the requirements of Article 230 apply:

- **Service Point.** The point of connection between the serving utility and the premises wiring.

- **Service Conductors.** The conductors from the service point to the service disconnecting means. Service-entrance conductors can either be overhead or underground.

- **Service Equipment.** The necessary equipment, usually consisting of circuit breakers or switches and fuses and their accessories, connected to the load end of service conductors at a building or other structure, and intended to constitute the main control and cutoff of the electrical supply. Service equipment doesn't include individual meter socket enclosures [230.66].

After reviewing these definitions, you should understand that service conductors originate at the serving utility (service point) and terminate on the line side of the service disconnecting means. Conductors and equipment on the load side of service equipment are considered feeder conductors or branch circuits, and must be installed in accordance with Articles 210 and 215. They must also comply with Article 225 if they're outside branch circuits and feeders, such as the supply to a building. Feeder conductors include: Figures 230–1 and 230–2

- Secondary conductors from customer-owned transformers,
- Conductors from generators, UPS systems, or PV systems, and
- Conductors to remote buildings

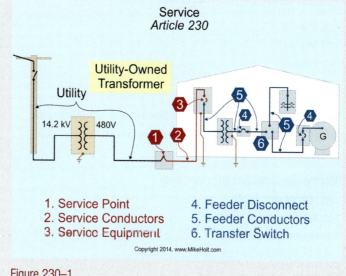

Figure 230–1

# Article 230 | Services

Article 230 consists of seven parts:

- Part I. General
- Part II. Overhead Service Conductors
- Part III. Underground Service Conductors
- Part IV. Service-Entrance Conductors
- Part V. Service Equipment
- Part VI. Disconnecting Means
- Part VIII. Overcurrent Protection

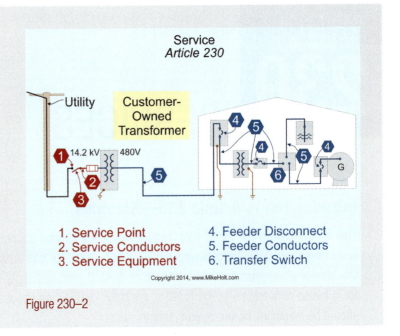

Figure 230–2

**Please use the 2014 *Code* book to answer the following questions.**

1. A building or structure shall be supplied by a maximum of _____ service(s), unless specifically permitted otherwise.

    (a) one
    (b) two
    (c) three
    (d) as many as desired

2. Additional services shall be permitted for a single building or other structure sufficiently large to make two or more services necessary if permitted by _____.

    (a) the registered design professional
    (b) special permission
    (c) the engineer of record
    (d) master electricians

3. Additional services shall be permitted for different voltages, frequencies, or phases, or for different uses such as for _____.

    (a) gymnasiums
    (b) different rate schedules
    (c) flea markets
    (d) special entertainment events

4. Where a building or structure is supplied by more than one service, a permanent plaque or directory shall be installed at each service disconnect location denoting all other services supplying that building or structure and the area served by each.

    (a) True
    (b) False

5. Service conductors supplying a building or other structure shall not _____ of another building or other structure.

   (a) be installed on the exterior walls
   (b) pass through the interior
   (c) a and b
   (d) none of these

6. Conductors are considered outside a building when they are installed _____.

   (a) Under not less than 2 in. of concrete beneath a building or structure
   (b) Within a building or structure in a raceway encased in not less than a 2 in. thickness of concrete or brick
   (c) Installed in a vault that meets the construction requirements of Article 450, Part III
   (d) all of these

7. Service conductors installed in overhead masts on the outside surface of the building traveling through the eave, but not the wall, of that building are considered to be outside of the building.

   (a) True
   (b) False

8. Conductors other than service conductors shall not be installed in the same _____.

   (a) service raceway
   (b) service cable
   (c) enclosure
   (d) a or b

9. Where a service raceway enters a building or structure from a(n) _____, it shall be sealed in accordance with 300.5(G).

   (a) transformer vault
   (b) underground distribution system
   (c) cable tray
   (d) overhead rack

10. Service conductors installed as unjacketed multiconductor cable shall have a minimum clearance of _____ ft from windows that are designed to be opened, doors, porches, stairs, fire escapes, or similar locations.

    (a) 3
    (b) 4
    (c) 6
    (d) 10

11. Overhead service conductors to a building shall maintain a vertical clearance of final spans above, or within, _____ ft measured horizontally from the platforms, projections, or surfaces from which they might be reached.

    (a) 3
    (b) 6
    (c) 8
    (d) 10

12. Service conductors shall not be installed beneath openings through which materials may be moved and shall not be installed where they will obstruct entrance to these buildings' openings.

    (a) True
    (b) False

13. Overhead service conductors can be supported to hardwood trees.

    (a) True
    (b) False

14. Service-drop conductors shall have _____.

    (a) sufficient ampacity to carry the load
    (b) adequate mechanical strength
    (c) a or b
    (d) a and b

15. The minimum size service-drop conductor permitted is _____ AWG copper or _____ AWG aluminum or copper-clad aluminum.

    (a) 8, 8
    (b) 8, 6
    (c) 6, 8
    (d) 6, 6

16. Overhead service conductors installed over roofs shall have a vertical clearance of _____ ft above the roof surface, unless a lesser distance is permitted by an exception.

    (a) 3
    (b) 8
    (c) 12
    (d) 15

17. If a set of 120/240V overhead service conductors terminate at a through-the-roof raceway or approved support, with less than 6 ft of these conductors passing over the roof overhang, the minimum clearance above the roof for these service conductors shall be _____.

    (a) 12 in.
    (b) 18 in.
    (c) 2 ft
    (d) 5 ft

18. The requirement to maintain a 3-foot vertical clearance from the edge of a roof does not apply to the final conductor span where the service drop is attached to _____.

    (a) a service pole
    (b) the side of a building
    (c) an antenna
    (d) the base of a building

19. If the voltage between overhead service conductors does not exceed 300V and the roof area is guarded or isolated, a reduction in clearance to 3 ft is permitted.

    (a) True
    (b) False

20. Overhead service conductors shall have a minimum of _____ ft vertical clearance from final grade over residential property and driveways, as well as over commercial areas not subject to truck traffic where the voltage is limited to 300 volts-to-ground.

    (a) 10
    (b) 12
    (c) 15
    (d) 18

21. The minimum clearance for overhead service conductors not exceeding 600V that pass over commercial areas subject to truck traffic is _____ ft.

    (a) 10
    (b) 12
    (c) 15
    (d) 18

22. Overhead service conductors shall have a horizontal clearance of not less than _____ ft from a pool.

    (a) 8
    (b) 10
    (c) 12
    (d) 14

23. Where communications cables and electric service drop conductors are supported by the same pole, communications cables must have a minimum separation of _____ in. at any point in the span, including the point of attachment to the building.

    (a) 2
    (b) 6
    (c) 12
    (d) 24

24. The minimum point of attachment of overhead service conductors to a building shall not be less than _____ above finished grade.

    (a) 8 ft
    (b) 10 ft
    (c) 12 ft
    (d) 15 ft

25. Where conduits are used as service masts, hubs shall be _____ for use with service entrance equipment.

    (a) identified
    (b) approved
    (c) of a heavy-duty type
    (d) listed

26. Underground service conductors shall have _____.

    (a) adequate mechanical strength
    (b) sufficient ampacity for the loads calculated
    (c) a and b
    (d) none of these

27. Underground copper service conductors supplying more than a single branch circuit shall not be smaller than _____ AWG copper.

    (a) 3
    (b) 4
    (c) 6
    (d) 8

28. Underground service conductors that supply power to limited loads of a single branch circuit shall not be smaller than _____.

    (a) 14 AWG copper
    (b) 14 AWG aluminum
    (c) 12 AWG copper
    (d) 12 AWG aluminum

29. Underground service conductors shall be protected from damage in accordance with _____ including minimum cover requirements.

    (a) 240.6(A)
    (b) 300.5
    (c) 310.15(B)(16)
    (d) 430.52

30. The general requirement for each service drop, set of overhead service conductors, set of underground service conductors, or service lateral is that it shall supply _____ set(s) of service-entrance conductors.

    (a) only one
    (b) only two
    (c) up to six
    (d) an unlimited number of

31. A single-family dwelling unit and its accessory structure(s) shall be permitted to have one set of service conductors run to each structure from a single service drop, set of overhead service conductors, set of underground service conductors, or service lateral.

    (a) True
    (b) False

32. Two-family dwellings, multifamily dwellings, and multiple occupancy buildings shall be permitted to have one set of service-entrance conductors to supply branch circuits for public or common areas.

    (a) True
    (b) False

33. One set of service-entrance conductors connected to the supply side of the normal service disconnecting means shall be permitted to supply standby power systems, fire pump equipment, and fire and sprinkler alarms covered by 230.82(5).

    (a) True
    (b) False

34. Ungrounded service-entrance conductors shall be sized not less than _____ percent of the continuous load, plus 100 percent of the noncontinuous load.

    (a) 100
    (b) 115
    (c) 125
    (d) 150

35. Wiring methods permitted for service-entrance conductors include _____.

    (a) rigid metal conduit
    (b) electrical metallic tubing
    (c) PVC conduit
    (d) all of these

36. Service-entrance conductors can be spliced or tapped by clamped or bolted connections at any time as long as _____.

    (a) the free ends of conductors are covered with an insulation that is equivalent to that of the conductors or with an insulating device identified for the purpose
    (b) wire connectors or other splicing means installed on conductors that are buried in the earth are listed for direct burial
    (c) no splice is made in a raceway
    (d) all of these

37. Underground service-entrance conductors shall be protected against physical damage.

    (a) True
    (b) False

38. Service-entrance cables which are not installed underground, where subject to physical damage, shall be protected by _____.

    (a) rigid metal conduit
    (b) IMC
    (c) Schedule 80 PVC conduit
    (d) any of these

39. Individual open conductors and cables, other than service-entrance cables, shall not be installed within _____ ft of grade level or where exposed to physical damage.

    (a) 8
    (b) 10
    (c) 12
    (d) 15

40. Service-entrance cables mounted in contact with a building shall be supported at intervals not exceeding _____.

    (a) 24 in.
    (b) 30 in.
    (c) 3 ft
    (d) 4 ft

41. Service raceways for overhead service drops or overhead service conductors shall have a service head listed for _____.

    (a) wet locations
    (b) damp locations
    (c) Class 2 locations
    (d) NEMA 3R

42. Overhead service-entrance cables shall be equipped with a _____.

    (a) raceway
    (b) service head
    (c) cover
    (d) all of these

43. Overhead service-entrance conductors of Type SE cable can be formed into a _____ and taped with self-sealing weather-resistant thermoplastic.

    (a) loop
    (b) circle
    (c) gooseneck
    (d) none of these

44. Service heads shall be located _____ the point of attachment, unless impracticable.

    (a) above
    (b) below
    (c) even with
    (d) none of these

45. To prevent moisture from entering service equipment, service-entrance conductors shall _____.

    (a) be connected to service-drop conductors below the level of the service head
    (b) have drip loops formed on the individual service-entrance conductors
    (c) a or b
    (d) a and b

46. Service-entrance and overhead service conductors shall be arranged so that _____ will not enter the service raceway or equipment.

    (a) dust
    (b) vapor
    (c) water
    (d) none of these

47. On a three-phase, 4-wire, delta-connected service where the midpoint of one phase winding is grounded, the service conductor having the higher phase voltage-to-ground shall be durably and permanently marked by an outer finish that is _____ in color, or by other effective means, at each termination or junction point.

    (a) orange
    (b) red
    (c) blue
    (d) any of these

48. The service disconnecting means shall be marked as suitable for use as service equipment and shall be _____.

    (a) weatherproof
    (b) listed
    (c) approved
    (d) acceptable

49. A service disconnecting means shall be installed at a(n) _____ location.

    (a) dry
    (b) readily accessible
    (c) outdoor
    (d) indoor

50. A service disconnecting means shall not be installed in bathrooms.

    (a) True
    (b) False

51. Where a remote-control device actuates the service disconnecting means, the service disconnecting means must still be at a readily accessible location either outside the building or structure, or nearest the point of entry of the service conductors.

    (a) True
    (b) False

52. Each service disconnecting means shall be permanently _____ to identify it as a service disconnect.

    (a) identified
    (b) positioned
    (c) marked
    (d) none of these

53. Each service disconnecting means shall be suitable for _____.

    (a) hazardous (classified) locations
    (b) wet locations
    (c) dry locations
    (d) the prevailing conditions

54. There shall be no more than _____ disconnects installed for each service or for each set of service-entrance conductors as permitted in 230.2 and 230.40.

    (a) two
    (b) four
    (c) six
    (d) eight

55. When the service contains two to six service disconnecting means, they shall be _____.

    (a) the same size
    (b) grouped
    (c) in the same enclosure
    (d) none of these

56. The additional service disconnecting means for fire pumps, emergency systems, legally required standby, or optional standby services, shall be installed remote from the one to six service disconnecting means for normal service to minimize the possibility of _____ interruption of supply.

    (a) intentional
    (b) accidental
    (c) simultaneous
    (d) prolonged

57. In a multiple-occupancy building, each occupant shall have access to the occupant's _____.

    (a) service disconnecting means
    (b) service drops
    (c) distribution transformer
    (d) lateral conductors

58. In a multiple-occupancy building where electric service and electrical maintenance are provided by the building management under continuous building management supervision, the service disconnecting means can be accessible to authorized _____ only.

    (a) inspectors
    (b) tenants
    (c) management personnel
    (d) qualified persons

59. When the service disconnecting means is a power-operated switch or circuit breaker, it shall be able to be opened by hand in the event of a _____.

    (a) ground fault
    (b) short circuit
    (c) power surge
    (d) power supply failure

60. The service disconnecting means shall plainly indicate whether it is in the _____ position.

    (a) open or closed
    (b) tripped
    (c) up or down
    (d) correct

61. For installations that supply only limited loads of a single branch circuit, the service disconnecting means shall have a rating not less than _____.

    (a) 15A
    (b) 20A
    (c) 25A
    (d) 30A

62. For installations consisting of not more than two 2-wire branch circuits, the service disconnecting means shall have a rating of not less than _____.

    (a) 15A
    (b) 20A
    (c) 25A
    (d) 30A

63. The service conductors shall be connected to the service disconnecting means by _____ or other approved means.

    (a) pressure connectors
    (b) clamps
    (c) solder
    (d) a or b

64. Electrical equipment shall not be connected to the supply side of the service disconnecting means, except for a few specific exceptions such as _____.

    (a) Type 1 surge protective devices
    (b) taps used to supply standby power systems, fire pump equipment, fire and sprinkler alarms, and load (energy) management devices
    (c) Solar photovoltaic systems
    (d) all of these

65. Each _____ service conductor shall have overload protection.

    (a) overhead
    (b) underground
    (c) ungrounded
    (d) none of these

# ARTICLE 240 — OVERCURRENT PROTECTION

## Introduction to Article 240—Overcurrent Protection

This article provides the requirements for selecting and installing overcurrent devices. Overcurrent exists when current exceeds the rating of equipment or the ampacity of a conductor, due to an overload, short circuit, or ground fault [Article 100].

- **Overload.** An overload is a condition where equipment or conductors carry current exceeding their current rating [Article 100]. A fault, such as a short circuit or ground fault, isn't an overload. An example of an overload is plugging two 12.50A (1,500W) hair dryers into a 20A branch circuit.

- **Short Circuit.** A short circuit is the unintentional electrical connection between any two normally current-carrying conductors of an electrical circuit, either line-to-line or line-to-neutral.

- **Ground Fault.** A ground fault is an unintentional, electrically conducting connection between an ungrounded conductor of an electrical circuit and the normally noncurrent-carrying conductors, metallic enclosures, metallic raceways, metallic equipment, or the earth [Article 100]. During the period of a ground fault, dangerous voltages will be present on metal parts until the circuit overcurrent device opens.

Overcurrent devices protect conductors and equipment. Selecting the proper overcurrent protection for a specific circuit can become more complicated than it sounds. The general rule for overcurrent protection is that conductors must be protected in accordance with their ampacities at the point where they receive their supply [240.4 and 240.21]. There are many special cases that deviate from this basic rule, such as the overcurrent protection limitations for small conductors [240.4(D)] and the rules for specific conductor applications found in other articles, as listed in Table 240.4(G). There are also a number of rules allowing tap conductors in specific situations [240.21(B)]. Article 240 even has limits on where overcurrent devices are allowed to be located [240.24].

An overcurrent protection device must be capable of opening a circuit when an overcurrent situation occurs, and must also have an interrupting rating sufficient to avoid damage in fault conditions [110.9]. Carefully study the provisions of this article to be sure you provide sufficient overcurrent protection in the correct location.

# Article 240 | Overcurrent Protection

Please use the 2014 Code book to answer the following questions.

1. Overcurrent protection for conductors and equipment is designed to _____ the circuit if the current reaches a value that will cause an excessive or dangerous temperature in conductors or conductor insulation.

   (a) open
   (b) close
   (c) monitor
   (d) record

2. A device that, when interrupting currents in its current-limiting range, reduces the current flowing in the faulted circuit to a magnitude substantially less than that obtainable in the same circuit if the device were replaced with a solid conductor having comparable impedance, is a(n) _____ protective device.

   (a) short-circuit
   (b) overload
   (c) ground-fault
   (d) current-limiting overcurrent

3. Conductor overload protection shall not be required where the interruption of the _____ would create a hazard, such as in a material-handling magnet circuit or fire pump circuit. However, short-circuit protection is required.

   (a) circuit
   (b) line
   (c) phase
   (d) system

4. The next higher standard rating overcurrent device above the ampacity of the ungrounded conductors being protected shall be permitted to be used, provided the _____.

   (a) conductors are not part of a branch circuit supplying more than one receptacle for cord-and-plug-connected portable loads
   (b) ampacity of the conductors doesn't correspond with the standard ampere rating of a fuse or circuit breaker
   (c) next higher standard rating selected doesn't exceed 800A
   (d) all of these

5. If the circuit's overcurrent device exceeds _____, the conductor ampacity must have a rating not less than the rating of the overcurrent device.

   (a) 800A
   (b) 1,000A
   (c) 1,200A
   (d) 2,000A

6. Overcurrent protection shall not exceed _____.

   (a) 15A for 14 AWG copper
   (b) 20A for 12 AWG copper
   (c) 30A for 10 AWG copper
   (d) all of these

7. Flexible cords approved for and used with a specific listed appliance or luminaire shall be considered to be protected by the branch-circuit overcurrent device when _____.

   (a) not more than 6 ft in length
   (b) 20 AWG and larger
   (c) applied within the listing requirements
   (d) 16 AWG and larger

8. Flexible cord used in listed extension cord sets shall be considered protected against overcurrent when used _____.

   (a) in indoor installations
   (b) in unclassified locations
   (c) within the extension cord's listing requirements
   (d) within 50 ft of the branch-circuit panelboard

9. Which of the following is not standard size fuses or inverse time circuit breakers?

   (a) 45A
   (b) 70A
   (c) 75A
   (d) 80A

10. The standard ampere ratings for fuses includes _____.

    (a) 1A
    (b) 6A
    (c) 601A
    (d) all of these

11. Supplementary overcurrent protection _____.

    (a) shall not be used in luminaires
    (b) may be used as a substitute for a branch-circuit overcurrent device
    (c) may be used to protect internal circuits of equipment
    (d) shall be readily accessible

12. Supplementary overcurrent devices used in luminaires or appliances are not required to be readily accessible.

    (a) True
    (b) False

13. Ground-fault protection of equipment shall be provided for solidly grounded wye electrical systems of more than 150 volts-to-ground, but not exceeding 1,000V phase-to-phase for each individual device used as a building or structure main disconnecting means rated _____ or more, unless specifically exempted.

    (a) 1,000A
    (b) 1,500A
    (c) 2,000A
    (d) 2,500A

14. A(n) _____ shall be considered equivalent to an overcurrent trip unit for the purpose of providing overcurrent protection of conductors.

    (a) current transformer
    (b) overcurrent relay
    (c) a and b
    (d) a or b

15. Circuit breakers shall _____ all ungrounded conductors of the circuit both manually and automatically unless specifically permitted otherwise.

    (a) open
    (b) close
    (c) isolate
    (d) inhibit

16. Single-pole breakers with identified handle ties can be used to protect each ungrounded conductor for line-to-line connected loads.

    (a) True
    (b) False

17. Conductors supplied under the tap rules are allowed to supply another conductor using the tap rules.

    (a) True
    (b) False

18. Outside feeder tap conductors can be of unlimited length without overcurrent protection at the point they receive their supply if the tap conductors _____.

    (a) are suitably protected from physical damage
    (b) terminate at a single circuit breaker or a single set of fuses that limits the load to the ampacity of the conductors
    (c) a and b
    (d) none of these

## Article 240 | Overcurrent Protection

19. Outside secondary conductors can be of unlimited length without overcurrent protection at the point they receive their supply if the conductors _____.

    (a) are suitably protected from physical damage
    (b) terminate at a single circuit breaker or a single set of fuses that limits the load to the ampacity of the conductors
    (c) a and b
    (d) none of these

20. Overcurrent devices shall be _____.

    (a) accessible (as applied to wiring methods)
    (b) accessible (as applied to equipment)
    (c) readily accessible
    (d) inaccessible to unauthorized personnel

21. Overcurrent devices shall be readily accessible and installed so the center of the grip of the operating handle of the switch or circuit breaker, when in its highest position, is not more than _____ above the floor or working platform.

    (a) 2 ft
    (b) 4 ft 6 in.
    (c) 5 ft
    (d) 6 ft 7 in.

22. Overcurrent devices shall not be located _____.

    (a) where exposed to physical damage
    (b) near easily ignitible materials, such as in clothes closets
    (c) in bathrooms of dwelling units
    (d) all of these

23. Overcurrent devices aren't permitted to be located in the bathrooms of _____.

    (a) dwelling units
    (b) dormitories
    (c) guest rooms or guest suites of hotels or motels
    (d) all of these

24. _____ shall not be located over the steps of a stairway.

    (a) Disconnect switches
    (b) Overcurrent devices
    (c) Knife switches
    (d) Transformers

25. Enclosures for overcurrent devices shall be mounted in a _____ position unless impracticable.

    (a) vertical
    (b) horizontal
    (c) vertical or horizontal
    (d) there are no requirements

26. Plug fuses of 15A or less shall be identified by a(n) _____ configuration of the window, cap, or other prominent part to distinguish them from fuses of higher ampere ratings.

    (a) octagonal
    (b) rectangular
    (c) hexagonal
    (d) triangular

27. Plug fuses of the Edison-base type shall have a maximum rating of _____.

    (a) 20A
    (b) 30A
    (c) 40A
    (d) 50A

28. Plug fuses of the Edison-base type shall be used _____.

    (a) where overfusing is necessary
    (b) as a replacement in existing installations
    (c) as a replacement for Type S fuses
    (d) 50A and above

29. Edison-base fuseholders shall be used only if they are made to accept _____ fuses by the use of adapters.

    (a) Edison-base
    (b) medium-base
    (c) heavy-duty base
    (d) Type S

30. Which of the following statements about Type S fuses are true?

    (a) Adapters shall fit Edison-base fuseholders.
    (b) Adapters are designed to be easily removed.
    (c) Type S fuses shall be classified as not over 125V and 30A.
    (d) a and c

31. Type _____ fuse adapters shall be designed so that once inserted in a fuseholder they cannot be removed.

    (a) A
    (b) E
    (c) S
    (d) P

32. Type S fuses, fuseholders, and adapters shall be designed so that _____ would be difficult.

    (a) installation
    (b) tampering
    (c) shunting
    (d) b or c

33. Dimensions of Type S fuses, fuseholders, and adapters shall be standardized to permit interchangeability regardless of the _____.

    (a) model
    (b) manufacturer
    (c) amperage
    (d) voltage

34. Fuseholders for cartridge fuses shall be so designed that it is difficult to put a fuse of any given class into a fuseholder that is designed for a _____ lower or a _____ higher than that of the class to which the fuse belongs.

    (a) voltage, wattage
    (b) wattage, voltage
    (c) voltage, current
    (d) current, voltage

35. Fuses shall be marked with their _____.

    (a) ampere and voltage rating
    (b) interrupting rating where other than 10,000A
    (c) name or trademark of the manufacturer
    (d) all of these

36. An 800A fuse rated at 1,000V _____ on a 250V system.

    (a) shall not be used
    (b) shall be used
    (c) can be used
    (d) none of these

37. Cartridge fuses and fuseholders shall be classified according to their _____ ranges.

    (a) voltage
    (b) amperage
    (c) a or b
    (d) a and b

38. Circuit breakers shall be capable of being closed and opened by manual operation. Operation by other means, such as electrical or pneumatic, shall be permitted if means for _____ operation is also provided.

    (a) automated
    (b) timed
    (c) manual
    (d) shunt trip

39. Where the circuit breaker handles are operated vertically, the up position of the handle shall be the _____ position.

    (a) on
    (b) off
    (c) tripped
    (d) any of these

40. A(n) _____ shall be of such design that any alteration of its trip point (calibration) or the time required for its operation requires dismantling of the device or breaking of a seal for other than intended adjustments.

    (a) Type S fuse
    (b) Edison-base fuse
    (c) circuit breaker
    (d) fuseholder

41. Circuit breakers shall be marked with their ampere rating in a manner that is durable and visible after installation. Such marking can be made visible by removal of a _____.

    (a) trim
    (b) cover
    (c) box
    (d) a or b

## Article 240 | Overcurrent Protection

42. A circuit breaker having an interrupting current rating of other than _____ shall have its interrupting rating marked on the circuit breaker.

    (a) 5,000A
    (b) 10,000A
    (c) 22,000A
    (d) 50,000A

43. Circuit breakers used to switch 120V or 277V fluorescent lighting circuits shall be listed and marked _____.

    (a) UL
    (b) SWD or HID
    (c) Amps
    (d) VA

44. Circuit breakers used to switch high-intensity discharge lighting circuits shall be listed and marked as _____.

    (a) SWD
    (b) HID
    (c) a or b
    (d) a and b

45. A circuit breaker with a _____ voltage rating, such as 240V or 480V, can be used where the nominal voltage between any two conductors does not exceed the circuit breaker's voltage rating.

    (a) straight
    (b) slash
    (c) high
    (d) low

46. A circuit breaker with a _____ rating, such as 120/240V or 277/480V can be used on a solidly grounded circuit where the nominal voltage of any conductor to ground does not exceed the lower of the two values, and the nominal voltage between any two conductors does not exceed the higher value.

    (a) straight
    (b) slash
    (c) high
    (d) low

# ARTICLE 250 — GROUNDING AND BONDING

## Introduction to Article 250—Grounding and Bonding

No other article can match Article 250 for misapplication, violation, and misinterpretation. Terminology used in this article has been a source for much confusion, but that has improved during the last few *NEC* revisions. It's very important to understand the difference between grounding and bonding in order to correctly apply the provisions of Article 250. Pay careful attention to the definitions that apply to grounding and bonding both here and in Article 100 as you begin the study of this important article. Article 250 covers the grounding requirements for providing a path to the earth to reduce overvoltage from lightning, and the bonding requirements for a low-impedance fault current path back to the source of the electrical supply to facilitate the operation of overcurrent devices in the event of a ground fault.

Over the past several *Code* cycles, this article was extensively revised to organize it better and make it easier to understand and implement. It's arranged in a logical manner, so it's a good idea to just read through Article 250 to get a big picture view—after you review the definitions. Next, study the article closely so you understand the details. The illustrations in *Mike Holt's Illustrated Guide to Understanding the National Electrical Code, Volume 1*, based on the 2014 *NEC* textbook will help you understand the key points.

Please use the 2014 *Code* book to answer the following questions.

1. A conductor installed on the supply side of a service or within a service equipment enclosure, or for a separately derived system, to ensure the electrical conductivity between metal parts required to be electrically connected is known as the _____.

    (a) supply-side bonding jumper
    (b) ungrounded conductor
    (c) the electrical supply source
    (d) grounding electrode conductor

2. Grounded electrical systems shall be connected to earth in a manner that will _____.

    (a) limit voltages due to lightning, line surges, or unintentional contact with higher-voltage lines
    (b) stabilize the voltage-to-ground during normal operation
    (c) facilitate overcurrent device operation in case of ground faults
    (d) a and b

## Article 250 | Grounding and Bonding

3. An important consideration for limiting imposed voltage on electrical systems is to remember that bonding and grounding electrode conductors shouldn't be any longer than necessary and unnecessary bends and loops should be avoided.

    (a) True
    (b) False

4. For grounded systems, normally noncurrent-carrying conductive materials enclosing electrical conductors or equipment shall be connected to earth so as to limit the voltage-to-ground on these materials.

    (a) True
    (b) False

5. For grounded systems, normally noncurrent-carrying conductive materials enclosing electrical conductors or equipment, or forming part of such equipment, shall be connected together and to the _____ to establish an effective ground-fault current path.

    (a) ground
    (b) earth
    (c) electrical supply source
    (d) none of these

6. In grounded systems, normally noncurrent-carrying electrically conductive materials that are likely to become energized shall be _____ in a manner that establishes an effective ground-fault current path.

    (a) connected together
    (b) connected to the electrical supply source
    (c) connected to the closest grounded conductor
    (d) a and b

7. For grounded systems, electrical equipment and other electrically conductive material likely to become energized, shall be installed in a manner that creates a _____ from any point on the wiring system where a ground fault may occur to the electrical supply source.

    (a) circuit facilitating the operation of the overcurrent device
    (b) low-impedance circuit
    (c) circuit capable of safely carrying the ground-fault current likely to be imposed on it
    (d) all of these

8. For grounded systems, electrical equipment and electrically conductive material likely to become energized, shall be installed in a manner that creates a low-impedance circuit capable of safely carrying the maximum ground-fault current likely to be imposed on it from where a ground fault may occur to the _____.

    (a) ground
    (b) earth
    (c) electrical supply source
    (d) none of these

9. For grounded systems, the earth is considered an effective ground-fault current path.

    (a) True
    (b) False

10. For ungrounded systems, noncurrent-carrying conductive materials enclosing electrical conductors or equipment shall be connected to the _____ in a manner that will limit the voltage imposed by lightning or unintentional contact with higher-voltage lines.

    (a) ground
    (b) earth
    (c) electrical supply source
    (d) none of these

11. For ungrounded systems, noncurrent-carrying conductive materials enclosing electrical conductors or equipment, or forming part of such equipment, shall be connected together and to the supply system equipment in a manner that creates a low-impedance path for ground-fault current that is capable of carrying _____.

    (a) the maximum branch-circuit current
    (b) at least twice the maximum ground-fault current
    (c) the maximum fault current likely to be imposed on it
    (d) the equivalent to the main service rating

12. Electrically conductive materials that are likely to _____ in ungrounded systems shall be connected together and to the supply system grounded equipment in a manner that creates a low-impedance path for ground-fault current that is capable of carrying the maximum fault current likely to be imposed on it.

    (a) become energized
    (b) require service
    (c) be removed
    (d) be coated with paint or nonconductive materials

13. In ungrounded systems, electrical equipment, wiring, and other electrically conductive material likely to become energized shall be installed in a manner that creates a low-impedance circuit from any point on the wiring system to the electrical supply source to facilitate the operation of overcurrent devices should a(n) _____ fault from a different phase occur on the wiring system.

    (a) isolated ground
    (b) second ground
    (c) arc
    (d) high impedance

14. The grounding of electrical systems, circuit conductors, surge arresters, surge-protective devices, and conductive normally noncurrent-carrying metal parts of equipment shall be installed and arranged in a manner that will prevent objectionable current.

    (a) True
    (b) False

15. Temporary currents resulting from abnormal conditions, such as ground faults, are not considered to be objectionable currents.

    (a) True
    (b) False

16. Currents that introduce noise or data errors in electronic equipment are considered objectionable currents in the context of 250.6(d) of the *NEC*.

    (a) True
    (b) False

17. Equipment grounding conductors, grounding electrode conductors, and bonding jumpers shall be connected by _____.

    (a) listed pressure connectors
    (b) terminal bars
    (c) exothermic welding
    (d) any of these

18. Grounding and bonding connection devices that depend solely on _____ shall not be used.

    (a) pressure connections
    (b) solder
    (c) lugs
    (d) approved clamps

19. Ground clamps and fittings that are exposed to physical damage shall be enclosed in _____.

    (a) metal
    (b) wood
    (c) the equivalent of a or b
    (d) none of these

20. _____ on equipment to be grounded shall be removed from contact surfaces to ensure good electrical continuity.

    (a) Paint
    (b) Lacquer
    (c) Enamel
    (d) any of these

21. Alternating-current circuits of less than 50V shall be grounded if supplied by a transformer whose supply system exceeds 150 volts-to-ground.

    (a) True
    (b) False

22. Alternating-current systems of 50V to 1,000V that supply premises wiring systems shall be grounded where the system is three-phase, 4-wire, wye connected with the neutral conductor used as a circuit conductor.

    (a) True
    (b) False

23. Alternating-current systems of 50V to 1,000V that supply premises wiring systems shall be grounded where supplied by a three-phase, 4-wire, delta-connected system in which the midpoint of one phase winding is used as a circuit conductor.

    (a) True
    (b) False

24. _____ alternating-current systems operating at 480V shall have ground detectors installed on the system.

    (a) Grounded
    (b) Solidly grounded
    (c) Effectively grounded
    (d) Ungrounded

25. Alternating current systems from 50V to less than 1,000V that aren't required to be grounded in accordance with 250.20(b) must have _____.

    (a) ground detectors installed
    (b) the ground detection sensing equipment connected as close as practicable to where the system receives its supply
    (c) a and b
    (d) ground fault protection for equipment

26. Ungrounded alternating current systems from 50V to less than 1,000V must be legibly marked "Caution: Ungrounded System — Operating _____ Volts Between Conductors" at _____ of the system, with sufficient durability to withstand the environment involved.

    (a) the source
    (b) the first disconnecting means
    (c) every junction box
    (d) a or b

27. The grounding electrode conductor shall be connected to the grounded service conductor at the _____.

    (a) load end of the service drop
    (b) load end of the service lateral
    (c) service disconnecting means
    (d) any of these

28. Where the main bonding jumper is installed from the grounded conductor terminal bar to the equipment grounding terminal bar in service equipment, the _____ conductor is permitted to be connected to the equipment grounding terminal bar.

    (a) grounding
    (b) grounded
    (c) grounding electrode
    (d) none of these

29. For a grounded system, an unspliced _____ shall be used to connect the equipment grounding conductor(s) and the service disconnecting means to the grounded conductor of the system within the enclosure for each service disconnect.

    (a) grounding electrode
    (b) main bonding jumper
    (c) busbar
    (d) insulated copper conductor

30. Where an alternating-current system operating at 1,000V or less is grounded at any point, the _____ conductor(s) shall be routed with the ungrounded conductors to each service disconnecting means and shall be connected to each disconnecting means grounded conductor(s) terminal or bus.

    (a) ungrounded
    (b) grounded
    (c) grounding
    (d) none of these

31. The grounded conductor of an alternating-current system operating at 1,000V or less shall be routed with the ungrounded conductors and connected to each disconnecting means grounded conductor terminal or bus, which is then connected to the service disconnecting means enclosure via a(n) _____ that's installed between the service neutral conductor and the service disconnecting means enclosure.

    (a) equipment bonding conductor
    (b) main bonding jumper
    (c) grounding electrode
    (d) intersystem bonding terminal

32. The grounded conductor brought to service equipment shall be routed with the phase conductors and shall not be smaller than specified in Table _____ when the service-entrance conductors are 1,100 kcmil copper and smaller.

    (a) 250.102(C)(1)
    (b) 250.122
    (c) 310.16
    (d) 430.52

33. When service-entrance conductors exceed 1,100 kcmil for copper, the required grounded conductor for the service shall be sized not less than _____ percent of the circular mil area of the largest set of ungrounded service-entrance conductor(s).

    (a) 9
    (b) 11
    (c) 12½
    (d) 15

34. Where service-entrance phase conductors are installed in parallel in two or more raceways, the size of the grounded conductor in each raceway shall be based on the total circular mil area of the parallel ungrounded service-entrance conductors in the raceway, sized in accordance with 250.24(C)(1), but not smaller than _____.

    (a) 1/0 AWG
    (b) 2/0 AWG
    (c) 3/0 AWG
    (d) 4/0 AWG

35. A grounding electrode conductor, sized in accordance with 250.66, shall be used to connect the equipment grounding conductors, the service-equipment enclosures, and, where the system is grounded, the grounded service conductor to the grounding electrode(s).

    (a) True
    (b) False

36. A main bonding jumper shall be a _____ or similar suitable conductor.

    (a) wire
    (b) bus
    (c) screw
    (d) any of these

37. Where a main bonding jumper is a screw only, the screw shall be identified by a(n) _____ that shall be visible with the screw installed.

    (a) silver or white finish
    (b) etched ground symbol
    (c) hexagonal head
    (d) green finish

38. Main bonding jumpers and system bonding jumpers shall not be smaller than specified in _____.

    (a) Table 250.102(C)(1)
    (b) Table 250.122
    (c) Table 310.15(B)(16)
    (d) Chapter 9, Table 8

39. Where the supply conductors are larger than 1,100 kcmil copper or 1,750 kcmil aluminum, the main bonding jumper shall have an area that is _____ the area of the largest phase conductor when of the same material.

    (a) at least equal to
    (b) at least 50 percent of
    (c) not less than 12½ percent of
    (d) not more than 12½ percent of

40. A grounded conductor shall not be connected to normally noncurrent-carrying metal parts of equipment on the _____ side of the system bonding jumper of a separately derived system except as otherwise permitted in Article 250.

    (a) supply
    (b) grounded
    (c) high-voltage
    (d) load

41. An unspliced _____ that is sized based on the derived phase conductors shall be used to connect the grounded conductor and the supply-side bonding jumper, or the equipment grounding conductor, or both, at a separately derived system.

    (a) system bonding jumper
    (b) equipment grounding conductor
    (c) grounded conductor
    (d) grounding electrode conductor

42. The connection of the system bonding jumper for a separately derived system shall be made _____ on the separately derived system from the source to the first system disconnecting means or overcurrent device.

    (a) in at least two locations
    (b) in every location that the grounded conductor is present
    (c) at any single point
    (d) none of these

43. Where a supply-side bonding jumper of the wire type is run with the derived phase conductors from the source of a separately derived system to the first disconnecting means, it shall be sized in accordance with 250.102(C), based on _____.

    (a) the size of the primary conductors
    (b) the size of the secondary overcurrent protection
    (c) the size of the derived ungrounded conductors
    (d) one third the size of the primary grounded conductor

44. The grounding electrode for a separately derived system shall be as near as practicable to, and preferably in the same area as, the grounding electrode conductor connection to the system.

    (a) True
    (b) False

45. For a single separately derived system, the grounding electrode conductor connects the grounded conductor of the derived system to the grounding electrode at the same point on the separately derived system where the _____ is connected.

    (a) metering equipment
    (b) transfer switch
    (c) system bonding jumper
    (d) largest circuit breaker

46. The grounding electrode conductor for a single separately derived system is used to connect the grounded conductor of the derived system to the grounding electrode.

    (a) True
    (b) False

47. Grounding electrode conductor taps from a separately derived system to a common grounding electrode conductor are permitted when a building or structure has multiple separately derived systems, provided that the taps terminate at the same point as the system bonding jumper.

    (a) True
    (b) False

48. The common grounding electrode conductor installed for multiple separately derived systems shall not be smaller than _____ copper when using a wire-type conductor.

    (a) 1/0 AWG
    (b) 2/0 AWG
    (c) 3/0 AWG
    (d) 4/0 AWG

49. Each tap conductor to a common grounding electrode conductor for multiple separately derived systems shall be sized in accordance with _____, based on the derived ungrounded conductors of the separately derived system it serves.

    (a) 250.66
    (b) 250.118
    (c) 250.122
    (d) 310.15

50. Tap connections to a common grounding electrode conductor for multiple separately derived systems shall be made at an accessible location by _____.

    (a) a connector listed as grounding and bonding equipment
    (b) listed connections to aluminum or copper busbars
    (c) the exothermic welding process
    (d) any of these

51. Tap connections to a common grounding electrode conductor for multiple separately derived systems may be made to a copper or aluminum busbar that is _____.

    (a) smaller than ¼ in. x 4 in.
    (b) not smaller than ¼ in. x 2 in.
    (c) not smaller than ½ in. x 2 in.
    (d) a and c

52. In an area served by a separately derived system, the _____ shall be connected to the grounded conductor of the separately derived system.

    (a) structural steel
    (b) metal piping
    (c) metal building skin
    (d) a and b

53. A grounding electrode shall be required if a building or structure is supplied by a feeder.

    (a) True
    (b) False

54. A grounding electrode at a separate building or structure shall be required where one multiwire branch circuit serves the building or structure.

    (a) True
    (b) False

55. The size of the grounding electrode conductor for a building or structure supplied by a feeder shall not be smaller than that identified in _____, based on the largest ungrounded supply conductor.

    (a) 250.66
    (b) 250.122
    (c) Table 310.15(B)(16)
    (d) none of these

56. The frame of a portable generator shall not be required to be connected to a(n) _____ if the generator only supplies equipment mounted on the generator, or cord-and-plug connected equipment using receptacles mounted on the generator, or both.

    (a) grounding electrode
    (b) grounded conductor
    (c) ungrounded conductor
    (d) equipment grounding conductor

57. The frame of a vehicle-mounted generator shall not be required to be connected to a(n) _____ if the generator only supplies equipment mounted on the vehicle or cord-and-plug connected equipment, using receptacles mounted on the vehicle.

    (a) grounding electrode
    (b) grounded conductor
    (c) ungrounded conductor
    (d) equipment grounding conductor

58. When a permanently installed generator _____, the requirements of 250.30 apply.

    (a) is a separately derived system
    (b) is not a separately derived system
    (c) supplies only cord and plug connected loads
    (d) none of these

59. High-impedance grounded neutral systems shall be permitted for three-phase ac systems of 480V to 1,000V where _____.

    (a) the conditions of maintenance ensure that only qualified persons service the installation
    (b) ground detectors are installed on the system
    (c) line-to-neutral loads are not served
    (d) all of these

60. Concrete-encased electrodes of _____ shall not be required to be part of the grounding electrode system where the steel reinforcing bars or rods aren't accessible for use without disturbing the concrete.

    (a) hazardous (classified) locations
    (b) health care facilities
    (c) existing buildings or structures
    (d) agricultural buildings with equipotential planes

61. In order for a metal underground water pipe to be used as a grounding electrode, it shall be in direct contact with the earth for _____.

    (a) 5 ft
    (b) 10 ft or more
    (c) less than 10 ft
    (d) 20 ft or more

62. The metal frame of a building shall be considered a grounding electrode where one of the *NEC*-prescribed methods for connection of the metal frame to earth has been met.

    (a) True
    (b) False

63. A bare 4 AWG copper conductor installed horizontally near the bottom or vertically, and within that portion of a concrete foundation or footing that is in direct contact with the earth can be used as a grounding electrode when the conductor is at least _____ ft in length.

    (a) 10
    (b) 15
    (c) 20
    (d) 25

64. An electrode encased by at least 2 in. of concrete, located horizontally near the bottom or vertically and within that portion of a concrete foundation or footing that is in direct contact with the earth, shall be permitted as a grounding electrode when it consists of _____.

    (a) at least 20 ft of ½ in. or larger steel reinforcing bars or rods
    (b) at least 20 ft of bare copper conductor of 4 AWG or larger
    (c) a or b
    (d) none of these

65. Reinforcing bars for use as a concrete-encased electrode can be bonded together by the usual steel tie wires or other effective means.

    (a) True
    (b) False

66. Where more than one concrete-encased electrode is present at a building or structure, it shall be permitted to connect to only one of them.

    (a) True
    (b) False

67. A ground ring encircling the building or structure can be used as a grounding electrode when _____.

    (a) the ring is in direct contact with the earth
    (b) the ring consists of at least 20 ft of bare copper conductor
    (c) the bare copper conductor is not smaller than 2 AWG
    (d) all of these

68. Grounding electrodes of the rod type less than _____ in. in diameter shall be listed.

    (a) ½ in.
    (b) ⅝ in.
    (c) ¾ in.
    (d) none of these

69. A buried iron or steel plate used as a grounding electrode shall expose not less than _____ of surface area to exterior soil.

    (a) 2 sq ft
    (b) 4 sq ft
    (c) 9 sq ft
    (d) 10 sq ft

70. Local metal underground systems or structures such as _____ are permitted to serve as grounding electrodes.

    (a) piping systems
    (b) underground tanks
    (c) underground metal well casings that are not bonded to a metal water pipe
    (d) all of these

71. Where practicable, rod, pipe, and plate electrodes shall be installed _____.

    (a) directly below the electrical meter
    (b) on the north side of the building
    (c) below permanent moisture level
    (d) all of these

72. Where the resistance-to-ground of 25 ohms or less is not achieved for a single rod electrode, _____.

(a) other means besides electrodes shall be used in order to provide grounding
(b) the single rod electrode shall be supplemented by one additional electrode
(c) no additional electrodes are required
(d) none of these

73. Two or more grounding electrodes bonded together are considered a single grounding electrode system.

(a) True
(b) False

74. Where a metal underground water pipe is used as a grounding electrode, the continuity of the grounding path or the bonding connection to interior piping shall not rely on _____ and similar equipment.

(a) bonding jumpers
(b) water meters or filtering devices
(c) grounding clamps
(d) all of these

75. Where the supplemental electrode is a rod, that portion of the bonding jumper that is the sole connection to the supplemental grounding electrode shall not be required to be larger than _____ AWG copper.

(a) 8
(b) 6
(c) 4
(d) 1

76. When a ground ring is used as a grounding electrode, it shall be buried at a depth below the earth's surface of not less than _____.

(a) 18 in.
(b) 24 in.
(c) 30 in.
(d) 0 ft

77. Ground rod electrodes shall be installed so that at least _____ of the length is in contact with the soil.

(a) 5 ft
(b) 8 ft
(c) one-half
(d) 80 percent

78. The upper end of a ground rod electrode shall be _____ ground level unless the aboveground end and the grounding electrode conductor attachment are protected against physical damage.

(a) above
(b) flush with
(c) below
(d) b or c

79. Where rock bottom is encountered when driving a ground rod at an angle up to 45 degrees, the electrode can be buried in a trench that is at least _____ deep.

(a) 18 in.
(b) 30 in.
(c) 4 ft
(d) 8 ft

80. Auxiliary grounding electrodes can be connected to the _____.

(a) equipment grounding conductor
(b) grounded conductor
(c) a and b
(d) none of these

81. When installing auxiliary electrodes, the earth shall not be used as an effective ground-fault current path.

(a) True
(b) False

82. The grounding electrode used for grounding strike termination devices of a lightning protection system can be used as a grounding electrode system for the buildings or structures.

(a) True
(b) False

83. Grounding electrode conductors of the wire type shall be _____.

    (a) solid
    (b) stranded
    (c) insulated or bare
    (d) any of these

84. Where used outside, aluminum or copper-clad aluminum grounding electrode conductors shall not be terminated within _____ of the earth.

    (a) 6 in.
    (b) 12 in.
    (c) 15 in.
    (d) 18 in.

85. Bare aluminum or copper-clad aluminum grounding electrode conductors shall not be used where in direct contact with _____ or where subject to corrosive conditions.

    (a) masonry or the earth
    (b) bare copper conductors
    (c) wooden framing members
    (d) all of these

86. Grounding electrode conductors _____ and larger that are not subject to physical damage can be run exposed along the surface of the building construction if it is securely fastened to the construction.

    (a) 10 AWG
    (b) 8 AWG
    (c) 6 AWG
    (d) 4 AWG

87. Grounding electrode conductors smaller than _____ shall be in rigid metal conduit, IMC, PVC conduit, electrical metallic tubing, or cable armor.

    (a) 10 AWG
    (b) 8 AWG
    (c) 6 AWG
    (d) 4 AWG

88. Grounding electrode conductors shall be installed in one continuous length without a splice or joint, unless spliced by _____.

    (a) connecting together sections of a busbar
    (b) irreversible compression-type connectors listed as grounding and bonding equipment
    (c) the exothermic welding process
    (d) any of these

89. Where service equipment consists of more than one enclosure, grounding electrode conductor connections shall be permitted to be _____.

    (a) multiple individual grounding electrode conductors
    (b) one grounding electrode conductor at a common location
    (c) a common grounding electrode conductor and taps
    (d) any of these

90. Ferrous metal raceways and enclosures for grounding electrode conductors shall be electrically continuous from the point of attachment to cabinets or equipment to the grounding electrode.

    (a) True
    (b) False

91. A grounding electrode conductor shall be permitted to be run to any convenient grounding electrode available in the grounding electrode system where the other electrode(s), if any, is connected by bonding jumpers in accordance with 250.53(C).

    (a) True
    (b) False

92. A service consisting of 12 AWG service-entrance conductors requires a grounding electrode conductor sized no less than _____.

    (a) 10 AWG
    (b) 8 AWG
    (c) 6 AWG
    (d) 4 AWG

93. The largest size grounding electrode conductor required is _____ copper.

   (a) 6 AWG
   (b) 1/0 AWG
   (c) 3/0 AWG
   (d) 250 kcmil

94. What size copper grounding electrode conductor is required for a service that has three sets of 600 kcmil copper conductors per phase?

   (a) 1 AWG
   (b) 1/0 AWG
   (c) 2/0 AWG
   (d) 3/0 AWG

95. In an ac system, the size of the grounding electrode conductor to a concrete-encased electrode shall not be required to be larger than a(n) _____ copper conductor.

   (a) 10 AWG
   (b) 8 AWG
   (c) 6 AWG
   (d) 4 AWG

96. Mechanical elements used to terminate a grounding electrode conductor to a grounding electrode shall be accessible.

   (a) True
   (b) False

97. An encased or buried connection to a concrete-encased, driven, or buried grounding electrode shall be accessible.

   (a) True
   (b) False

98. The connection of the grounding electrode conductor to a buried grounding electrode (driven ground rod) shall be made with a listed terminal device that is accessible.

   (a) True
   (b) False

99. Exothermic or irreversible compression connections, together with the mechanical means used to attach to fireproofed structural metal, shall not be required to be accessible.

   (a) True
   (b) False

100. When an underground metal water piping system is used as a grounding electrode, bonding shall be provided around insulated joints and around any equipment that is likely to be disconnected for repairs or replacement.

   (a) True
   (b) False

101. Interior metal water piping located not more than _____ from the point of entrance to the building shall be permitted to be used as a conductor to interconnect electrodes that are part of the grounding electrode system.

   (a) 2 ft
   (b) 4 ft
   (c) 5 ft
   (d) 6 ft

102. The grounding conductor connection to the grounding electrode shall be made by _____.

   (a) listed lugs
   (b) exothermic welding
   (c) listed pressure connectors
   (d) any of these

103. Metal enclosures and raceways containing service conductors shall be connected to the grounded system conductor if the electrical system is grounded.

   (a) True
   (b) False

104. Metal enclosures and raceways for other than service conductors shall be connected to the neutral conductor.

   (a) True
   (b) False

105. Short sections of metal enclosures or raceways used to provide support or protection of _____ from physical damage shall not be required to be connected to the equipment grounding conductor.

    (a) conduit
    (b) feeders under 600V
    (c) cable assemblies
    (d) none of these

106. Bonding shall be provided where necessary to ensure _____ and the capacity to conduct safely any fault current likely to be imposed.

    (a) electrical continuity
    (b) fiduciary responsibility
    (c) listing requirements
    (d) electrical demand

107. The normally noncurrent-carrying metal parts of service equipment, such as _____, shall be bonded together.

    (a) service raceways or service cable armor
    (b) service equipment enclosures containing service conductors, including meter fittings, boxes, or the like, interposed in the service raceway or armor
    (c) service cable trays
    (d) all of these

108. Bonding jumpers for service raceways shall be used around impaired connections such as _____.

    (a) oversized concentric knockouts
    (b) oversized eccentric knockouts
    (c) reducing washers
    (d) any of these

109. Electrical continuity at service equipment, service raceways, and service conductor enclosures shall be ensured by _____.

    (a) bonding equipment to the grounded service conductor
    (b) connections utilizing threaded couplings on enclosures, if made up wrenchtight
    (c) other listed bonding devices, such as bonding-type locknuts, bushings, or bushings with bonding jumpers
    (d) any of these

110. Service raceways threaded into metal service equipment such as bosses (hubs) are considered to be effectively _____ to the service metal enclosure.

    (a) attached
    (b) bonded
    (c) grounded
    (d) none of these

111. Service metal raceways and metal-clad cables are considered effectively bonded when using threadless couplings and connectors that are _____.

    (a) nonmetallic
    (b) made up tight
    (c) sealed
    (d) classified

112. A means external to enclosures for connecting intersystem _____ conductors shall be provided at service equipment or metering equipment enclosure and disconnecting means of buildings or structures supplied by a feeder.

    (a) bonding
    (b) ungrounded
    (c) secondary
    (d) a and b

113. The intersystem bonding termination shall _____.

    (a) be accessible for connection and inspection
    (b) consist of a set of terminals with the capacity for connection of not less than three intersystem bonding conductors
    (c) not interfere with opening the enclosure for a service, building/structure disconnecting means, or metering equipment
    (d) all of these

114. The intersystem bonding termination shall _____.

    (a) be securely mounted and electrically connected to service equipment, the meter enclosure, or exposed nonflexible metallic service raceway, or be mounted at one of these enclosures and be connected to the enclosure or grounding electrode conductor with a minimum 6 AWG copper conductor
    (b) be securely mounted to the building/structure disconnecting means, or be mounted at the disconnecting means and be connected to the metallic enclosure or grounding electrode conductor with a minimum 6 AWG copper conductor
    (c) have terminals that are listed as grounding and bonding equipment
    (d) all of these

115. At existing buildings or structures, an intersystem bonding termination is not required if other acceptable means of bonding exits. An external accessible means for bonding communications systems together can be by the use of a(n) _____.

    (a) nonflexible metallic raceway
    (b) exposed grounding electrode conductor
    (c) connection to a grounded raceway or equipment approved by the authority having jurisdiction
    (d) any of these

116. When bonding enclosures, metal raceways, frames, and fittings, any nonconductive paint, enamel, or similar coating shall be removed at _____.

    (a) contact surfaces
    (b) threads
    (c) contact points
    (d) all of these

117. Equipment bonding jumpers shall be of copper or other corrosion-resistant material.

    (a) True
    (b) False

118. Equipment bonding jumpers on the supply side of the service shall be no smaller than the sizes shown in _____.

    (a) Table 250.102(C)(1)
    (b) Table 250.122
    (c) Table 310.15(B)(16)
    (d) Table 310.15(B)(6)

119. The supply-side bonding jumper on the supply side of services shall be sized according to the _____.

    (a) overcurrent device rating
    (b) ungrounded supply conductor size
    (c) service-drop size
    (d) load to be served

120. What is the minimum size copper supply-side bonding jumper for a service raceway containing 4/0 THHN aluminum conductors?

    (a) 6 AWG aluminum
    (b) 4 AWG aluminum
    (c) 4 AWG copper
    (d) 3 AWG copper

121. Where ungrounded supply conductors are paralleled in two or more raceways or cables, the bonding jumper for each raceway or cable shall be based on the size of the _____ in each raceway or cable.

    (a) overcurrent protection for conductors
    (b) grounded conductors
    (c) ungrounded supply conductors
    (d) sum of all conductors

122. A service is supplied by three metal raceways, each containing 600 kcmil ungrounded conductors. Determine the copper supply-side bonding jumper size for each service raceway.

    (a) 1/0 AWG
    (b) 3/0 AWG
    (c) 250 kcmil
    (d) 500 kcmil

123. What is the minimum size copper equipment bonding jumper for a 40A rated circuit?

    (a) 14 AWG
    (b) 12 AWG
    (c) 10 AWG
    (d) 8 AWG

## Article 250 | Grounding and Bonding

124. An equipment bonding jumper can be installed on the outside of a raceway, providing the length of the equipment bonding jumper is not more than _____ and the equipment bonding jumper is routed with the raceway.

    (a) 12 in.
    (b) 24 in.
    (c) 36 in.
    (d) 72 in.

125. Metal water piping system(s) shall be bonded to the _____.

    (a) grounded conductor at the service
    (b) service equipment enclosure
    (c) equipment grounding bar or bus at any panelboard within a single occupancy building
    (d) a or b

126. The bonding jumper used to bond the metal water piping system shall be sized in accordance with _____.

    (a) Table 250.66
    (b) Table 250.122
    (c) Table 310.15(B)(16)
    (d) Table 310.15(B)(6)

127. Where isolated metal water piping systems are installed in a multiple-occupancy building, the water pipes can be bonded with bonding jumpers sized in accordance with Table 250.122, based on the size of the _____.

    (a) service-entrance conductors
    (b) feeder conductors
    (c) rating of the service equipment overcurrent device
    (d) rating of the overcurrent device supplying the occupancy

128. A building or structure shall have the interior metal water piping system bonded with a conductor sized in accordance with _____.

    (a) Table 250.66
    (b) Table 250.122
    (c) Table 310.15(B)(16)
    (d) none of these

129. Metal gas piping shall be considered bonded by the equipment grounding conductor for the circuit that is likely to energize the piping.

    (a) True
    (b) False

130. Exposed structural metal interconnected to form a metal building frame that is not intentionally grounded and is likely to become energized, shall be bonded to the _____.

    (a) service equipment enclosure or building disconnecting means
    (b) grounded conductor at the service
    (c) grounding electrode conductor where of sufficient size
    (d) any of these

131. Lightning protection system ground terminals _____ be bonded to the building or structure grounding electrode system.

    (a) shall
    (b) shall not
    (c) shall be permitted to
    (d) none of these

132. Exposed normally noncurrent-carrying metal parts of fixed equipment likely to become energized shall be connected to the equipment grounding conductor where located _____.

    (a) within 8 ft vertically or 5 ft horizontally of ground or grounded metal objects and subject to contact by persons
    (b) in wet or damp locations and not isolated
    (c) in electrical contact with metal
    (d) any of these

133. Electrical equipment permanently mounted on skids, and the skids themselves, shall be connected to the equipment grounding conductor sized as required by _____.

    (a) 250.50
    (b) 250.66
    (c) 250.122
    (d) 310.15

134. Listed FMC can be used as the equipment grounding conductor if the length in any ground return path does not exceed 6 ft and the circuit conductors contained in the conduit are protected by overcurrent devices rated at _____ or less.

    (a) 15A
    (b) 20A
    (c) 30A
    (d) 60A

135. Listed FMC and LFMC shall contain an equipment grounding conductor if the raceway is installed for the reason of _____.

    (a) physical protection
    (b) flexibility after installation
    (c) minimizing transmission of vibration from equipment
    (d) b or c

136. The *Code* requires the installation of an equipment grounding conductor of the wire type in _____.

    (a) Rigid metal conduit (RMC)
    (b) Intermediate metal conduit (IMC)
    (c) Electrical metallic tubing (EMT)
    (d) Listed flexible metal conduit over 6 ft in length

137. Listed liquidtight flexible metal conduit (LFMC) is acceptable as an equipment grounding conductor when it terminates in listed fittings and is protected by an overcurrent device rated 60A or less for trade sizes ⅜ through ½.

    (a) True
    (b) False

138. The armor of Type AC cable containing an aluminum bonding strip is recognized by the *NEC* as an equipment grounding conductor.

    (a) True
    (b) False

139. Type MC cable provides an effective ground-fault current path and is recognized by the *NEC* as an equipment grounding conductor when _____.

    (a) it contains an insulated or uninsulated equipment grounding conductor in compliance with 250.118(1)
    (b) the combined metallic sheath and uninsulated equipment grounding/bonding conductor of interlocked metal tape–type MC cable is listed and identified as an equipment grounding conductor
    (c) only when it is hospital grade Type MC cable
    (d) a or b

140. An equipment grounding conductor shall be identified by _____.

    (a) a continuous outer finish that is green
    (b) being bare
    (c) a continuous outer finish that is green with one or more yellow stripes
    (d) any of these

141. Conductors with the color _____ insulation shall not be used for ungrounded or grounded conductors.

    (a) green
    (b) green with one or more yellow stripes
    (c) a or b
    (d) white

142. A wire-type equipment grounding conductor is permitted to be used as a grounding electrode conductor if it meets all the requirements of Parts II, III, and IV of Article 250.

    (a) True
    (b) False

143. The equipment grounding conductor shall not be required to be larger than the circuit conductors.

    (a) True
    (b) False

144. When ungrounded circuit conductors are increased in size from the minimum size that has sufficient ampacity for the intended installation, the equipment grounding conductor must be proportionately increased in size according to the _____ of the ungrounded conductors.

    (a) ampacity
    (b) circular mil area
    (c) diameter
    (d) none of these

145. When a single equipment grounding conductor is used for multiple circuits in the same raceway, cable, or cable tray, the single equipment grounding conductor shall be sized according to the _____.

    (a) combined rating of all the overcurrent devices
    (b) largest overcurrent device of the multiple circuits
    (c) combined rating of all the loads
    (d) any of these

146. Equipment grounding conductors for motor branch circuits shall be sized in accordance with Table 250.122, based on the rating of the _____ device.

    (a) motor overload
    (b) motor over-temperature
    (c) branch-circuit short-circuit and ground-fault protective
    (d) feeder overcurrent protection

147. Where conductors are run in parallel in multiple raceways or cables and include an EGC of the wire type, the equipment grounding conductor must be installed in parallel in each raceway or cable, sized in compliance with 250.122.

    (a) True
    (b) False

148. Equipment grounding conductors for feeder taps are not required to be larger than the tap conductors.

    (a) True
    (b) False

149. The structural metal frame of a building can be used as the required equipment grounding conductor for ac equipment.

    (a) True
    (b) False

150. Metal parts of cord-and-plug-connected equipment shall be connected to an equipment grounding conductor that terminates to a grounding-type attachment plug.

    (a) True
    (b) False

151. A grounded circuit conductor is permitted to ground noncurrent-carrying metal parts of equipment, raceways, and other enclosures on the supply side or within the enclosure of the ac service-disconnecting means.

    (a) True
    (b) False

152. It shall be permissible to ground meter enclosures located near the service disconnecting means to the _____ circuit conductor on the load side of the service disconnect, if service ground-fault protection is not provided.

    (a) grounding
    (b) bonding
    (c) grounded
    (d) phase

153. A(n) _____ shall be used to connect the grounding terminal of a grounding-type receptacle to a grounded box.

    (a) equipment bonding jumper
    (b) grounded conductor jumper
    (c) a or b
    (d) a and b

154. Where the box is mounted on the surface, direct metal-to-metal contact between the device yoke and the box shall be permitted to ground the receptacle to the box if at least _____ of the insulating washers of the receptacle is (are) removed.

    (a) one
    (b) two
    (c) three
    (d) none of these

155. A listed exposed work cover can be the grounding and bonding means when the device is attached to the cover with at least _____ permanent fastener(s) and the cover mounting holes are located on a non-raised portion of the cover.

    (a) one
    (b) two
    (c) three
    (d) none of these

156. Receptacle yokes designed and _____ as self-grounding can, in conjunction with the supporting screws, establish the equipment bonding between the device yoke and a flush-type box.

    (a) approved
    (b) advertised
    (c) listed
    (d) installed

157. The receptacle grounding terminal of an isolated ground receptacle shall be connected to a(n) _____ equipment grounding conductor run with the circuit conductors.

    (a) insulated
    (b) covered
    (c) bare
    (d) solid

158. Where circuit conductors are spliced or terminated on equipment within a box, any equipment grounding conductors associated with those circuit conductors shall be connected to the box with devices suitable for the use.

    (a) True
    (b) False

159. The arrangement of grounding connections shall be such that the disconnection or the removal of a receptacle, luminaire, or other device fed from the box does not interrupt the grounding continuity.

    (a) True
    (b) False

160. A connection between equipment grounding conductors and a metal box shall be by _____.

    (a) a grounding screw used for no other purpose
    (b) equipment listed for grounding
    (c) a listed grounding device
    (d) any of these

## Notes

# ARTICLE 285 SURGE PROTECTIVE DEVICES (SPDS)

## Introduction to Article 285—Surge Protective Devices (SPDs)

This article covers the general requirements, installation requirements, and connection requirements for surge protective devices (SPDs) rated 1kV or less that are permanently installed on premises wiring systems. The *NEC* doesn't require surge protective devices to be installed, but if they are, they must comply with this article.

Surge protective devices are designed to reduce transient voltages present on premises power distribution wiring and load-side equipment, particularly electronic equipment such as computers, telecommunications equipment, security systems, and electronic appliances.

These transient voltages can originate from a number of sources, including anything from lightning to laser printers. The best line of defense for all types of electronic equipment may be the installation of surge protective devices at the electrical service and source of power, as well as at the location of the utilization equipment. Figures 285–1 and 285–2

The intent of a surge protection device is to limit transient voltages by diverting or limiting surge current and preventing continued flow of current while remaining capable of repeating these functions [Article 100]. Figure 285–3

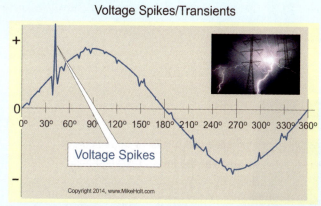

Voltage spikes/transients caused by the switching of utility power lines or power factor correction capacitors, or lightning can reach thousands of volts and amperes.

Figure 285–1

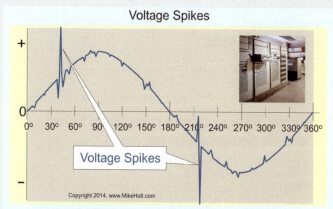

Voltage spikes (transients) produced by premises equipment such as photocopiers, laser printers, and other high reactive loads cycling off, can be in the hundreds of volts.

Figure 285–2

# Article 285 | Surge Protective Devices (SPDs)

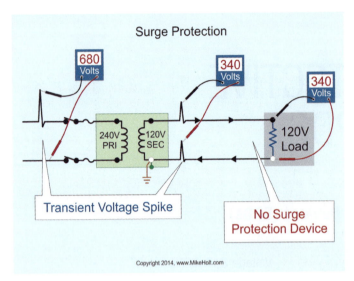

Figure 285–3

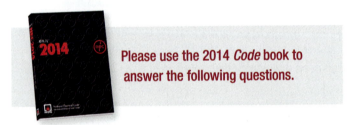

1. Article 285 covers surge protective devices rated over 1 kV.

   (a) True
   (b) False

2. Surge arrestors 1,000V or less are also known as Type 1 surge protective devices (SPDs).

   (a) True
   (b) False

3. Where used, the surge protective device shall be connected to the grounded conductor of the circuit.

   (a) True
   (b) False

4. Surge protective devices shall be listed.

   (a) True
   (b) False

5. Surge protective devices shall be marked with a short-circuit current rating and shall not be installed where the available fault current is in excess of that rating.

   (a) True
   (b) False

6. Surge protective devices shall only be located outdoors.

   (a) True
   (b) False

7. The conductors used to connect the surge protective device to the line or bus and to ground shall not be any longer than _____ and shall avoid unnecessary bends

   (a) 6 in.
   (b) 12 in.
   (c) 18 in.
   (d) necessary

8. A Type 2 surge protective device is permitted to be connected on either the line or load side of the service equipment.

   (a) True
   (b) False

9. Type 3 surge protective devices can be installed on the load side of a branch-circuit overcurrent device up to the equipment served. If _____, the Type 3 SPD connection must be a minimum 30 ft of conductor distance from the service or separately derived system disconnect.

   (a) voltage drop is excessive
   (b) installed in a metal raceway or cable
   (c) included in the manufacturer's instructions
   (d) b and c

# CHAPTER 3
# WIRING METHODS AND MATERIALS

## Introduction to Chapter 3—Wiring Methods and Materials

Chapter 3 covers wiring methods and materials, and provides some very specific installation requirements for conductors, cables, boxes, raceways, and fittings. This chapter includes detailed information about the installation and restrictions involved with wiring methods.

It may be because of those details that many people incorrectly apply the rules from this chapter. Be sure to pay careful attention to the details, and be sure that you make your installation comply with the rules in the *NEC*, not just completing it in the manner that you may have been taught or because "it's always been done that way." This is especially true when it comes to applying the Tables.

Violations of the rules for wiring methods found in Chapter 3 can result in problems with power quality and can lead to fire, shock, and other hazards.

The type of wiring method you'll use depends on several factors; job specifications, *Code* requirements, the environment, need, and cost are among them.

Chapter 3 begins with rules that are common to most wiring methods [Article 300]. It then covers conductors [Article 310] and enclosures [Articles 312 and 314]. The articles that follow become more specific and deal more in-depth with individual wiring methods such as specific types of cables [Articles 320 through 340] and various raceways [Articles 342 through 390]. The chapter winds up with Article 392, a support system, and the final articles [Articles 394 through 398] for open wiring.

Notice as you read through the various wiring methods that the *Code* attempts to use similar subsection numbering for similar topics from one article to the next, using the same digits after the decimal point in the section number for the same topic. This makes it easier to locate specific requirements in a particular article. For example, the rules for securing and supporting can be found in the section that ends with .30 of each article. In addition to this, you'll find a "uses permitted" and "uses not permitted" section in nearly every article.

### Wiring Method Articles

- **Article 300—General Requirements for Wiring Methods and Materials.** Article 300 contains the general requirements for all wiring methods included in the *NEC*, except for signaling and communications systems, which are covered in Chapters 7 and 8.

- **Article 310—Conductors for General Wiring.** This article contains the general requirements for conductors, such as insulation markings, ampacity ratings, and conductor use. Article 310 doesn't apply to conductors that are part of flexible cords, fixture wires, or conductors that are an integral part of equipment [90.6 and 300.1(B)].

- **Article 312—Cabinet and Cutout Boxes.** Article 312 covers the installation and construction specifications for cabinet.

- **Article 314—Outlet, Device, Pull, and Junction Boxes; Conduit Bodies, Fittings; and Handhole Enclosures.** Installation requirements for outlet boxes, pull and junction boxes, as well as conduit bodies, and handhole enclosures are contained in this article.

**Cable Articles**

Articles 320 through 340 address specific types of cables. If you take the time to become familiar with the various types of cables, you'll:

- Understand what's available for doing the work.
- Recognize cable types that have special *NEC* requirements.
- Avoid buying cable that you can't install due to *Code* requirements you can't meet with that particular wiring method.

Here's a brief overview of each one:

- **Article 320—Armored Cable (Type AC).** Armored cable is an assembly of insulated conductors, 14 AWG through 1 AWG, individually wrapped with waxed paper. The conductors are contained within a flexible spiral metal (steel or aluminum) sheath that interlocks at the edges. Armored cable looks like flexible metal conduit. Many electricians call this metal cable "BX®."

- **Article 330—Metal-Clad Cable (Type MC).** Metal-clad cable encloses insulated conductors in a metal sheath of either corrugated or smooth copper or aluminum tubing, or spiral interlocked steel or aluminum. The physical characteristics of Type MC cable make it a versatile wiring method permitted in almost any location and for almost any application. The most commonly used Type MC cable is the interlocking kind, which looks similar to armored cable or flexible metal conduit.

- **Article 334—Nonmetallic-Sheathed Cable (Type NM).** Nonmetallic-sheathed cable encloses two, three, or four insulated conductors, 14 AWG through 2 AWG, within a nonmetallic outer jacket. Because this cable is nonmetallic, it contains a separate equipment grounding conductor. Nonmetallic-sheathed cable is a common wiring method used for residential and commercial branch circuits. Many electricians call this plastic-sheathed cable "Romex®."

- **Article 336—Power and Control Tray Cable (Type TC).** Power and control tray cable is a factory assembly of two or more insulated conductors under a nonmetallic sheath for installation in cable trays, in raceways, or supported by a messenger wire.

- **Article 338—Service-Entrance Cable (Types SE and USE).** Service-entrance cable can be a single-conductor or a multiconductor assembly within an overall nonmetallic covering. This cable is used primarily for services not over 600V, but is also permitted for feeders and branch circuits.

- **Article 340—Underground Feeder and Branch-Circuit Cable (Type UF).** Underground feeder cable is a moisture-, fungus-, and corrosion-resistant cable suitable for direct burial in the earth, and it comes in sizes 14 AWG through 4/0 AWG [340.104]. Multiconductor UF cable is covered in molded plastic that surrounds the insulated conductors.

**Raceway Articles**

Articles 342 through 390 address specific types of raceways. Refer to Article 100 for the definition of a raceway. If you take the time to become familiar with the various types of raceways, you'll:

- Understand what's available for doing the work.
- Recognize raceway types that have special *Code* requirements.
- Avoid buying a raceway that you can't install due to *NEC* requirements you can't meet with that particular wiring method.

Here's a brief overview of each one:

- **Article 342—Intermediate Metal Conduit (Type IMC).** Intermediate metal conduit is a circular metal raceway with the same outside diameter as rigid metal conduit. The wall thickness of intermediate metal conduit is less than that of rigid metal conduit, so it has a greater interior cross-sectional area for holding conductors. Intermediate metal conduit is lighter and less expensive than rigid metal conduit, but it's permitted in all the same locations as rigid metal conduit. Intermediate metal conduit also uses a different steel alloy, which makes it stronger than rigid metal conduit, even though the walls are thinner.

- **Article 344—Rigid Metal Conduit (Type RMC).** Rigid metal conduit is similar to intermediate metal conduit, except the wall thickness is greater, so it has a smaller interior cross-sectional area. Rigid metal conduit is heavier than intermediate metal conduit and it's permitted to be installed in any location, just like intermediate metal conduit.

- **Article 348—Flexible Metal Conduit (Type FMC).** Flexible metal conduit is a raceway of circular cross section made of a helically wound, interlocked metal strip of either steel or aluminum. It's commonly called "Greenfield" or "Flex."

- **Article 350—Liquidtight Flexible Metal Conduit (Type LFMC).** Liquidtight flexible metal conduit is a raceway of circular cross section with an outer liquidtight, nonmetallic, sunlight-resistant jacket over an inner flexible metal core, with associated couplings, connectors, and fittings. It's listed for the installation of electrical conductors. Liquidtight flexible metal conduit is commonly called "Sealtite®" or simply "liquidtight." Liquidtight flexible metal conduit is of similar construction to flexible metal conduit, but it has an outer thermoplastic covering.

- **Article 352—Rigid Polyvinyl Chloride Conduit (Type PVC).** Rigid polyvinyl chloride conduit is a nonmetallic raceway of circular cross section with integral or associated couplings, connectors, and fittings. It's listed for the installation of electrical conductors.

- **Article 356—Liquidtight Flexible Nonmetallic Conduit (Type LFNC).** Liquidtight flexible nonmetallic conduit is a raceway of circular cross section with an outer liquidtight, nonmetallic, sunlight-resistant jacket over an inner flexible core, with associated couplings, connectors, and fittings.

    - Type LFNC-A (orange). A smooth seamless inner core and cover bonded together with reinforcement layers inserted between the core and covers.
    - Type LFNC-B (gray). A smooth inner surface with integral reinforcement within the conduit wall.
    - Type LFNC-C (black). A corrugated internal and external surface without integral reinforcement within the conduit wall.

- **Article 358—Electrical Metallic Tubing (EMT).** Electrical metallic tubing is a nonthreaded thinwall raceway of circular cross section designed for the physical protection and routing of conductors and cables. Compared to rigid metal conduit and intermediate metal conduit, electrical metallic tubing is relatively easy to bend, cut, and ream. EMT isn't threaded, so all connectors and couplings are of the threadless type. Today, it's available in a range of colors, such as red and blue.

- **Article 362—Electrical Nonmetallic Tubing (ENT).** Electrical nonmetallic tubing is a pliable, corrugated, circular raceway made of PVC. It's often called "Smurf Pipe" or "Smurf Tube," because it was available only in blue when it came out and at the time the children's cartoon characters "The Smurfs" were popular. It's now available in multiple colors such as red and yellow as well as blue.

- **Article 376—Metal Wireways.** A metal wireway is a sheet metal trough with hinged or removable covers for housing and protecting electrical conductors and cable, in which conductors are placed after the wireway has been installed as a complete system.

- **Article 380—Multioutlet Assemblies.** A multioutlet assembly is a surface, flush, or freestanding raceway designed to hold conductors and receptacles. It's assembled in the field or at the factory.

- **Article 386—Surface Metal Raceways.** A surface metal raceway is a metallic raceway intended to be mounted to the surface with associated accessories, in which conductors are placed after the raceway has been installed as a complete system.

- **Article 388—Surface Nonmetallic Raceways.** A surface nonmetallic raceway is intended to be surface mounted with associated accessories. Conductors are placed inside after the raceway has been installed as a complete system.

**Cable Tray**

- **Article 392—Cable Trays.** A cable tray system is a unit or assembly of units or sections with associated fittings that form a structural system used to securely fasten or support cables and raceways. A cable tray isn't a raceway; it's a support system for raceways, cables, and enclosures.

# ARTICLE 300 — GENERAL REQUIREMENTS FOR WIRING METHODS AND MATERIALS

## Introduction to Article 300—General Requirements for Wiring Methods and Materials

Article 300 contains the general requirements for all wiring methods included in the *NEC*. However, the article doesn't apply to communications systems, which are covered in Chapter 8, except when Article 300 is specifically referenced in Chapter 8.

This article is primarily concerned with how to install, route, splice, protect, and secure conductors and raceways. How well you conform to the requirements of Article 300 will generally be evident in the finished work, because many of the requirements tend to determine the appearance of the installation. Because of this, it's often easy to spot Article 300 problems if you're looking for *Code* violations. For example, you can easily see when someone runs an equipment grounding conductor outside a raceway instead of grouping all conductors of a circuit together, as required by 300.3(B).

A good understanding of Article 300 will start you on the path to correctly installing the wiring methods included in Chapter 3. Be sure to refer to the definitions in Article 100 as needed.

**Please use the 2014 *Code* book to answer the following questions.**

1. All conductors of the same circuit, including the grounded and equipment grounding conductors, shall be contained within the same _____, unless otherwise permitted elsewhere in the *Code*.

   (a) raceway
   (b) cable
   (c) trench
   (d) all of these

2. Conductors of ac and dc circuits, rated 1,000V or less, shall be permitted to occupy the same _____ provided that all conductors have an insulation rating equal to the maximum voltage applied to any conductor.

   (a) enclosure
   (b) cable
   (c) raceway
   (d) any of these

3. Where cables or nonmetallic raceways are installed through bored holes in joists, rafters, or wood members, holes shall be bored so that the edge of the hole is _____ the nearest edge of the wood member.

   (a) not less than 1¼ in. from
   (b) immediately adjacent to
   (c) not less than 1⁄16 in. from
   (d) 90° away from

4. Cables laid in wood notches require protection against nails or screws by using a steel plate at least _____ thick, installed before the building finish is applied.

   (a) 1⁄16 in.
   (b) 1⁄8 in.
   (c) ¼ in.
   (d) ½ in.

5. Where Type NM cable passes through factory or field openings in metal members, it shall be protected by _____ bushings or _____ grommets that cover metal edges.

   (a) approved
   (b) identified
   (c) listed
   (d) none of these

6. Where Type NM cables pass through cut or drilled slots or holes in metal members, the cable shall be protected by _____ which are installed in the opening prior to the installation of the cable and which securely cover all metal edges.

   (a) listed bushings
   (b) listed grommets
   (c) plates
   (d) a or b

7. Where nails or screws are likely to penetrate nonmetallic-sheathed cable or ENT installed through metal framing members, a steel sleeve, steel plate, or steel clip not less than _____ in thickness shall be used to protect the cable or tubing.

   (a) 1⁄16 in.
   (b) 1⁄8 in.
   (c) ½ in.
   (d) ¾ in.

8. Wiring methods installed behind panels that allow access shall be _____ according to their applicable articles.

   (a) supported
   (b) painted
   (c) in a metal raceway
   (d) all of these

9. Where cables and nonmetallic raceways are installed parallel to framing members, the nearest outside surface of the cable or raceway shall be _____ the nearest edge of the framing member where nails or screws are likely to penetrate.

   (a) not less than 1¼ in. from
   (b) immediately adjacent to
   (c) not less than 1⁄16 in. from
   (d) 90° away from

10. A cable, raceway, or box installed under metal-corrugated sheet roof decking shall be supported so the top of the cable, raceway, or box is not less than _____ from the lowest surface of the roof decking to the top of the cable, raceway, or box.

    (a) ½ in.
    (b) 1 in.
    (c) 1½ in.
    (d) 2 in.

11. When installed under metal-corrugated sheet roof decking, cables, raceways, and enclosures are permitted in concealed locations of metal-corrugated sheet decking type roofing if they are at least 2 in. away from a structural support member.

    (a) True
    (b) False

12. When installed under metal-corrugated sheet roof decking, the rules for spacing from roof decking apply equally to rigid metal conduit and intermediate metal conduit.

    (a) True
    (b) False

General Requirements for Wiring Methods and Materials | Article 300

13. Where raceways contain insulated circuit conductors _____ AWG and larger, the conductors shall be protected from abrasion during and after installation by a fitting that provides a smooth, rounded insulating surface.

    (a) 8
    (b) 6
    (c) 4
    (d) 2

14. A listed expansion/deflection fitting or other approved means must be used where a raceway crosses a _____ intended for expansion, contraction or deflection used in buildings, bridges, parking garages, or other structures.

    (a) junction box
    (b) structural joint
    (c) cable tray
    (d) unistrut hanger

15. What is the minimum cover requirement for direct burial Type UF cable installed outdoors that supplies a 120V, 30A circuit?

    (a) 6 in.
    (b) 12 in.
    (c) 18 in.
    (d) 24 in.

16. Rigid metal conduit that is directly buried outdoors shall have at least _____ in. of cover.

    (a) 6
    (b) 12
    (c) 18
    (d) 24

17. When installing PVC conduit underground without concrete cover, there shall be a minimum of _____ in. of cover.

    (a) 6
    (b) 12
    (c) 18
    (d) 22

18. What is the minimum cover requirement for Type UF cable supplying power to a 120V, 15A GFCI-protected circuit outdoors under a driveway of a one-family dwelling?

    (a) 6 in.
    (b) 12 in.
    (c) 16 in.
    (d) 24 in.

19. Type UF cable used with a 24V landscape lighting system can have a minimum cover of _____ in.

    (a) 6
    (b) 12
    (c) 18
    (d) 24

20. _____ is defined as the area between the top of direct-burial cable and the top surface of the finished grade.

    (a) Notch
    (b) Cover
    (c) Gap
    (d) none of these

21. The interior of underground raceways shall be considered a _____ location.

    (a) wet
    (b) dry
    (c) damp
    (d) corrosive

22. Type MC Cable listed for _____ is permitted to be installed underground under a building without installation in a raceway.

    (a) direct burial
    (b) damp and wet locations
    (c) rough service
    (d) b and c

23. Where direct-buried conductors and cables emerge from grade, they shall be protected by enclosures or raceways to a point at least _____ ft above finished grade.

    (a) 3
    (b) 6
    (c) 8
    (d) 10

Article 300 | General Requirements for Wiring Methods and Materials

24. Direct-buried service conductors that are not encased in concrete and that are buried 18 in. or more below grade shall have their location identified by a warning ribbon placed in the trench at least _____ in. above the underground installation.

    (a) 6
    (b) 10
    (c) 12
    (d) 18

25. Direct-buried conductors or cables can be spliced or tapped without the use of splice boxes when the splice or tap is made in accordance with 110.14(B).

    (a) True
    (b) False

26. Backfill used for underground wiring shall not _____.

    (a) damage the wiring method
    (b) prevent compaction of the fill
    (c) contribute to the corrosion of the raceway
    (d) all of these

27. Conduits or raceways through which moisture may contact live parts shall be _____ at either or both ends.

    (a) sealed
    (b) plugged
    (c) bushed
    (d) a or b

28. When installing direct-buried cables, a _____ shall be used at the end of a conduit that terminates underground.

    (a) splice kit
    (b) terminal fitting
    (c) bushing
    (d) b or c

29. All conductors of the same circuit shall be _____, unless otherwise specifically permitted in the *Code*.

    (a) in the same raceway or cable
    (b) in close proximity in the same trench
    (c) the same size
    (d) a or b

30. Each direct-buried single conductor cable must be located _____ in the trench to the other single conductor cables in the same parallel set of conductors, including equipment grounding conductors.

    (a) perpendicular
    (b) bundled together
    (c) in close proximity
    (d) spaced apart

31. Direct-buried conductors, cables, or raceways, which are subject to movement by settlement or frost, shall be arranged to prevent damage to the _____ or to equipment connected to the raceways.

    (a) siding of the building mounted on
    (b) landscaping around the cable or raceway
    (c) enclosed conductors
    (d) expansion fitting

32. Cables or raceways installed using directional boring equipment shall be _____ for this purpose.

    (a) marked
    (b) listed
    (c) labeled
    (d) approved

33. Raceways, cable trays, cablebus, auxiliary gutters, cable armor, boxes, cable sheathing, cabinets, elbows, couplings, fittings, supports, and support hardware shall be of materials suitable for _____.

    (a) corrosive locations
    (b) wet locations
    (c) the environment in which they are to be installed
    (d) none of these

34. Where corrosion protection is necessary for ferrous metal equipment and the conduit is threaded in the field, the threads shall be coated with a(n) _____ electrically conductive, corrosion-resistant compound.

    (a) marked
    (b) listed
    (c) labeled
    (d) approved

35. Which of the following metal parts shall be protected from corrosion?

    (a) Ferrous metal raceways.
    (b) Ferrous metal elbows.
    (c) Ferrous boxes.
    (d) all of these

36. Ferrous metal raceways, boxes, fittings, supports, and support hardware can be installed in concrete or in direct contact with the earth or other areas subject to severe corrosive influences, where _____ approved for the conditions.

    (a) the soil is
    (b) made of material
    (c) the qualified installer is
    (d) none of these

37. Aluminum raceways, cable trays, cablebus, auxiliary gutters, cable armor, boxes, cable sheathing, cabinets, elbows, couplings, nipples, fittings, supports, and support hardware _____ shall be provided with supplementary corrosion protection.

    (a) embedded or encased in concrete
    (b) in direct contact with the earth
    (c) likely to become energized
    (d) a or b

38. Where exposed to sunlight, nonmetallic raceways, cable trays, boxes, cables with a nonmetallic outer jacket, fittings, and support hardware shall be _____.

    (a) listed as sunlight resistant
    (b) identified as sunlight resistant
    (c) a and b
    (d) a or b

39. Where nonmetallic wiring methods are subject to exposure to chemical solvents or vapors, they shall be inherently resistant to chemicals based upon their being _____.

    (a) listed for the chemical
    (b) identified for the chemical
    (c) a and b
    (d) a or b

40. An exposed wiring system for indoor wet locations where walls are frequently washed shall be mounted so that there is at least a _____ between the mounting surface and the electrical equipment.

    (a) ¼ in. airspace
    (b) separation by insulated bushings
    (c) separation by noncombustible tubing
    (d) none of these

41. In general, areas where acids and alkali chemicals are handled and stored may present corrosive conditions, particularly when wet or damp.

    (a) True
    (b) False

42. Where portions of a cable raceway or sleeve are subjected to different temperatures and condensation is known to be a problem, the _____ shall be filled with an approved material to prevent the circulation of warm air to a colder section of the raceway or sleeve.

    (a) raceway
    (b) sleeve
    (c) a or b
    (d) none of these

43. Raceways shall be provided with expansion fittings where necessary to compensate for thermal expansion and contraction.

    (a) True
    (b) False

44. Raceways or cable trays containing electric conductors shall not contain any pipe or tube for steam, water, air, gas, drainage, or any service other than _____.

    (a) as permitted by the authority having jurisdiction
    (b) electrical
    (c) pneumatic
    (d) as designed by the engineer

45. Where raceways are installed in wet locations above grade, the interior of these raceways shall be considered a _____ location.

    (a) wet
    (b) dry
    (c) damp
    (d) corrosive

46. Metal raceways, cable armor, and other metal enclosures shall be _____ joined together into a continuous electric conductor so as to provide effective electrical continuity.

    (a) electrically
    (b) permanently
    (c) metallically
    (d) none of these

47. Raceways, cable assemblies, boxes, cabinets, and fittings shall be securely fastened in place.

    (a) True
    (b) False

48. Electrical wiring within the cavity of a fire-rated floor-ceiling or roof-ceiling assembly shall not be supported by the ceiling assembly or ceiling support wires.

    (a) True
    (b) False

49. The independent support wires for supporting electrical wiring methods in a fire-rated ceiling assembly shall be distinguishable from fire-rated suspended-ceiling framing support wires by _____.

    (a) color
    (b) tagging
    (c) other effective means
    (d) any of these

50. Independent support wires used for the support of electrical raceways and cables within nonfire-rated assemblies shall be distinguishable from the suspended-ceiling framing support wires.

    (a) True
    (b) False

51. Raceways can be used as a means of support of Class 2 circuit conductors or cables that connect to the same equipment.

    (a) True
    (b) False

52. Cable wiring methods shall not be used as a means of support for _____.

    (a) other cables
    (b) raceways
    (c) nonelectrical equipment
    (d) all of these

53. Metal or nonmetallic raceways, cable armors, and cable sheaths _____ between cabinets, boxes, fittings, or other enclosures or outlets.

    (a) can be attached with electrical tape
    (b) are allowed gaps for expansion
    (c) shall be continuous
    (d) none of these

54. Raceways and cables installed into the _____ of open bottom equipment shall not be required to be mechanically secured to the equipment.

    (a) bottom
    (b) sides
    (c) top
    (d) any of these

55. Conductors in raceways shall be _____ between outlets, boxes, devices, and so forth.

    (a) continuous
    (b) installed
    (c) copper
    (d) in conduit

56. In multiwire branch circuits, the continuity of the _____ conductor shall not be dependent upon the device connections.

    (a) ungrounded
    (b) grounded
    (c) grounding electrode
    (d) a and b

57. When the opening to an outlet, junction, or switch point is less than 8 in. in any dimension, each conductor shall be long enough to extend at least _____ in. outside the opening of the enclosure.

    (a) 0
    (b) 3
    (c) 6
    (d) 12

58. Fittings and connectors shall be used only with the specific wiring methods for which they are designed and listed.

    (a) True
    (b) False

59. A box or conduit body shall not be required where cables enter or exit from conduit or tubing that is used to provide cable support or protection against physical damage.

    (a) True
    (b) False

60. A box or conduit body shall not be required for splices and taps in direct-buried conductors and cables as long as the splice is made with a splicing device that is identified for the purpose.

    (a) True
    (b) False

61. A box or conduit body shall not be required for conductors in handhole enclosures, except where connected to electrical equipment.

    (a) True
    (b) False

62. A bushing shall be permitted in lieu of a box or terminal where the conductors emerge from a raceway and enter or terminate at equipment such as open switchboards, unenclosed control equipment, or similar equipment.

    (a) True
    (b) False

63. The number and size of conductors permitted in a raceway is limited to _____.

    (a) permit heat to dissipate
    (b) prevent damage to insulation during installation
    (c) prevent damage to insulation during removal of conductors
    (d) all of these

64. Raceways shall be _____ between outlet, junction, or splicing points prior to the installation of conductors.

    (a) installed complete
    (b) tested for ground faults
    (c) a minimum of 80 percent complete
    (d) none of these

65. Prewired raceway assemblies shall be used only where specifically permitted in the *NEC* for the applicable wiring method.

    (a) True
    (b) False

66. Short sections of raceways used for _____ shall not be required to be installed complete between outlet, junction, or splicing points.

    (a) meter to service enclosure connection
    (b) protection of cables from physical damage
    (c) nipples
    (d) separately derived systems

67. Metal raceways shall not be _____ by welding to the raceway.

    (a) supported
    (b) terminated
    (c) connected
    (d) all of these

68. A vertical run of 4/0 AWG copper shall be supported at intervals not exceeding _____.

    (a) 40 ft
    (b) 80 ft
    (c) 100 ft
    (d) 120 ft

69. Conductors in ferrous metal raceways and enclosures shall be arranged so as to avoid heating the surrounding ferrous metal by alternating-current induction. To accomplish this, the _____ conductor(s) shall be grouped together.

    (a) phase
    (b) grounded
    (c) equipment grounding
    (d) all of these

70. _____ is a nonferrous, nonmagnetic metal that has no heating due to hysteresis heating.

    (a) Steel
    (b) Iron
    (c) Aluminum
    (d) all of these

71. Electrical installations in hollow spaces, vertical shafts, and ventilation or air-handling ducts shall be made so that the possible spread of fire or products of combustion is not _____.

    (a) substantially increased
    (b) allowed
    (c) inherent
    (d) possible

72. Openings around electrical penetrations into or through fire-resistant-rated walls, partitions, floors, or ceilings shall _____ to maintain the fire-resistance rating.

    (a) be documented
    (b) not be permitted
    (c) be firestopped using approved methods
    (d) be enlarged

73. No wiring of any type shall be installed in ducts used to transport _____.

    (a) dust
    (b) flammable vapors
    (c) loose stock
    (d) all of these

74. Equipment and devices shall only be permitted within ducts or plenum chambers specifically fabricated to transport environmental air if necessary for their direct action upon, or sensing of, the _____.

    (a) contained air
    (b) air quality
    (c) air temperature
    (d) none of these

75. The space above a hung ceiling used for environmental air-handling purposes is an example of _____, and the wiring limitations of _____ apply.

    (a) a specifically fabricated duct used for environmental air, 300.22(B)
    (b) other space used for environmental air (plenum), 300.22(C)
    (c) a supply duct used for environmental air, 300.22(B)
    (d) none of these

76. Wiring methods permitted in the ceiling areas used for environmental air include _____.

    (a) electrical metallic tubing
    (b) FMC of any length
    (c) RMC without an overall nonmetallic covering
    (d) all of these

77. _____ shall be permitted to support the wiring methods and equipment permitted to be used in other spaces used for environmental air (plenum).

    (a) Metal cable tray systems
    (b) Nonmetallic wireways
    (c) PVC conduit
    (d) Surface nonmetallic raceways

78. Electrical equipment with _____ and having adequate fire-resistant and low-smoke-producing characteristics can be installed within an air-handling space (plenum).

    (a) a metal enclosure
    (b) a nonmetallic enclosure listed for use within an air-handling (plenum) space
    (c) any type of enclosure
    (d) a or b

79. Wiring methods and equipment installed behind suspended-ceiling panels shall be arranged and secured to allow access to the electrical equipment.

    (a) True
    (b) False

# ARTICLE 310 CONDUCTORS FOR GENERAL WIRING

## Introduction to Article 310—Conductors for General Wiring

This article contains the general requirements for conductors, such as insulation markings, ampacity ratings, and conditions of use. Article 310 doesn't apply to conductors that are part of flexible cords, fixture wires, or to conductors that are an integral part of equipment [90.7 and 300.1(B)].

People often make mistakes in applying the ampacity tables contained in Article 310. If you study the explanations carefully, you'll avoid common errors such as applying Table 310.15(B)(17) when you should be applying Table 310.15(B)(16).

Why so many tables? Why does Table 310.15(B)(17) list the ampacity of 6 THHN as 105 amperes, while Table 310.15(B)(16) lists the same conductor as having an ampacity of only 75 amperes? To answer that, go back to Article 100 and review the definition of ampacity. Notice the phrase "conditions of use." These tables set a maximum current value at which premature failure of the conductor insulation shouldn't occur during normal use, under the conditions described in the tables.

The designations THHN, THHW, RHH, and so on, are insulation types. Every type of insulation has a limit to how much heat it can withstand. When current flows through a conductor, it creates heat. How well the insulation around a conductor can dissipate that heat depends on factors such as whether that conductor is in free air or not. Think about what happens when you put on a sweater, a jacket, and then a coat—all at the same time. You heat up. Your skin can't dissipate heat with all that clothing on nearly as well as it dissipates heat in free air. The same principal applies to conductors.

Conductor insulation also fails with age. That's why we conduct cable testing and take other measures to predict failure and replace certain conductors (for example, feeders or critical equipment conductors) while they're still within design specifications. But conductor insulation failure takes decades under normal use—and it's a maintenance issue. However, if a conductor is forced to exceed the ampacity listed in the appropriate table, and as a result its design temperature is exceeded, insulation failure happens much more rapidly—often catastrophically. Consequently, exceeding the allowable ampacity of a conductor is a serious safety issue.

# Article 310 | Conductors for General Wiring

Please use the 2014 *Code* book to answer the following questions.

1. Conductors shall be permitted for use in any of the wiring methods recognized in Chapter 3 and as permitted in the *NEC*.

    (a) True
    (b) False

2. In general, the minimum size conductor permitted for use in parallel installations is _____ AWG.

    (a) 10
    (b) 4
    (c) 1
    (d) 1/0

3. Parallel conductors shall have the same _____.

    (a) length
    (b) material
    (c) size in circular mil area
    (d) all of these

4. Where conductors in parallel are run in separate raceways, the raceways shall have the same electrical characteristics.

    (a) True
    (b) False

5. No conductor shall be used where its operating temperature exceeds that designated for the type of insulated conductor involved.

    (a) True
    (b) False

6. The _____ rating of a conductor is the maximum temperature, at any location along its length, which the conductor can withstand over a prolonged period of time without serious degradation.

    (a) ambient
    (b) temperature
    (c) maximum withstand
    (d) short-circuit

7. There are four principal determinants of conductor operating temperature, one of which is _____ generated internally in the conductor as the result of load current flow, including fundamental and harmonic currents.

    (a) friction
    (b) magnetism
    (c) heat
    (d) none of these

8. The ampacities listed in 310.15 do not take _____ into consideration.

    (a) continuous loads
    (b) voltage drop
    (c) insulation
    (d) wet locations

9. The ampacity of a conductor can be different along the length of the conductor. The higher ampacity can be used beyond the point of transition for a distance of no more than _____ ft, or no more than _____ percent of the circuit length figured at the higher ampacity, whichever is less.

    (a) 10, 10
    (b) 10, 20
    (c) 15, 15
    (d) 20, 10

10. Each current-carrying conductor of a paralleled set of conductors shall be counted as a current-carrying conductor for the purpose of applying the adjustment factors of 310.15(B)(3)(a).

    (a) True
    (b) False

11. Where six current-carrying conductors are run in the same conduit or cable, the ampacity of each conductor shall be adjusted by a factor of _____ percent.

    (a) 40
    (b) 60
    (c) 80
    (d) 90

12. Conductor adjustment factors shall not apply to conductors in raceways having a length not exceeding _____ in.

    (a) 12
    (b) 24
    (c) 36
    (d) 48

13. The ampacity adjustment factors of Table 310.15(B)(3)(a) do not apply to Type AC or Type MC cable without an overall outer jacket, if which of the following conditions are met?

    (a) Each cable has not more than three current-carrying conductors.
    (b) The conductors are 12 AWG copper.
    (c) No more than 20 current-carrying conductors are installed without maintaining spacing.
    (d) all of these

14. Where conductors are installed in raceways or cables exposed to direct sunlight on or above rooftops, the ambient temperature shall be increased by _____ where the conduits are less than ½ in. from the rooftop.

    (a) 30°F
    (b) 40°F
    (c) 50°F
    (d) 60°F

15. A _____ conductor that carries only the unbalanced current from other conductors of the same circuit shall not be required to be counted when applying the provisions of 310.15(B)(3)(a).

    (a) neutral
    (b) ungrounded
    (c) grounding
    (d) none of these

16. On a three-phase, 4-wire, wye circuit, where the major portion of the load consists of nonlinear loads, the neutral conductor shall be counted when applying 310.15(B)(3)(a) adjustment factors.

    (a) True
    (b) False

17. When determining the number of current-carrying conductors, a grounding or bonding conductor shall not be counted when applying the provisions of 310.15(B)(3)(a).

    (a) True
    (b) False

18. THWN insulated conductors are rated _____.

    (a) 75°C
    (b) for wet locations
    (c) a and b
    (d) not enough information

19. THW insulation has a _____ rating when installed within electric-discharge lighting equipment, such as through fluorescent luminaires.

    (a) 60°C
    (b) 75°C
    (c) 90°C
    (d) 105°C

20. Which conductor type has an insulation temperature rating of 90°C?

    (a) THWN
    (b) RHW
    (c) THHN
    (d) TW

21. The minimum size conductor permitted for branch circuits under 600V is _____ AWG.

    (a) 14
    (b) 12
    (c) 10
    (d) 8

## Article 310 | Conductors for General Wiring

22. Where installed in raceways, conductors _____ AWG and larger shall be stranded.

    (a) 10
    (b) 8
    (c) 6
    (d) 4

# ARTICLE 312 — CABINET AND CUTOUT BOXES

## Introduction to Article 312—Cabinet and Cutout Boxes

This article addresses the installation and construction specifications for the items mentioned in its title. In Article 310, we observed that the conditions of use have an effect on the ampacity of a conductor. Likewise, the conditions of use have an effect on the selection and application of cabinet. For example, you can't use just any enclosure in a wet location or in a hazardous location. The conditions of use impose special requirements for these situations.

For all such enclosures, certain requirements apply—regardless of the use. For example, you must cover any openings, protect conductors from abrasion, and allow sufficient bending room for conductors.

Notice that Article 408 covers switchboards and panelboards, with primary emphasis on the interior, or "guts," while the cabinet that'd be used to enclose a panelboard is covered here in Article 312. Therefore you'll find that some important considerations such as wire-bending space at terminals of panelboards are included in this article.

Article 312 covers the installation and construction specifications for cabinets and cutout boxes. [312.1].

Please use the 2014 *Code* book to answer the following questions.

1. Surface-type cabinets, cutout boxes, and meter socket enclosures in damp or wet locations shall be mounted so there is at least _____ in. airspace between the enclosure and the wall or supporting surface.

    (a) 1/16
    (b) 1/4
    (c) 1¼
    (d) 6

2. Cabinets, cutout boxes, and meter socket enclosures installed in wet locations shall be _____.

    (a) waterproof
    (b) raintight
    (c) weatherproof
    (d) watertight

## Article 312 | Cabinet and Cutout Boxes

3. Where raceways or cables enter above the level of uninsulated live parts of cabinets, cutout boxes, and meter socket enclosures in a wet location, a(n) _____ shall be used.

   (a) fitting listed for wet locations
   (b) explosionproof seal
   (c) fitting listed for damp locations
   (d) insulated fitting

4. In walls constructed of wood or other _____ material, electrical cabinets shall be flush with the finished surface or project there from.

   (a) nonconductive
   (b) porous
   (c) fibrous
   (d) combustible

5. Noncombustible surfaces that are broken or incomplete shall be repaired so there will be no gaps or open spaces greater than _____ in. at the edge of a cabinet or cutout box employing a flush-type cover.

   (a) 1/32
   (b) 1/16
   (c) 1/8
   (d) 1/4

6. Openings in cabinets, cutout boxes, and meter socket enclosures through which conductors enter shall be _____.

   (a) closed in an approved manner
   (b) made using concentric knockouts only
   (c) centered in the cabinet wall
   (d) identified

7. Each cable entering a cutout box _____.

   (a) shall be secured to the cutout box
   (b) can be sleeved through a chase
   (c) shall have a maximum of two cables per connector
   (d) all of these

8. Nonmetallic cables can enter the top of surface-mounted cabinets, cutout boxes, and meter socket enclosures through nonflexible raceways not less than 18 in. or more than _____ ft in length if all of the required conditions are met.

   (a) 3
   (b) 10
   (c) 25
   (d) 100

9. Enclosures for switches or overcurrent devices are allowed to have conductors feeding through where the wiring space at any cross section is not filled to more than _____ percent of the cross-sectional area of the space.

   (a) 20
   (b) 30
   (c) 40
   (d) 60

10. Cabinets, cutout boxes, and meter socket enclosures can be used for conductors feeding through, spliced, or tapping off to other enclosures, switches, or overcurrent devices where _____.

    (a) the total area of the conductors at any cross section doesn't exceed 40 percent of the cross-sectional area of the space
    (b) the total area of conductors, splices, and taps installed at any cross section doesn't exceed 75 percent of the cross-sectional area of that space
    (c) a warning label on the enclosure identifies the closest disconnecting means for any feed-through conductors
    (d) all of these

# ARTICLE 314 — OUTLET, DEVICE, PULL, AND JUNCTION BOXES; CONDUIT BODIES; AND HANDHOLE ENCLOSURES

## Introduction to Article 314—Outlet, Device, Pull, and Junction Boxes; Conduit Bodies; and Handhole Enclosures

Article 314 contains installation requirements for outlet boxes, pull and junction boxes, conduit bodies, and handhole enclosures. As with the cabinet covered in Article 312, the conditions of use have a bearing on the type of material and equipment selected for a particular installation. If a raceway is installed in a wet location, for example, the correct fittings and the proper installation methods must be used.

The information here will help you size an outlet box using the proper cubic-inch capacity as well as calculating the minimum dimensions for larger pull boxes. There are limits on the amount of weight that can be supported by an outlet box and rules on how to support a device or outlet box to various surfaces. Article 314 will help you understand these types of rules so that your installation will be compliant with the *NEC*.

Please use the 2014 *Code* book to answer the following questions.

1. Nonmetallic boxes can be used with _____.
   (a) nonmetallic sheaths
   (b) nonmetallic raceways
   (c) flexible cords
   (d) all of these

2. Metal boxes shall be _____ in accordance with Article 250.
   (a) grounded
   (b) bonded
   (c) a and b
   (d) none of these

3. Boxes, conduit bodies, and fittings installed in wet locations shall be required to be listed for use in wet locations.
   (a) True
   (b) False

4. The total volume occupied by two internal cable clamps, six 12 AWG conductors, and a single-pole switch is _____ cu in.
   (a) 2.00
   (b) 4.50
   (c) 14.50
   (d) 20.25

## Article 314 | Outlet, Device, Pull, and Junction Boxes; Conduit Bodies; and Handhole Enclosures

5. According to the *NEC*, the volume of a 3 x 2 x 2 in. device box is _____ cu in.

    (a) 8
    (b) 10
    (c) 12
    (d) 14

6. When counting the number of conductors in a box, a conductor running through the box with an unbroken loop or coil not less than twice the minimum length required for free conductors shall be counted as _____ conductor(s).

    (a) one
    (b) two
    (c) three
    (d) four

7. Equipment grounding conductor(s), and not more than _____ fixture wires smaller than 14 AWG shall be omitted from the calculations where they enter the box from a domed luminaire or similar canopy and terminate within that box.

    (a) one
    (b) two
    (c) three
    (d) four

8. Where one or more internal cable clamps are present in the box, a single volume allowance in accordance with Table 314.16(b) shall be made based on the largest conductor present in the box.

    (a) True
    (b) False

9. Where a luminaire stud or hickey is present in the box, a _____ volume allowance in accordance with Table 314.16(b) shall be made for each type of fitting, based on the largest conductor present in the box.

    (a) single
    (b) double
    (c) single allowance for each gang
    (d) none of these

10. For the purposes of determining box fill, each device or utilization equipment in the box which is wider than a single device box counts as two conductors for each _____ required for the mounting.

    (a) inch
    (b) kilometer
    (c) gang
    (d) box

11. Each strap containing one or more devices shall count as a _____ volume allowance in accordance with Table 314.16(B), based on the largest conductor connected to a device(s) or equipment supported by the strap.

    (a) single
    (b) double
    (c) triple
    (d) none of these

12. A device or utilization equipment wider than a single 2 in. device box shall have _____ volume allowances provided for each gang required for mounting.

    (a) single
    (b) double
    (c) triple
    (d) none of these

13. Where one or more equipment grounding conductors enter a box, a _____ volume allowance in accordance with Table 314.16(b) shall be made based on the largest equipment grounding conductor.

    (a) single
    (b) double
    (c) triple
    (d) none of these

14. Conduit bodies that are durably and legibly marked by the manufacturer with their volume can contain splices, taps, or devices

    (a) True
    (b) False

15. Short-radius conduit bodies such as capped elbows, and service-entrance elbows that enclose conductors 6 AWG or smaller shall not contain _____.

    (a) splices
    (b) taps
    (c) devices
    (d) any of these

16. When Type NM cable is used with nonmetallic boxes not larger than 2¼ x 4 in., securing the cable to the box shall not be required if the cable is fastened within _____ in. of that box.

    (a) 6
    (b) 8
    (c) 10
    (d) 12

17. In noncombustible walls or ceilings, the front edge of a box, plaster ring, extension ring, or listed extender employing a flush-type cover, shall be set back not more than _____ in. from the finished surface.

    (a) ⅛
    (b) ¼
    (c) ⅜
    (d) ½

18. In walls or ceilings constructed of wood or other combustible surface material, boxes, plaster rings, extension rings, or listed extenders shall _____.

    (a) be flush with the surface
    (b) project from the surface
    (c) a or b
    (d) be set back no more than ¼ in.

19. Noncombustible surfaces that are broken or incomplete around boxes employing a flush-type cover or faceplate shall be repaired so there will be no gaps or open spaces larger than _____ in. at the edge of the box.

    (a) 1/16
    (b) ⅛
    (c) ¼
    (d) ½

20. A surface extension can be made from the cover of a box where the cover is designed so it is unlikely to fall off or be removed if its securing means becomes loose. The wiring method shall be _____ for an approved length that permits removal of the cover and provide access to the box interior, and arranged so that any grounding continuity is independent of the connection between the box and cover.

    (a) solid
    (b) flexible
    (c) rigid
    (d) cord

21. Surface-mounted outlet boxes shall be _____.

    (a) rigidly and securely fastened in place
    (b) supported by cables that protrude from the box
    (c) supported by cable entries from the top and permitted to rest against the supporting surface
    (d) none of these

22. _____ can be used to fasten boxes to a structural member using brackets on the outside of the enclosure.

    (a) Nails
    (b) Screws
    (c) Bolts
    (d) a and b

23. A wood brace used for supporting a box for structural mounting shall have a cross-section not less than nominal _____.

    (a) 1 in. x 2 in.
    (b) 2 in. x 2 in.
    (c) 2 in. x 3 in.
    (d) 2 in. x 4 in.

24. When mounting an enclosure in a finished surface, the enclosure shall be _____ secured to the surface by clamps, anchors, or fittings identified for the application.

    (a) temporarily
    (b) partially
    (c) never
    (d) rigidly

25. Outlet boxes can be secured to suspended-ceiling framing members by mechanical means such as _____, or by other means identified for the suspended-ceiling framing member(s).

    (a) bolts
    (b) screws
    (c) rivets
    (d) any of these

26. Enclosures not over 100 cu in. having threaded entries and not containing a device shall be considered to be adequately supported where _____ or more conduits are threaded wrenchtight into the enclosure and each conduit is secured within 3 ft of the enclosure.

    (a) one
    (b) two
    (c) three
    (d) none of these

27. Two intermediate metal or rigid metal conduits threaded wrenchtight into an enclosure can be used to support an outlet box containing devices or luminaires, if each raceway is supported within _____ in. of the box.

    (a) 12
    (b) 18
    (c) 24
    (d) 36

28. In completed installations, each outlet box shall have a _____.

    (a) cover
    (b) faceplate
    (c) canopy
    (d) any of these

29. A vertically mounted luminaire weighing not more than _____ can be supported to a device box or plaster ring with no fewer than two No. 6 or larger screws.

    (a) 4 lb
    (b) 6 lb
    (c) 8 lb
    (d) 10 lb

30. Boxes used at luminaire or lampholder outlets in a ceiling shall be designed so that a luminaire or lampholder can be attached and the boxes shall be required to support a luminaire weighing a minimum of _____ lb.

    (a) 20
    (b) 30
    (c) 40
    (d) 50

31. A luminaire that weighs more than _____ lb can be supported by an outlet box that is listed and marked for the weight of the luminaire.

    (a) 20
    (b) 30
    (c) 40
    (d) 50

32. Floor boxes _____ specifically for the application shall be used for receptacles located in the floor.

    (a) identified
    (b) listed
    (c) approved
    (d) none of these

33. Listed outlet boxes to support ceiling-suspended fans that weigh more than _____ lb shall have the maximum allowable weight marked on the box.

    (a) 35
    (b) 50
    (c) 60
    (d) 70

34. Utilization equipment weighing not more than 6 lb can be supported to any box or plaster ring secured to a box, provided the equipment is secured with at least two _____ or larger screws.

    (a) No. 6
    (b) No. 8
    (c) No. 10
    (d) self tapping

35. In straight pulls, the length of the box or conduit body shall not be less than _____ times the trade size of the largest raceway.

    (a) six
    (b) eight
    (c) twelve
    (d) none of these

36. Where angle or U pulls are made, the distance between each raceway entry inside the box or conduit body and the opposite wall of the box or conduit body shall not be less than _____ times the trade size of the largest raceway in a row plus the sum of the trade sizes of the remaining raceways in the same wall and row.

    (a) six
    (b) eight
    (c) twelve
    (d) none of these

37. Pull boxes or junction boxes with any dimension over _____ ft shall have all conductors cabled or racked in an approved manner.

    (a) 3
    (b) 6
    (c) 9
    (d) 12

38. Power distribution blocks shall be permitted in pull and junction boxes over 100 cubic inches when they comply with the provisions of 314.28(E)(1) through (5).

    (a) True
    (b) False

39. Power distribution blocks shall be permitted in pull and junction boxes over 100 cubic inches when _____.

    (a) they are listed as a power distribution block.
    (b) they are installed in a box not smaller than required by the installation instructions of the power distribution block.
    (c) the junction box is sized so that the wire-bending space requirements of 312.6 can be met.
    (d) all of these

40. Exposed live parts on the power distribution block are allowed when the junction box cover is removed.

    (a) True
    (b) False

41. Where the junction box contains a power distribution block, and it has conductors that don't terminate on the power distribution block(s), the through conductors must be arranged so the power distribution block terminals are _____ following installation.

    (a) unobstructed
    (b) above the through conductors
    (c) visible
    (d) labeled

42. _____ shall be installed so that the wiring contained in them can be rendered accessible without removing any part of the building or structure or, in underground circuits, without excavating sidewalks, paving, or earth.

    (a) Boxes
    (b) Conduit bodies
    (c) Handhole enclosures
    (d) all of these

43. Listed boxes and handhole enclosures designed for underground installation can be directly buried when covered by _____, if their location is effectively identified and accessible.

    (a) concrete
    (b) gravel
    (c) noncohesive granulated soil
    (d) b or c

44. Handhole enclosures shall be designed and installed to withstand _____.

    (a) 600 lb
    (b) 3,000 lb
    (c) 6,000 lb
    (d) all loads likely to be imposed

45. Underground raceways and cable assemblies entering a handhole enclosure shall extend into the enclosure, but they are not required to be _____.

    (a) bonded
    (b) insulated
    (c) mechanically connected to the handhole enclosure
    (d) below minimum cover requirements after leaving the handhole

46. Conductors, splices or terminations in a handhole enclosure shall be listed as suitable for _____.

    (a) wet locations
    (b) damp locations
    (c) direct burial in the earth
    (d) none of these

47. Handhole enclosure covers shall have an identifying _____ that prominently identifies the function of the enclosure, such as "electric."

    (a) mark
    (b) logo
    (c) manual
    (d) a or b

48. Handhole enclosure covers shall require the use of tools to open, or they shall weigh over _____.

    (a) 45 lb
    (b) 70 lb
    (c) 100 lb
    (d) 200 lb

# ARTICLE 320
# ARMORED CABLE (TYPE AC)

## Introduction to Article 320—Armored Cable (Type AC)

Armored cable is an assembly of insulated conductors, 14 AWG through 1 AWG, individually wrapped within waxed paper and contained within a flexible spiral metal sheath. The outside appearance of armored cable looks like flexible metal conduit as well as metal-clad cable to the casual observer. This cable has been referred to as "BX®" cable over the years and used in residential wiring in some areas of the country.

**Please use the 2014 *Code* book to answer the following questions.**

1. Type _____ cable is a fabricated assembly of insulated conductors in a flexible interlocked metallic armor.
   (a) AC
   (b) MC
   (c) NM
   (d) b and c

2. Type AC cable is permitted in _____ installations.
   (a) wet
   (b) cable trays
   (c) exposed
   (d) b and c

3. Armored cable shall not be installed _____.
   (a) in damp or wet locations
   (b) where subject to physical damage
   (c) where exposed to corrosive conditions
   (d) all of these

4. Exposed runs of Type AC cable can be installed on the underside of joists where supported at each joist and located so it is not subject to physical damage.
   (a) True
   (b) False

5. Type AC cable installed through, or parallel to, framing members shall be protected against physical damage from penetration by screws or nails.
   (a) True
   (b) False

6. When Type AC cable is run across the top of a floor joist in an attic without permanent ladders or stairs, guard strips within _____ of the scuttle hole or attic entrance shall protect the cable.
   (a) 3 ft
   (b) 4 ft
   (c) 5 ft
   (d) 6 ft

## Article 320 | Armored Cable (Type AC)

7. When armored cable is run parallel to the sides of rafters, studs, or floor joists in an accessible attic, the cable shall be protected with running boards.

   (a) True
   (b) False

8. The radius of the curve of the inner edge of any bend shall not be less than _____ for Type AC cable.

   (a) five times the largest conductor within the cable
   (b) three times the diameter of the cable
   (c) five times the diameter of the cable
   (d) six times the outside diameter of the conductors

9. Type AC cable shall be supported and secured by _____.

   (a) staples
   (b) cable ties
   (c) straps
   (d) any of these

10. Type AC cable shall be secured at intervals not exceeding 4½ ft and within _____ in. of every outlet box, cabinet, conduit body, or fitting.

    (a) 6
    (b) 8
    (c) 10
    (d) 12

11. Type AC cable installed horizontally through wooden or metal framing members is considered supported where support doesn't exceed _____ ft intervals.

    (a) 2
    (b) 3
    (c) 4½
    (d) 6

12. Armored cable used to connect recessed luminaires or equipment within an accessible ceiling can be unsecured for lengths up to _____ ft.

    (a) 2
    (b) 3
    (c) 4½
    (d) 6

13. At Type AC cable terminations, a(n) _____ shall be provided.

    (a) fitting (or box design) that protects the conductors from abrasion
    (b) insulating bushing between the conductors and the cable armor
    (c) a and b
    (d) none of these

14. Type AC cable installed in thermal insulation shall have conductors that are rated at 90°C. The ampacity of the cable in this application shall not exceed that of a _____ rated conductor.

    (a) 60°C
    (b) 75°C
    (c) 90°C
    (d) none of these

# ARTICLE 330 — METAL-CLAD CABLE (TYPE MC)

## Introduction to Article 330—Metal-Clad Cable (Type MC)

Metal-clad cable encloses insulated conductors in a metal sheath of either corrugated or smooth copper or aluminum tubing, or spiral interlocked steel or aluminum. The physical characteristics of Type MC cable make it a versatile wiring method that you can use in almost any location, and for almost any application. The most commonly used Type MC cable is the interlocking kind, which looks similar to armored cable or flexible metal conduit. Traditional interlocked Type MC cable isn't permitted to serve as an equipment grounding conductor, therefore this cable must contain an equipment grounding conductor in accordance with 250.118(1). There's a fairly new product available called interlocked Type MC$^{AP}$ cable that contains a bare aluminum grounding/bonding conductor running just below the metal armor, which allows the sheath to serve as an equipment grounding conductor [250.118(10)(b)].

**Please use the 2014 Code book to answer the following questions.**

1. Type _____ cable is a factory assembly of insulated circuit conductors within an armor of interlocking metal tape, or a smooth or corrugated metallic sheath.

   (a) AC
   (b) MC
   (c) NM
   (d) b and c

2. Type MC cable shall not be _____ unless the metallic sheath or armor is resistant to the conditions, or is protected by material resistant to the conditions.

   (a) used for direct burial in the earth
   (b) embedded in concrete
   (c) exposed to cinder fill
   (d) all of these

3. Type MC cable installed through, or parallel to, framing members shall be protected against physical damage from penetration by screws or nails by 1¼ in. separation or protected by a suitable metal plate.

   (a) True
   (b) False

4. Smooth-sheath Type MC cable with an external diameter not greater than ¾ in. shall have a bending radius not more than _____ times the cable external diameter.

   (a) five
   (b) 10
   (c) 12
   (d) 13

## Article 330 | Metal-Clad Cable (Type MC)

5. Bends made in interlocked or corrugated sheath Type MC cable shall have a radius of at least _____ times the external diameter of the metallic sheath.

    (a) 5
    (b) 7
    (c) 10
    (d) 12

6. Type MC cable containing four or fewer conductors, sized no larger than 10 AWG, shall be secured within _____ in. of every box, cabinet, fitting, or other cable termination.

    (a) 8
    (b) 12
    (c) 18
    (d) 24

7. Type MC cable shall be secured at intervals not exceeding _____ ft.

    (a) 3
    (b) 4
    (c) 6
    (d) 8

8. Type MC cable installed horizontally through wooden or metal framing members are considered secured and supported where such support doesn't exceed _____ ft intervals.

    (a) 3
    (b) 4
    (c) 6
    (d) 8

9. Type MC cable can be unsupported where the cable is _____.

    (a) fished between concealed access points in finished buildings or structures and support is impracticable
    (b) not more than 2 ft in length at terminals where flexibility is necessary
    (c) not more than 6 ft from the last point of support within an accessible ceiling for the connection of luminaires or other electrical equipment
    (d) a or c

10. Fittings used for connecting Type MC cable to boxes, cabinets, or other equipment shall _____.

    (a) be nonmetallic only
    (b) be listed and identified for such use
    (c) be listed and identified as weatherproof
    (d) include anti-shorting bushings

# ARTICLE 334 — NONMETALLIC-SHEATHED CABLE (TYPES NM AND NMC)

## Introduction to Article 334—Nonmetallic-Sheathed Cable (Types NM and NMC)

Nonmetallic-sheathed cable is flexible, inexpensive, and easily installed. It provides very limited physical protection for the conductors, so the installation restrictions are strict. Its low cost and relative ease of installation make it a common wiring method for residential and commercial branch circuits. In the field, Type NM cable is typically referred to as "Romex®."

Please use the 2014 *Code* book to answer the following questions.

1. Type _____ cable is a factory assembly that encloses two or more insulated conductors within a nonmetallic jacket.

   (a) AC
   (b) MC
   (c) NM
   (d) b and c

2. Type NM cable shall be _____.

   (a) marked
   (b) approved
   (c) identified
   (d) listed

3. Type NM cables shall not be used in one- and two-family dwellings exceeding three floors above grade.

   (a) True
   (b) False

4. Type NM and Type NMC cables shall be permitted in _____.

   (a) one- and two-family dwellings and their attached/detached garages and storage buildings
   (b) multifamily dwellings permitted to be of Types III, IV, and V construction
   (c) other structures permitted to be of Types III, IV, and V construction, except as prohibited in 334.12
   (d) any of these

5. Type NM cable can be installed as open runs in dropped or suspended ceilings in other than one- and two-family and multifamily dwellings.

   (a) True
   (b) False

## Article 334 | Nonmetallic-Sheathed Cable (Types NM and NMC)

6. Type NM cable shall not be used _____.

    (a) in other than dwelling units
    (b) in the air void of masonry block not subject to excessive moisture
    (c) for exposed work
    (d) embedded in poured cement, concrete, or aggregate

7. Type NM cable shall closely follow the surface of the building finish or running boards when run exposed.

    (a) True
    (b) False

8. Type NM cable shall be protected from physical damage by _____.

    (a) EMT
    (b) Schedule 80 PVC conduit
    (c) RMC
    (d) any of these

9. Type NM cable on a wall of an unfinished basement installed in a listed raceway shall have a(n) _____ installed at the point where the cable enters the raceway.

    (a) insulating bushing or adapter
    (b) sealing fitting
    (c) bonding bushing
    (d) junction box

10. Where Type NM cable is run at angles with joists in unfinished basements and crawl spaces, it is permissible to secure cables not smaller than _____ conductors directly to the lower edges of the joist.

    (a) two, 6 AWG
    (b) three, 8 AWG
    (c) three, 10 AWG
    (d) a or b

11. Grommets or bushings for the protection of Type NM cable shall be _____ for the purpose.

    (a) marked
    (b) approved
    (c) identified
    (d) listed

12. Type NM cable can be supported and secured by _____.

    (a) staples
    (b) cable ties
    (c) straps
    (d) any of these

13. Type NM cable protected from physical damage by a raceway shall not be required to be _____ within the raceway.

    (a) covered
    (b) insulated
    (c) secured
    (d) unspliced

14. Flat Type NM cables shall not be stapled on edge.

    (a) True
    (b) False

15. Where more than two Type NM cables are installed through the same opening in wood framing that is to be sealed with thermal insulation, caulk, or sealing foam, the allowable ampacity of each conductor shall be _____.

    (a) no more than 20A
    (b) adjusted in accordance with Table 310.15(B)(3)(a)
    (c) limited to 30A
    (d) calculated by an engineer

16. For Type NM and NMC cable, the conductor ampacity used for ambient temperature correction [310.15(B)(2)(a)], conductor bundling adjustment [310.15(B)(3)(a)], or both, is based on the 90°C conductor insulation rating [310.15(B)(2)], provided the adjusted or corrected ampacity doesn't exceed that of a _____ rated conductor.

    (a) 60°C
    (b) 75°C
    (c) 90°C
    (d) 120°C

17. The insulation temperature rating of conductors in Type NM cable shall be _____.

    (a) 60°C
    (b) 75°C
    (c) 90°C
    (d) 105°C

# ARTICLE 338 — SERVICE-ENTRANCE CABLE (TYPES SE AND USE)

## Introduction to Article 338—Service-Entrance Cable (Types SE and USE)

Service-entrance cable is a single conductor or multiconductor assembly with or without an overall moisture-resistant covering. This cable is used primarily for services, but can also be used for feeders and branch circuits when the limitations of this article are observed.

Please use the 2014 *Code* book to answer the following questions.

1. Type _____ cable is an assembly primarily used for services.

    (a) NM
    (b) TC
    (c) SE
    (d) none of these

2. Type _____ is a multiconductor cable identified for use as underground service-entrance cable.

    (a) SE
    (b) NM
    (c) UF
    (d) USE

3. Type SE cable shall be permitted to be used as _____ in wiring systems where all of the circuit conductors of the cable are of the thermoset or thermoplastic type.

    (a) branch circuits
    (b) feeders
    (c) a or b
    (d) neither a or b

4. Type SE cables shall be permitted to be used for branch circuits or feeders where the insulated conductors are used for circuit wiring and the uninsulated conductor is used only for _____ purposes.

    (a) grounded connection
    (b) equipment grounding
    (c) remote control and signaling
    (d) none of these

5. Type SE cable can be used for interior wiring as long as it complies with the installation requirements of Part II of Article 334, excluding 334.80.

    (a) True
    (b) False

6. Type USE cable is not permitted for _____ wiring.

    (a) underground
    (b) interior
    (c) a or b
    (d) a and b

## Article 338 | Service-Entrance Cable (Types SE and USE)

7. Type USE cable used for service laterals shall be permitted to emerge from the ground if terminated in an enclosure at an outside location and protected in accordance with 300.5(D).

   (a) True
   (b) False

8. The radius of the curve of the inner edge of any bend, during or after installation, shall not be less than _____ times the diameter of Type USE or SE cable.

   (a) five
   (b) seven
   (c) 10
   (d) 12

# ARTICLE 340 — UNDERGROUND FEEDER AND BRANCH-CIRCUIT CABLE (TYPE UF)

## Introduction to Article 340—Underground Feeder and Branch-Circuit Cable (Type UF)
UF cable is a moisture-, fungus-, and corrosion-resistant cable suitable for direct burial in the earth.

Please use the 2014 *Code* book to answer the following questions.

1. Type _____ cable is a factory assembly of conductors with an overall covering of nonmetallic material suitable for direct burial in the earth.
   (a) NM
   (b) UF
   (c) SE
   (d) TC

2. Type UF cable is permitted to be used for inside wiring.
   (a) True
   (b) False

3. Type UF cable can be used for service conductors.
   (a) True
   (b) False

4. Type UF cable can be used in commercial garages.
   (a) True
   (b) False

5. Type UF cable shall not be used in _____.
   (a) motion picture studios
   (b) storage battery rooms
   (c) hoistways
   (d) all of these

6. Type UF cable shall not be used _____.
   (a) in any hazardous (classified) location except as otherwise permitted in this *Code*
   (b) embedded in poured cement, concrete, or aggregate
   (c) where exposed to direct rays of the sun, unless identified as sunlight resistant
   (d) all of these

7. Type UF cable shall not be used where subject to physical damage.
   (a) True
   (b) False

### Article 340 | Underground Feeder and Branch-Circuit Cable (Type UF)

8. The ampacity of Type UF cable shall be that of _____ conductors in accordance with 310.15.

   (a) 60°C
   (b) 75°C
   (c) 90°C
   (d) 105°C

# ARTICLE 342 — INTERMEDIATE METAL CONDUIT (TYPE IMC)

## Introduction to Article 342—Intermediate Metal Conduit (Type IMC)

Intermediate metal conduit (IMC) is a circular metal raceway with an outside diameter equal to that of rigid metal conduit. The wall thickness of intermediate metal conduit is less than that of rigid metal conduit (RMC), so it's a greater interior cross-sectional area for containing conductors. Intermediate metal conduit is lighter and less expensive than rigid metal conduit, but it can be used in all of the same locations as rigid metal conduit. Intermediate metal conduit also uses a different steel alloy that makes it stronger than rigid metal conduit, even though the walls are thinner. Intermediate metal conduit is manufactured in both galvanized steel and aluminum; the steel type is much more common.

Please use the 2014 *Code* book to answer the following questions.

1. IMC can be installed in or under cinder fill subject to permanent moisture _____.

   (a) where the conduit is not less than 18 in. under the fill
   (b) when protected on all sides by 2 in. of noncinder concrete
   (c) where protected by corrosion protection and judged suitable for the condition
   (d) any of these

2. Materials such as straps, bolts, screws, and so forth, which are associated with the installation of IMC in wet locations shall be _____.

   (a) weatherproof
   (b) weathertight
   (c) corrosion resistant
   (d) none of these

3. Where practicable, contact of dissimilar metals shall be avoided in an IMC raceway installation to prevent _____.

   (a) corrosion
   (b) galvanic action
   (c) shorts
   (d) none of these

4. A run of IMC shall not contain more than the equivalent of _____ quarter bend(s) between pull points such as conduit bodies and boxes.

   (a) one
   (b) two
   (c) three
   (d) four

## Article 342 | Intermediate Metal Conduit (Type IMC)

5. When IMC is cut in the field, reaming is required to remove the burrs and rough edges.

    (a) True
    (b) False

6. IMC must be secured _____.

    (a) by fastening within 3 ft of each outlet box, junction box, device box, cabinet, conduit body, or other conduit termination
    (b) within 5 ft of a box or termination fitting when structural members don't permit the raceway to be secured within 3 ft of the termination
    (c) except when the IMC is within 3 ft of the service head for an above-the-roof termination of a mast
    (d) a, b, or c

7. Trade size 1 IMC shall be supported at intervals not exceeding _____ ft.

    (a) 8
    (b) 10
    (c) 12
    (d) 14

8. Horizontal runs of IMC supported by openings through framing members at intervals not exceeding 10 ft and securely fastened within 3 ft of terminations shall be permitted.

    (a) True
    (b) False

9. Threadless couplings and connectors used on threaded IMC ends shall be listed for the purpose.

    (a) True
    (b) False

10. Threadless couplings approved for use with IMC in wet locations shall be _____.

    (a) rainproof
    (b) listed for wet locations
    (c) moistureproof
    (d) concrete-tight

11. Running threads shall not be used on IMC for connection at couplings.

    (a) True
    (b) False

12. Where IMC enters a box, fitting, or other enclosure, _____ shall be provided to protect the wire from abrasion unless the design of the box, fitting, or enclosure affords equivalent protection.

    (a) a bushing
    (b) duct seal
    (c) electrical tape
    (d) seal fittings

# ARTICLE 344 — RIGID METAL CONDUIT (TYPE RMC)

## Introduction to Article 344—Rigid Metal Conduit (Type RMC)

Rigid metal conduit, commonly called "rigid," has long been the standard raceway for providing protection from physical impact and from difficult environments. The outside diameter of rigid metal conduit is the same as intermediate metal conduit. However, the wall thickness of rigid metal conduit is greater than intermediate metal conduit; therefore the interior cross-sectional area is smaller. Rigid metal conduit is heavier and more expensive than intermediate metal conduit, and it can be used in any location. Rigid metal conduit is manufactured in both galvanized steel and aluminum; the steel type is much more common.

Please use the 2014 *Code* book to answer the following questions.

1. Galvanized steel, stainless steel and red brass RMC can be installed in concrete, in direct contact with the earth, or in areas subject to severe corrosive influences when protected by _____ and judged suitable for the condition.

   (a) ceramic
   (b) corrosion protection
   (c) backfill
   (d) a natural barrier

2. Galvanized steel, stainless steel, and red brass RMC shall be permitted in or under cinder fill subject to permanent moisture, when protected on all sides by a layer of noncinder concrete not less than _____ in. thick.

   (a) 2
   (b) 4
   (c) 6
   (d) 18

3. Materials such as straps, bolts, and so forth, associated with the installation of RMC in wet locations shall be _____.

   (a) weatherproof
   (b) weathertight
   (c) corrosion resistant
   (d) none of these

4. Aluminum fittings and enclosures can be used with _____ conduit where not subject to severe corrosive influences.

   (a) steel rigid metal
   (b) aluminum rigid metal
   (c) PVC-coated rigid conduit only
   (d) a and b

## Article 344 | Rigid Metal Conduit (Type RMC)

5. The minimum radius of a field bend on trade size 1¼ RMC is _____ in.

   (a) 7
   (b) 8
   (c) 10
   (d) 14

6. A run of RMC shall not contain more than the equivalent of _____ quarter bend(s) between pull points such as conduit bodies and boxes.

   (a) one
   (b) two
   (c) three
   (d) four

7. Cut ends of RMC shall be _____ or otherwise finished to remove rough edges.

   (a) threaded
   (b) reamed
   (c) painted
   (d) galvanized

8. Horizontal runs of RMC supported by openings through _____ at intervals not exceeding 10 ft and securely fastened within 3 ft of termination points shall be permitted.

   (a) walls
   (b) trusses
   (c) rafters
   (d) framing members

9. Threadless couplings and connectors used with RMC in wet locations shall be _____.

   (a) listed for wet locations
   (b) listed for damp locations
   (c) nonabsorbent
   (d) weatherproof

10. Threadless couplings and connectors used with RMC buried in masonry or concrete shall be the _____ type.

    (a) raintight
    (b) wet and damp location
    (c) nonabsorbent
    (d) concrete tight

11. Running threads shall not be used on RMC for connection at _____.

    (a) boxes
    (b) cabinets
    (c) couplings
    (d) meter sockets

12. Where RMC enters a box, fitting, or other enclosure, _____ shall be provided to protect the wire from abrasion, unless the design of the box, fitting, or enclosure affords equivalent protection.

    (a) a bushing
    (b) duct seal
    (c) electrical tape
    (d) seal fittings

13. The standard length of RMC shall _____.

    (a) be 10 ft
    (b) include a coupling on each length
    (c) be threaded on each end
    (d) all of these

# ARTICLE 348 — FLEXIBLE METAL CONDUIT (TYPE FMC)

## Introduction to Article 348—Flexible Metal Conduit (Type FMC)

Flexible metal conduit (FMC), commonly called "Greenfield" or "flex," is a raceway of an interlocked metal strip of either steel or aluminum. It's primarily used for the final 6 ft or less of raceways between a more rigid raceway system and equipment that moves, shakes, or vibrates. Examples of such equipment include pump motors and industrial machinery.

Please use the 2014 *Code* book to answer the following questions.

1. _____ is a raceway of circular cross section made of a helically wound, formed, interlocked metal strip.

   (a) Type MC cable
   (b) Type AC Cable
   (c) LFMC
   (d) FMC

2. FMC shall not be installed _____.

   (a) in wet locations
   (b) embedded in poured concrete
   (c) where subject to physical damage
   (d) all of these

3. FMC can be installed exposed or concealed where not subject to physical damage.

   (a) True
   (b) False

4. Bends in FMC shall be made so that the conduit is not damaged and the internal diameter of the conduit is _____.

   (a) larger than ⅜ in.
   (b) not effectively reduced
   (c) increased
   (d) larger than 1 in.

5. Bends in FMC _____ between pull points.

   (a) shall not be made
   (b) need not be limited (in degrees)
   (c) shall not exceed 360 degrees
   (d) shall not exceed 180 degrees

6. Cut ends of FMC shall be trimmed or otherwise finished to remove rough edges, except where fittings _____.

   (a) are the crimp-on type
   (b) thread into the convolutions
   (c) contain insulated throats
   (d) are listed for grounding

## Article 348 | Flexible Metal Conduit (Type FMC)

7. FMC shall be supported and secured _____.

   (a) at intervals not exceeding 4½ ft
   (b) within 8 in. on each side of a box where fished
   (c) where fished
   (d) at intervals not exceeding 6 ft

8. Flexible metal conduit must be securely fastened by a means approved by the authority having jurisdiction within _____ of termination.

   (a) 6 in.
   (b) 10 in.
   (c) 1 ft
   (d) 10 ft

9. Flexible metal conduit shall not be required to be _____ where fished between access points through concealed spaces in finished buildings or structures and supporting is impracticable.

   (a) secured
   (b) supported
   (c) complete
   (d) a and b

10. FMC to a luminaire or electrical equipment within an accessible ceiling is permitted to be unsupported for not more than 6 ft from the last point where the raceway is securely fastened, including securing by listed FMC fittings.

    (a) True
    (b) False

11. In an FMC installation, _____ connectors shall not be concealed.

    (a) straight
    (b) angle
    (c) grounding-type
    (d) none of these

12. When FMC is used where flexibility is necessary to minimize the transmission of vibration from equipment or to provide flexibility for equipment that requires movement after installation, _____ shall be installed.

    (a) an equipment grounding conductor
    (b) an expansion fitting
    (c) flexible nonmetallic connectors
    (d) none of these

# ARTICLE 350 — LIQUIDTIGHT FLEXIBLE METAL CONDUIT (TYPE LFMC)

## Introduction to Article 350—Liquidtight Flexible Metal Conduit (Type LFMC)

Liquidtight flexible metal conduit (LFMC), with its associated connectors and fittings, is a flexible raceway commonly used for connections to equipment that vibrates or is required to move occasionally. Liquidtight flexible metal conduit is commonly called "Sealtight®" or "liquidtight." Liquidtight flexible metal conduit is of similar construction to flexible metal conduit, but it also has an outer liquidtight thermoplastic covering. It has the same primary purpose as flexible metal conduit, but it also provides protection from moisture and some corrosive effects.

**Please use the 2014 *Code* book to answer the following questions.**

1. _____ is a raceway of circular cross section having an outer liquidtight, nonmetallic, sunlight-resistant jacket over an inner flexible metal core.

    (a) FMC
    (b) LFNMC
    (c) LFMC
    (d) none of these

2. The use of LFMC shall be permitted for _____.

    (a) direct burial where listed and marked for the purpose
    (b) exposed work
    (c) concealed work
    (d) all of these

3. Liquidtight flexible metal conduit must be securely fastened by a means approved by the authority having jurisdiction within _____ of termination.

    (a) 6 in.
    (b) 10 in.
    (c) 1 ft
    (d) 10 ft

4. LFMC shall be supported and secured _____.

    (a) at intervals not exceeding 4½ ft
    (b) within 8 in. on each side of a box where fished
    (c) where fished
    (d) at intervals not exceeding 6 ft

## Article 350 | Liquidtight Flexible Metal Conduit (Type LFMC)

5. LFMC shall not be required to be secured or supported where fished between access points through _____ spaces in finished buildings or structures and supporting is impractical.

    (a) concealed
    (b) exposed
    (c) hazardous
    (d) completed

6. For liquidtight flexible metal conduit, if flexibility is necessary after installation, unsecured lengths from the last point the raceway is securely fastened must not exceed _____.

    (a) 3 ft for trade sizes ½ through 1¼
    (b) 4 ft for trade sizes 1½ through 2
    (c) 5 ft for trade sizes 2½ and larger
    (d) all of these

7. _____ connectors shall not be concealed when used in installations of LFMC.

    (a) Straight
    (b) Angle
    (c) Grounding-type
    (d) none of these

8. When LFMC is used to connect equipment where flexibility is necessary to minimize the transmission of vibration from equipment of for equipment requiring movement after installation, a(n) _____ conductor shall be installed.

    (a) main bonding
    (b) grounded
    (c) equipment grounding
    (d) none of these

9. Where flexibility _____, liquidtight flexible metal conduit shall be permitted to be used as an equipment grounding conductor when installed in accordance with 250.118(6).

    (a) is required after installation
    (b) is not required after installation
    (c) either a or d
    (d) is optional

# ARTICLE 352 — RIGID POLYVINYL CHLORIDE CONDUIT (TYPE PVC)

## Introduction to Article 352—Rigid Polyvinyl Chloride Conduit (Type PVC)

Rigid polyvinyl chloride conduit (PVC) is a rigid nonmetallic conduit that provides many of the advantages of rigid metal conduit, while allowing installation in areas that are wet or corrosive. It's an inexpensive raceway, and easily installed. It's lightweight, easily cut and glued together, and relatively strong. However, conduits manufactured from polyvinyl chloride (PVC) are brittle when cold, and they sag when hot. This type of conduit is commonly used as an underground raceway because of its low cost, ease of installation, and resistance to corrosion and decay.

Please use the 2014 *Code* book to answer the following questions.

1. Extreme _____ may cause PVC conduit to become brittle, and therefore more susceptible to damage from physical contact.

    (a) sunlight
    (b) corrosive conditions
    (c) heat
    (d) cold

2. PVC conduit shall be permitted for exposed work where subject to physical damage if identified for such use.

    (a) True
    (b) False

3. PVC conduit can support nonmetallic conduit bodies not larger than the largest entering raceway, but the conduit bodies shall not contain devices, luminaires, or other equipment.

    (a) True
    (b) False

4. Conductors rated at a temperature _____ than the listed temperature rating of PVC conduit shall be permitted to be installed in PVC conduit, provided the conductors are not operated at a temperature above the raceway's listed temperature rating.

    (a) lower
    (b) the same as
    (c) higher
    (d) a or b

5. PVC conduit shall not be used _____, unless specifically permitted.

    (a) in hazardous (classified) locations
    (b) for the support of luminaires or other equipment
    (c) where subject to physical damage unless identified for such use
    (d) all of these

6. The number of conductors permitted in PVC conduit shall not exceed the percentage fill specified in _____.

   (a) Chapter 9, Table 1
   (b) Table 250.66
   (c) Table 310.15(B)(16)
   (d) 240.6

7. Bends in PVC conduit shall be made only _____.

   (a) by hand forming the bend
   (b) with bending equipment identified for the purpose
   (c) with a truck exhaust pipe
   (d) by use of an open flame torch

8. Bends in PVC conduit shall _____ between pull points.

   (a) not be made
   (b) not be limited in degrees
   (c) be limited to 360 degrees
   (d) be limited to 180 degrees

9. The cut ends of PVC conduit must be trimmed to remove the burrs and rough edges.

   (a) True
   (b) False

10. PVC conduit shall be securely fastened within _____ in. of each box.

    (a) 6
    (b) 12
    (c) 24
    (d) 36

11. Where PVC conduit enters a box, fitting, or other enclosure, a bushing or adapter shall be provided to protect the conductor from abrasion unless the design of the box, fitting, or enclosure affords equivalent protection.

    (a) True
    (b) False

12. Joints between PVC conduit, couplings, fittings, and boxes shall be made by _____.

    (a) the authority having jurisdiction
    (b) set screw fittings
    (c) an approved method
    (d) expansion fittings

# ARTICLE 356 — LIQUIDTIGHT FLEXIBLE NONMETALLIC CONDUIT (TYPE LFNC)

## Introduction to Article 356—Liquidtight Flexible Nonmetallic Conduit (Type LFNC)

Liquidtight flexible nonmetallic conduit (LFNC) is a listed raceway of circular cross section having an outer liquidtight, nonmetallic, sunlight-resistant jacket over an inner flexible core with associated couplings, connectors, and fittings.

Please use the 2014 *Code* book to answer the following questions.

1. LFNC shall be permitted for _____.

   (a) direct burial where listed and marked for the purpose
   (b) exposed work
   (c) outdoors where listed and marked for this purpose
   (d) all of these

2. The number of conductors permitted in LFNC shall not exceed the percentage fill specified in _____.

   (a) Chapter 9, Table 1
   (b) Table 250.66
   (c) Table 310.15(B)(16)
   (d) 240.6

3. Bends in LFNC shall be made so that the conduit will not be damaged and the internal diameter of the conduit will not be effectively reduced. Bends can be made _____.

   (a) manually without auxiliary equipment
   (b) with bending equipment identified for the purpose
   (c) with any kind of conduit bending tool that will work
   (d) by the use of an open flame torch

4. Bends in LFNC shall _____ between pull points.

   (a) not be made
   (b) not be limited in degrees
   (c) be limited to 360 degrees
   (d) be limited to 180 degrees

5. When LFNC is used, and equipment grounding is required, a separate _____ shall be installed in the conduit.

   (a) equipment grounding conductor
   (b) expansion fitting
   (c) flexible nonmetallic connector
   (d) none of these

Notes

# ARTICLE 358 ELECTRICAL METALLIC TUBING (TYPE EMT)

## Introduction to Article 358—Electrical Metallic Tubing (Type EMT)

Electrical metallic tubing (EMT) is a lightweight raceway that's relatively easy to bend, cut, and ream. Because it isn't threaded, all connectors and couplings are of the threadless type and provide quick, easy, and inexpensive installation when compared to other metallic conduit systems, which makes it very popular. Electrical metallic tubing is manufactured in both galvanized steel and aluminum; the steel type is used the most.

Please use the 2014 *Code* book to answer the following questions.

1. _____ is a listed thin-wall, metallic tubing of circular cross section used for the installation and physical protection of electrical conductors when joined together with listed fittings.

    (a) LFNC
    (b) EMT
    (c) NUCC
    (d) RTRC

2. EMT, elbows, couplings, and fittings can be installed in concrete, in direct contact with the earth, or in areas subject to severe corrosive influences if _____.

    (a) protected by corrosion protection
    (b) approved as suitable for the condition
    (c) a and b
    (d) listed for wet locations

3. When EMT is installed in wet locations, all supports, bolts, straps, and screws shall be _____.

    (a) of corrosion-resistant materials
    (b) protected against corrosion
    (c) a or b
    (d) of nonmetallic materials only

4. EMT shall not be used where _____.

    (a) subject to severe physical damage
    (b) protected from corrosion only by enamel
    (c) used for the support of luminaires
    (d) any of these

5. EMT shall not be threaded.

    (a) True
    (b) False

## Article 358 | Electrical Metallic Tubing (Type EMT)

6. EMT couplings and connectors shall be made up _____.

   (a) of metal
   (b) in accordance with industry standards
   (c) tight
   (d) none of these

# ARTICLE 362 — ELECTRICAL NONMETALLIC TUBING (TYPE ENT)

## Introduction to Article 362—Electrical Nonmetallic Tubing (Type ENT)

Electrical nonmetallic tubing (ENT) is a pliable, corrugated, circular raceway made of polyvinyl chloride. In some parts of the country, the field name for electrical nonmetallic tubing is "Smurf Pipe" or "Smurf Tube," because it was only available in blue when it originally came out at the time the children's cartoon characters "The Smurfs" were most popular. Today, the raceway is available in many colors such as white, yellow, red, green, and orange, and is sold in both fixed lengths and on reels.

Please use the 2014 *Code* book to answer the following questions.

1. ENT is composed of a material resistant to moisture and chemical atmospheres, and is _____.

    (a) flexible
    (b) flame retardant
    (c) fireproof
    (d) flammable

2. When a building is supplied with a(n) _____ fire sprinkler system, ENT shall be permitted to be used within walls, floors, and ceilings, exposed or concealed, in buildings exceeding three floors above grade.

    (a) listed
    (b) identified
    (c) NFPA 13-2013
    (d) none of these

3. When a building is supplied with a fire sprinkler system, ENT can be installed above any suspended ceiling.

    (a) True
    (b) False

4. ENT and fittings can be _____, provided fittings identified for this purpose are used.

    (a) encased in poured concrete
    (b) embedded in a concrete slab on grade where the tubing is placed on sand or approved screenings
    (c) a or b
    (d) none of these

5. ENT is not permitted in hazardous (classified) locations, unless permitted in other articles of the *Code*.

    (a) True
    (b) False

6. ENT shall be permitted for direct earth burial when used with fittings listed for this purpose.

   (a) True
   (b) False

7. ENT shall not be used where exposed to the direct rays of the sun, unless identified as _____.

   (a) high-temperature rated
   (b) sunlight resistant
   (c) Schedule 80
   (d) never can be

8. The number of conductors permitted in ENT shall not exceed the percentage fill specified in _____.

   (a) Chapter 9, Table 1
   (b) Table 250.66
   (c) Table 310.15(B)(16)
   (d) 240.6

9. Cut ends of ENT shall be trimmed inside and _____ to remove rough edges.

   (a) outside
   (b) tapered
   (c) filed
   (d) beveled

10. Unbroken lengths of electric nonmetallic tubing shall not be required to be secured where fished between access points for _____ work in finished buildings or structures and supporting is impractical.

    (a) concealed
    (b) exposed
    (c) hazardous
    (d) completed

11. Bushings or adapters shall be provided at ENT terminations to protect the conductors from abrasion, unless the box, fitting, or enclosure design provides equivalent protection.

    (a) True
    (b) False

12. Joints between lengths of ENT, couplings, fittings, and boxes shall be made by _____.

    (a) a qualified person
    (b) set screw fittings
    (c) an approved method
    (d) exothermic welding

# ARTICLE 376 — METAL WIREWAYS

## Introduction to Article 376—Metal Wireways

Metal wireways are commonly used where access to the conductors within a raceway is required to make terminations, splices, or taps to several devices at a single location. High cost precludes their use for other than short distances, except in some commercial or industrial occupancies where the wiring is frequently revised.

### Author's Comment:

- Both metal wireways and nonmetallic wireways are often incorrectly called "troughs," "auxiliary gutters," "auxiliary wireways," or "gutters" in the field.

Please use the 2014 *Code* book to answer the following questions.

1. Metal wireways are sheet metal troughs with _____ for housing and protecting electric conductors and cable.

   (a) removable covers
   (b) hinged covers
   (c) a or b
   (d) none of these

2. Wireways shall be permitted for _____.

   (a) exposed work
   (b) totally concealed work
   (c) wet locations if listed for the purpose
   (d) a and c

3. Wireways can pass transversely through a wall _____.

   (a) if the length passing through the wall is unbroken
   (b) if the wall is of fire-rated construction
   (c) in hazardous (classified) locations
   (d) if the wall is not of fire-rated construction

4. Conductors larger than that for which the wireway is designed can be installed in any wireway.

   (a) True
   (b) False

## Article 376 | Metal Wireways

5. The sum of the cross-sectional areas of all contained conductors at any cross-section of a metal wireway shall not exceed _____ percent.

    (a) 50
    (b) 20
    (c) 25
    (d) 80

6. The ampacity adjustment factors in 310.15(B)(3)(a) shall be applied to a metal wireway only where the number of current-carrying conductors in any cross section of the wireway exceeds _____.

    (a) 30
    (b) 40
    (c) 50
    (d) 60

7. Where insulated conductors are deflected within a metal wireway, the wireway shall be sized to meet the bending requirements corresponding to _____ wire per terminal in Table 312.6(A).

    (a) one
    (b) two
    (c) three
    (d) four

8. Power distribution blocks installed in metal wireways on the line side of the service equipment shall be listed for the purpose.

    (a) True
    (b) False

9. Power distribution blocks installed in metal wireways shall _____.

    (a) allow for sufficient wire-bending space at terminals
    (b) not have uninsulated exposed live parts
    (c) a or b
    (d) a and b

# ARTICLE 380 — MULTIOUTLET ASSEMBLIES

## Introduction to Article 380—Multioutlet Assemblies

A multioutlet assembly is a surface, flush, or freestanding raceway designed to hold conductors and receptacles, and is assembled in the field or at the factory [Article 100]. It's not limited to systems commonly referred to by the trade names "Plugtrak®" or "Plugmold®."

Please use the 2014 *Code* book to answer the following questions.

1. A multioutlet assembly can be installed in _____.

   (a) dry locations
   (b) wet locations
   (c) a and b
   (d) damp locations

2. A multioutlet assembly shall not be installed _____.

   (a) in hoistways
   (b) where subject to severe physical damage
   (c) where subject to corrosive vapors
   (d) all of these

3. Metal multioutlet assemblies can pass through a dry partition, provided no receptacle is concealed in the partition and the cover of the exposed portion of the system can be removed.

   (a) True
   (b) False

## Notes

# ARTICLE 386 SURFACE METAL RACEWAYS

## Introduction to Article 386—Surface Metal Raceways

A surface metal raceway is a common method of adding a raceway when exposed traditional raceway systems aren't acceptable, and concealing the raceway isn't economically feasible. It comes in several colors, and is now available with colored or real wood inserts designed to make it look like molding rather than a raceway. A surface metal raceway is commonly known as "Wiremold®" in the field.

Please use the 2014 *Code* book to answer the following questions.

1. A surface metal raceway is a metallic raceway that is intended to be mounted to the surface of a structure, with associated couplings, connectors, boxes, and fittings for the installation of electrical conductors.

    (a) True
    (b) False

2. Unbroken lengths of surface metal raceways can be run through dry _____.

    (a) walls
    (b) partitions
    (c) floors
    (d) all of these

3. Surface metal raceways shall not be used _____.

    (a) where subject to severe physical damage
    (b) where subject to corrosive vapors
    (c) in hoistways
    (d) all of these

4. The voltage between conductors in a surface metal raceway shall not exceed _____ unless the metal has a thickness of not less than 0.040 in. nominal.

    (a) 150V
    (b) 300V
    (c) 600V
    (d) 1,000V

## Article 386 | Surface Metal Raceways

5. The maximum size conductors permitted in a metal surface raceway shall not be larger than that for which the wireway is designed.

   (a) True
   (b) False

6. The maximum number of conductors permitted in any surface raceway shall be _____.

   (a) no more than 30 percent of the inside diameter
   (b) no greater than the number for which it was designed
   (c) no more than 75 percent of the cross-sectional area
   (d) that which is permitted in Table 312.6(A)

7. The ampacity adjustment factors of 310.15(B)(3)(a) shall not apply to conductors installed in surface metal raceways where the _____.

   (a) cross-sectional area exceeds 4 sq in.
   (b) current-carrying conductors do not exceed 30 in number
   (c) total cross-sectional area of all conductors does not exceed 20 percent of the interior cross-sectional area of the raceway
   (d) all of these

8. Surface metal raceways and associated fittings shall be supported _____.

   (a) in accordance with the manufacturer's installation instructions
   (b) at intervals appropriate for the building design
   (c) at intervals not exceeding 4 ft
   (d) at intervals not exceeding 8 ft

9. The conductors, including splices and taps, in a metal surface raceway having a removable cover shall not fill the raceway to more than _____ percent of its cross-sectional area at that point.

   (a) 38
   (b) 40
   (c) 53
   (d) 75

10. Surface metal raceway enclosures providing a transition from other wiring methods shall have a means for connecting a(n) _____.

    (a) grounded conductor
    (b) ungrounded conductor
    (c) equipment grounding conductor
    (d) all of these

11. Where combination surface metal raceways are used for both signaling conductors and lighting and power circuits, the different systems shall be run in separate compartments identified by _____ of the interior finish.

    (a) stamping
    (b) imprinting
    (c) color coding
    (d) any of these

# ARTICLE 392 CABLE TRAYS

## Introduction to Article 392—Cable Trays

A cable tray system is a unit or an assembly of units or sections with associated fittings that forms a structural system used to securely fasten or support cables and raceways. A cable tray isn't a raceway.

Cable tray systems include ladder, ventilated trough, ventilated channel, solid bottom, and other similar structures. Cable trays are manufactured in many forms, from a simple hanger or wire mesh to a substantial, rigid, steel support system. Cable trays are designed and manufactured to support specific wiring methods, as identified in 392.10(A).

Please use the 2014 *Code* book to answer the following questions.

1. A cable tray is a unit or assembly of units or sections and associated fittings forming a _____ system used to securely fasten or support cables and raceways.

    (a) structural
    (b) flexible
    (c) movable
    (d) secure

2. Cable trays can be used as a support system for _____.

    (a) service conductors, feeders, and branch circuits
    (b) communications circuits
    (c) control and signaling circuits
    (d) all of these

3. Where exposed to the direct rays of the sun, insulated conductors and jacketed cables installed in cable trays shall be _____ as being sunlight resistant.

    (a) listed
    (b) approved
    (c) identified
    (d) none of these

4. Cable trays and their associated fittings shall be _____ for the intended use.

    (a) listed
    (b) approved
    (c) identified
    (d) none of these

5. _____ wiring methods can be installed in a cable tray.

    (a) Metal raceway
    (b) Nonmetallic raceway
    (c) Cable
    (d) all of these

6. Cable tray systems shall not be used _____.

    (a) in hoistways
    (b) where subject to severe physical damage
    (c) in hazardous (classified) locations
    (d) a or b

7. Each run of cable tray shall be _____ before the installation of cables.

    (a) tested for 25 ohms resistance
    (b) insulated
    (c) completed
    (d) all of these

8. Cable trays shall be _____ except as permitted by 392.10(D).

    (a) exposed
    (b) accessible
    (c) concealed
    (d) a and b

9. In industrial facilities where conditions of maintenance and supervision ensure that only qualified persons will service the installation, cable tray systems can be used to support _____.

    (a) raceways
    (b) cables
    (c) boxes and conduit bodies
    (d) all of these

10. For raceways terminating at a cable tray, a(n) _____ cable tray clamp or adapter shall be used to securely fasten the raceway to the cable tray system.

    (a) listed
    (b) approved
    (c) identified
    (d) none of these

11. Where single conductor cables comprising each phase, neutral, or grounded conductor of a circuit are connected in parallel in a cable tray, the conductors shall be installed _____, to prevent current unbalance in the paralleled conductors due to inductive reactance.

    (a) in groups consisting of not more than three conductors per phase or neutral
    (b) in groups consisting of not more than one conductor per phase or neutral
    (c) as individual conductors securely bound to the cable tray
    (d) in separate groups

12. Cable trays shall be supported at intervals in accordance with the installation instructions.

    (a) True
    (b) False

13. A box shall not be required where cables or conductors from cable trays are installed in bushed conduit and tubing used as support or for protection against _____.

    (a) abuse
    (b) unauthorized access
    (c) physical damage
    (d) tampering

14. Cable _____ made and insulated by approved methods can be located within a cable tray provided they are accessible, and do not project above the side rails where the splices are subject to physical damage.

    (a) connections
    (b) jumpers
    (c) splices
    (d) conductors

15. Metal cable trays containing only non-power conductors (such as communication, data, and signal conductors and cables) must be electrically continuous through approved connections or the use of a(n) _____.

    (a) grounding electrode conductor
    (b) bonding jumper
    (c) equipment grounding conductor
    (d) grounded conductor

16. Steel or aluminum cable tray systems shall be permitted to be used as an equipment grounding conductor, provided the cable tray sections and fittings are identified as _____, among other requirements.

    (a) an equipment grounding conductor
    (b) special
    (c) industrial
    (d) all of these

17. The conductor ampacity adjustment factors only apply to the number of current-carrying conductors in the cable and not to the number of conductors in the cable tray.

    (a) True
    (b) False

Notes

# CHAPTER 4
# EQUIPMENT FOR GENERAL USE

## Introduction to Chapter 4—Equipment for General Use

With the first three chapters behind you, the final chapter in the *NEC* necessary for building a solid foundation in general work is Chapter 4. This chapter helps you apply the first three to installations involving general equipment. These first four chapters follow a natural sequential progression. Each of the next four chapters—5, 6, 7, and 8—build upon the first four, but in no particular order. You need to understand all of the first four chapters to properly apply any of the next ones.

As in the preceding chapters, Chapter 4 is also arranged logically. Here are the groupings:

- Flexible cords and cables, and fixture wires.
- Switches and receptacles.
- Switchboards, switchgear, and panelboards.
- Lamps and luminaires.
- Appliances and space heaters.
- Motors, refrigeration equipment, generators, and transformers.
- Batteries, capacitors, and other components.

This logical arrangement of the *NEC* is something to keep in mind when you're searching for a particular item. You know, for example, that transformers are general equipment. So you'll find the *Code* requirements for them in Chapter 4. You know they're wound devices, so you'll find transformer requirements located somewhere near motor requirements.

- **Article 400—Flexible Cords and Flexible Cables.** Article 400 covers the general requirements, applications, and construction specifications for flexible cords and flexible cables.

- **Article 402—Fixture Wires.** This article covers the general requirements and construction specifications for fixture wires.

- **Article 404—Switches.** The requirements of Article 404 apply to switches of all types. These include snap (toggle) switches, dimmer switches, fan switches, knife switches, circuit breakers used as switches, and automatic switches such as time clocks, timers, and switches and circuit breakers used for disconnecting means.

- **Article 406—Receptacles, Cord Connectors, and Attachment Plugs (Caps).** This article covers the rating, type, and installation of receptacles, cord connectors, and attachment plugs (cord caps). It also covers flanged surface inlets.

**Chapter 4** | Equipment for General Use

- **Article 408—Switchboards, Switchgear, and Panelboards.** Article 408 covers specific requirements for switchboards, panelboards, switchgear, and distribution boards that supply lighting and power circuits.

    **Author's Comment:**
    - See Article 100 for the definitions of "Panelboard," "Switchboard," and "Switchgear."

- **Article 410—Luminaires, Lampholders, and Lamps.** This article contains the requirements for luminaires, lampholders, and lamps. Because of the many types and applications of luminaires, manufacturer's instructions are very important and helpful for proper installation. Underwriters Laboratories produces a pamphlet called the *Luminaire Marking Guide*, which provides information for properly installing common types of incandescent, fluorescent, and high-intensity discharge (HID) luminaires.

- **Article 411—Lighting Systems Operating at 30V or Less and Lighting Equipment Connected to Class-2 Power Sources.** Article 411 covers lighting systems, and their associated components, that operate at 30V or less, or that are connected to a Class-2 power source.

- **Article 422—Appliances.** This article covers electric appliances used in any occupancy.

- **Article 424—Fixed Electric Space-Heating Equipment.** Article 424 covers fixed electric equipment used for space heating. For the purpose of this article, heating equipment includes heating cable, unit heaters, boilers, central systems, and other fixed electric space-heating equipment. Article 424 doesn't apply to process heating and room air-conditioning.

- **Article 430—Motors, Motor Circuits, and Controllers.** This article contains the specific requirements for conductor sizing, overcurrent protection, control circuit conductors, motor controllers, and disconnecting means. The installation requirements for motor control centers are covered in Article 430, Part VIII.

- **Article 440—Air-Conditioning and Refrigeration Equipment.** Article 440 applies to electrically driven air-conditioning and refrigeration equipment with a motorized hermetic refrigerant compressor. The requirements in this article are in addition to, or amend, the requirements in Article 430 and others.

- **Article 445—Generators.** Article 445 contains the electrical installation requirements for generators and other requirements, such as where they can be installed, nameplate markings, conductor ampacity, and disconnecting means.

- **Article 450—Transformers.** This article covers the installation of transformers.

- **Article 480—Batteries.** Article 480 covers stationary installations of storage batteries.

# ARTICLE 400 — FLEXIBLE CORDS AND FLEXIBLE CABLES

## Introduction to Article 400—Flexible Cords and Flexible Cables

This article covers the general requirements, applications, and construction specifications for flexible cords and flexible cables. The *NEC* doesn't consider flexible cords to be wiring methods like those defined in Chapter 3.

Always use a cord (and fittings) identified for the application. Table 400.4 will help you in that regard. For example, use cords listed for a wet location if you're using them outdoors. The jacket material of any cord is tested to maintain its insulation properties and other characteristics in the environments for which it's been listed. Tables 400.5(A)(1) and 400.5(A)(2) are also important tables to turn to when looking for the ampacity of flexible cords and cables.

Please use the 2014 *Code* book to answer the following questions.

1. HPD cord shall be permitted for _____.
   (a) not hard usage
   (b) hard usage
   (c) extra-hard usage
   (d) all of these

2. TPT and TST cords shall be permitted in lengths not exceeding _____ ft when attached directly to a portable appliance rated 50W or less.
   (a) 8
   (b) 10
   (c) 15
   (d) 20

3. The allowable ampacity of flexible cords and cables is found in _____.
   (a) Table 310.15(B)(16)
   (b) Tables 400.5(A)(1) and (2)
   (c) Chapter 9, Table 1
   (d) Table 430.52

4. Where flexible cords are used in ambient temperatures other than _____ the temperature correction factors from Table 310.15(B)(2)(a) shall be applied to the ampacity in Table 400.5(A)(1) and Tables 400.5(A)(2).
   (a) 30°C
   (b) 60°C
   (c) 75°C
   (d) 90°C

## Article 400 | Flexible Cords and Flexible Cables

5. A 3-conductor SJE cable (one conductor is used for grounding) has a maximum ampacity of _____ for each 16 AWG conductor.

   (a) 9A
   (b) 11A
   (c) 13A
   (d) 15A

6. Flexible cords and cables can be used for _____.

   (a) wiring of luminaires
   (b) connection of portable luminaires or appliances
   (c) connection of utilization equipment to facilitate frequent interchange
   (d) all of these

7. Flexible cords shall not be used as a substitute for _____ wiring.

   (a) temporary
   (b) fixed
   (c) overhead
   (d) none of these

8. Flexible cords and cables shall not be concealed behind building _____, or run through doorways, windows, or similar openings.

   (a) structural ceilings
   (b) suspended or dropped ceilings
   (c) floors or walls
   (d) all of these

9. Flexible cords and cables shall be connected to fittings so that tension will not be transmitted to joints or terminal screws by _____.

   (a) knotting the cord
   (b) winding the cord with tape
   (c) fittings designed for the purpose
   (d) any of these

10. Flexible cords and cables shall be protected by _____ where passing through holes in covers, outlet boxes, or similar enclosures.

    (a) bushings
    (b) fittings
    (c) a or b
    (d) none of these

11. In industrial establishments where conditions of maintenance and supervision ensure that only qualified persons service the installation, flexible cords and cables can be installed in aboveground raceways that are no longer than _____ ft, to protect the flexible cord or cable from physical damage.

    (a) 25
    (b) 50
    (c) 100
    (d) 150

# ARTICLE 402 — FIXTURE WIRES

## Introduction to Article 402—Fixture Wires

This article covers the general requirements and construction specifications for fixture wires. One such requirement is that no fixture wire can be smaller than 18 AWG. Another requirement is that fixture wires must be of a type listed in Table 402.3. That table makes up the bulk of Article 402. Table 402.5 lists the allowable ampacity for fixture wires.

Please use the 2014 *Code* book to answer the following questions.

1. The allowable ampacity of 18 TFFN is _____.

    (a) 6A
    (b) 8A
    (c) 10A
    (d) 14A

2. The smallest size fixture wire permitted by the *NEC* is _____ AWG.

    (a) 22
    (b) 20
    (c) 18
    (d) 16

3. The number of fixture wires in a single conduit or tubing shall not exceed the percentage fill specified in _____.

    (a) Chapter 9, Table 1
    (b) Table 250.66
    (c) Table 310.15(B)(16)
    (d) 240.6

4. Fixture wires are used to connect luminaires to the _____ conductors supplying the luminaires.

    (a) service
    (b) branch-circuit
    (c) feeder
    (d) none of these

5. Fixture wires shall not be used for branch-circuit wiring, except as permitted in other articles of the *Code*.

    (a) True
    (b) False

Notes

# ARTICLE 404 SWITCHES

## Introduction to Article 404—Switches

The requirements of Article 404 apply to switches of all types, including snap (toggle) switches, dimmer switches, fan switches, knife switches, circuit breakers used as switches, and automatic switches, such as time clocks and timers.

Please use the 2014 *Code* book to answer the following questions.

1. Three-way and four-way switches shall be wired so that all switching is done only in the _____ circuit conductor.

    (a) ungrounded
    (b) grounded
    (c) equipment ground
    (d) neutral

2. When grouping conductors of switch loops in the same raceway, it is not required to include a grounded conductor in every switch loop.

    (a) True
    (b) False

3. Switches or circuit breakers shall not disconnect the grounded conductor of a circuit unless the switch or circuit breaker _____.

    (a) can be opened and closed by hand levers only
    (b) simultaneously disconnects all conductors of the circuit
    (c) opens the grounded conductor before it disconnects the ungrounded conductors
    (d) none of these

4. As a general rule, the grounded circuit conductor for the controlled lighting circuit shall be provided at the location where switches control lighting loads that are supplied by a grounded general-purpose branch circuit.

    (a) True
    (b) False

5. Switches controlling line-to-neutral lighting loads must have a grounded conductor provided at the switch location unless the _____.

    (a) conductors enter the device box through a raceway that has sufficient area to accommodate a grounded conductor
    (b) box enclosing the switch is accessible for the installation of an additional or replacement cable without removing finish materials
    (c) lighting consists of all fluorescent fixtures with integral disconnects for the ballasts
    (d) a or b

## Article 404 | Switches

6. Surface-mounted switches or circuit breakers in a damp or wet location shall be enclosed in a _____ enclosure or cabinet that complies with 312.2.

    (a) weatherproof
    (b) rainproof
    (c) watertight
    (d) raintight

7. Switches shall not be installed within tubs or shower spaces unless installed as part of a listed tub or shower assembly.

    (a) True
    (b) False

8. Single-throw knife switches shall be installed so that gravity will tend to close the switch.

    (a) True
    (b) False

9. Which of the following switches must indicate whether they are in the open (off) or closed (on) position?

    (a) General-use switches
    (b) Motor-circuit switches
    (c) Circuit breakers
    (d) all of these

10. Switches and circuit breakers used as switches shall be installed so that they may be operated from a readily accessible place.

    (a) True
    (b) False

11. Switches and circuit breakers used as switches can be mounted _____ if they are installed adjacent to motors, appliances, or other equipment that they supply and are accessible by portable means.

    (a) not higher than 6 ft 7 in.
    (b) higher than 6 ft 7 in.
    (c) in the mechanical equipment room
    (d) up to 8 ft high

12. Snap switches shall not be grouped or ganged in enclosures unless the voltage between adjacent devices does not exceed _____.

    (a) 100V
    (b) 200V
    (c) 300V
    (d) 400V

13. Snap switches, including dimmer and similar control switches, shall be connected to an equipment grounding conductor and shall provide a means to connect metal faceplates to the equipment grounding conductor, whether or not a metal faceplate is installed.

    (a) True
    (b) False

14. Snap switches are considered to be part of the effective ground-fault current path when _____.

    (a) the switch is connected to the intersystem bonding termination
    (b) the switch is mounted with metal screws to a metal box or a metal cover that's connected to an equipment grounding conductor
    (c) an equipment grounding conductor or equipment bonding jumper is connected to the equipment grounding termination of the snap switch
    (d) b or c

15. A snap switch that does not have means for connection to an equipment grounding conductor shall be permitted for replacement purposes only where the wiring method does not include an equipment grounding conductor and the switch is _____.

    (a) provided with a faceplate of nonconducting, noncombustible material with nonmetallic screws
    (b) GFCI protected
    (c) a or b
    (d) none of these

16. The metal mounting yoke of a replacement switch isn't required to be connected to an equipment grounding conductor if the wiring at the existing switch doesn't contain an equipment grounding conductor, and _____

    (a) the switch faceplate is nonmetallic with nonmetallic screws
    (b) the replacement switch is GFCI protected
    (c) a or b
    (d) the circuit is AFCI protected

17. Snap switches in listed assemblies aren't required to be connected to an equipment grounding conductor if _____.

    (a) the device is provided with a nonmetallic faceplate that cannot be installed on any other type of device and the device does not have mounting means to accept other configurations of faceplates
    (b) the device is equipped with a nonmetallic yoke
    (c) all parts of the device that are accessible after installation of the faceplate are manufactured of nonmetallic material
    (d) all of these

18. A snap switch with integral nonmetallic enclosure complying with 300.15(E) is required to be connected to an equipment grounding conductor.

    (a) True
    (b) False

19. Snap switches installed in boxes shall have the _____ seated against the finished wall surface.

    (a) extension plaster ears
    (b) body
    (c) toggle
    (d) all of these

20. Nonmetallic boxes for switches shall be installed with a wiring method that provides or includes _____.

    (a) a grounded conductor
    (b) an equipment grounding conductor
    (c) an inductive balance
    (d) none of these

21. Metal enclosures for switches or circuit breakers shall be connected to the circuit _____.

    (a) grounded conductor
    (b) grounding conductor
    (c) equipment grounding conductor
    (d) any of these

22. Alternating-current general-use snap switches are permitted to control _____.

    (a) resistive and inductive loads that do not exceed the ampere and voltage rating of the switch
    (b) tungsten-filament lamp loads that do not exceed the ampere rating of the switch at 120V
    (c) motor loads that do not exceed 80 percent of the ampere and voltage rating of the switch
    (d) all of these

23. AC or dc general-use snap switches may be used for control of inductive loads not exceeding _____ percent of the ampere rating of the switch at the applied voltage.

    (a) 50
    (b) 75
    (c) 90
    (d) 100

24. Snap switches rated _____ or less directly connected to aluminum conductors shall be listed and marked CO/ALR.

    (a) 15A
    (b) 20A
    (c) 25A
    (d) 30A

25. General-use _____ switches shall be used only to control permanently installed incandescent luminaires unless listed for control of other loads and installed accordingly.

    (a) dimmer
    (b) fan speed control
    (c) timer
    (d) all of these

26. Switches shall be marked with _____.

(a) current
(b) voltage
(c) maximum horsepower, if horsepower rated
(d) all of these

27. A switching device with a marked OFF position shall completely disconnect all _____ conductors of the load it controls.

(a) grounded
(b) ungrounded
(c) grounding
(d) all of these

# ARTICLE 406 — RECEPTACLES, CORD CONNECTORS, AND ATTACHMENT PLUGS (CAPS)

## Introduction to Article 406—Receptacles, Cord Connectors, and Attachment Plugs (Caps)

This article covers the rating, type, and installation of receptacles, cord connectors, and attachment plugs (cord caps). It also addresses their grounding requirements. Some key points to remember include:

- Following the grounding requirements of the specific type of device you're using.
- Providing GFCI protection where specified by 406.4(D)(3).
- Mounting receptacles according to the requirements of 406.5, which are highly detailed.

Please use the 2014 *Code* book to answer the following questions.

1. A child care facility is a building or structure, or portion thereof, used for educational, supervision, or personal care services for more than _____ children seven years in age or less.

   (a) two
   (b) three
   (c) four
   (d) six

2. Receptacles rated _____ or less directly connected to aluminum conductors shall be listed and marked CO/ALR.

   (a) 15A
   (b) 20A
   (c) 25A
   (d) 30A

3. Receptacles incorporating an isolated grounding conductor connection intended for the reduction of electrical noise shall be identified by _____ on the face of the receptacle.

   (a) an orange triangle
   (b) a green triangle
   (c) the color orange
   (d) the engraved word ISOLATED

4. Where a grounding means exists in the receptacle enclosure a(n) _____-type receptacle shall be used.

   (a) isolated ground
   (b) grounding
   (c) GFCI
   (d) dedicated

## Article 406 | Receptacles, Cord Connectors, and Attachment Plugs (Caps)

5. When replacing a nongrounding-type receptacle where attachment to an equipment grounding conductor does not exist in the receptacle enclosure, the receptacle can use a _____.

   (a) nongrounding-type receptacle
   (b) grounding receptacle
   (c) GFCI-type receptacle
   (d) a or c

6. When replacing receptacles in locations that would require GFCI protection under the current *NEC*, _____ receptacles shall be installed.

   (a) dedicated
   (b) isolated ground
   (c) GFCI-protected
   (d) grounding

7. Effective January 1, 2014, where a receptacle outlet is supplied by a branch circuit that requires arc-fault circuit-interrupter protection [210.12(A)], a replacement receptacle at this outlet shall be _____.

   (a) a listed (receptacle) outlet branch circuit type arc-fault circuit-interrupter receptacle
   (b) a receptacle protected by a listed (receptacle) outlet branch-circuit type arc-fault circuit-interrupter type receptacle
   (c) a receptacle protected by a listed combination type arc-fault circuit-interrupter type circuit breaker
   (d) all of these

8. Listed tamper-resistant receptacles shall be provided where replacements are made at receptacle outlets that are required to be tamper resistant elsewhere in this *Code*.

   (a) True
   (b) False

9. Weather-resistant receptacles _____ where replacements are made at receptacle outlets that are required to be so protected elsewhere in the *Code*.

   (a) shall be provided
   (b) are not required
   (c) are optional
   (d) are not allowed

10. Receptacles mounted in boxes set back from the wall surface shall be installed so that the mounting _____ of the receptacle is held rigidly at the finished surface.

    (a) screws or nails
    (b) yoke or strap
    (c) faceplate
    (d) none of these

11. Receptacles mounted in boxes flush with the finished surface or projecting beyond it shall be installed so that the mounting yoke or strap of the receptacle is _____.

    (a) held rigidly against the box or box cover
    (b) mounted behind the wall surface
    (c) held rigidly at the finished surface
    (d) none of these

12. Receptacles mounted to and supported by a cover shall be secured by more than one screw unless listed and identified for securing by a single screw.

    (a) True
    (b) False

13. Receptacles in countertops and similar work surfaces shall not be installed _____, unless listed as receptacle assemblies for countertop applications.

    (a) in the sides of cabinets
    (b) in a face-up position
    (c) on GFCI circuits
    (d) on the kitchen small-appliance circuit

14. Receptacles shall not be grouped or ganged in enclosures unless the voltage between adjacent devices does not exceed _____.

    (a) 100V
    (b) 200V
    (c) 300V
    (d) 400V

15. Metal faceplates for receptacles shall be grounded.

    (a) True
    (b) False

16. Attachment plugs and cord connectors shall be listed and marked with the _____.

    (a) manufacturer's name or identification
    (b) voltage rating
    (c) amperage rating
    (d) all of these

17. An outdoor receptacle in a location protected from the weather, or in another damp location, shall be installed in an enclosure that is weatherproof when the receptacle is _____.

    (a) covered
    (b) enclosed
    (c) protected
    (d) none of these

18. Receptacles installed outdoors, in a location protected from the weather or other damp locations, shall be in an enclosure that is _____ when the receptacle is covered.

    (a) raintight
    (b) weatherproof
    (c) rainproof
    (d) weathertight

19. A receptacle is considered to be in a location protected from the weather when located under roofed open porches, canopies, marquees, and the like, where it will not be subjected to _____.

    (a) spray from a hose
    (b) a direct lightning hit
    (c) beating rain or water runoff
    (d) falling or wind-blown debris

20. Nonlocking 15A and 20A, 125V and 250V receptacles installed in damp locations shall be listed as _____.

    (a) raintight
    (b) watertight
    (c) weatherproof
    (d) weather resistant

21. _____, 125V and 250V receptacles installed in a wet location shall have an enclosure that is weatherproof whether or not the attachment plug cap is inserted.

    (a) 15A
    (b) 20A
    (c) a and b
    (d) none of these

22. When 15A and 20A receptacles are installed in a wet location, the outlet box _____ must be listed for extra-duty use.

    (a) sleeve
    (b) hood
    (c) threaded entry
    (d) mounting

23. Where installed in a wet location, all _____ receptacle(s) shall be listed as weather resistant.

    (a) 125V, 30A nonlocking
    (b) 250V, 15A nonlocking
    (c) 125V, 30A locking
    (d) 250V, 15A locking

24. 20A, 125V receptacles subject to _____ can have an enclosure that is weatherproof when the attachment plug is removed.

    (a) shower spray
    (b) beating rain
    (c) corrosive conditions
    (d) routine high-pressure spray washing

25. A 30A, 208V receptacle installed in a wet location, where the product intended to be plugged into it is not attended while in use, shall have an enclosure that is weatherproof with the attachment plug cap inserted or removed.

    (a) True
    (b) False

26. A receptacle shall not be installed within, or directly over, a bathtub or shower space.

    (a) True
    (b) False

27. A receptacle installed in an outlet box flush-mounted in a finished surface in a damp or wet location shall be made weatherproof by means of a weatherproof faceplate assembly that provides a _____ connection between the plate and the finished surface.

    (a) sealed
    (b) weathertight
    (c) sealed and protected
    (d) watertight

28. In dwelling units, all nonlocking type 125V, 15A and 20A receptacles installed _____ shall be listed as tamper resistant.

    (a) in bedrooms
    (b) outdoors, at grade level
    (c) above counter tops
    (d) in all areas specified in 210.52, except as covered by exceptions

29. Nonlocking type 15A and 20A, 125V receptacles in a dwelling unit shall be listed as tamper resistant except _____.

    (a) receptacles located more than 5½ ft above the floor
    (b) receptacles that are part of a luminaire or appliance
    (c) a receptacle located within dedicated space for an appliance that, in normal use, is not easily moved from one place to another
    (d) all of these

30. Nongrounding, nonlocking type, 15A and 20A, 125V receptacles used for replacements in a dwelling unit shall not be required to be listed as tamper resistant.

    (a) True
    (b) False

31. Nonlocking type 15A and 20A, 125V receptacles in _____ must be listed as tamper resistant.

    (a) restaurants
    (b) guest rooms and guest suites of hotels and motels
    (c) office buildings
    (d) b and c

32. Nonlocking type 15A and 20A, 125V receptacles in _____ must be listed as tamper resistant.

    (a) theatres
    (b) arcades
    (c) child care facilities
    (d) major repair garages

# ARTICLE 408 — SWITCHBOARDS, SWITCHGEAR, AND PANELBOARDS

## Introduction to Article 408—Switchboards, Switchgear, and Panelboards

Article 408 covers the specific requirements for switchboards, switchgear, and panelboards that control power and lighting circuits.

There's a tendency among some people in the industry to use the terms switchboard and switchgear interchangeably. Switchgear is manufactured and tested to more exacting standards and is configured differently than switchboards. For example, in switchgear there are physical barriers between breakers, and between the breakers and the bus. Switchgear is more durable and fault resistant, and is commonly selected for larger applications where low-voltage power circuit breakers and selective coordination are applied, such as computer data centers, manufacturing, and process facilities [Source NCCER].

As you study this article, remember some of these key points:

- One objective of Article 408 is that the installation prevents contact between current-carrying conductors and people or equipment.
- The circuit directory of a panelboard must clearly identify the purpose or use of each circuit that originates in the panelboard.
- You must understand the detailed grounding and overcurrent protection requirements for panelboards.

**Please use the 2014 *Code* book to answer the following questions.**

1. In switchboards and panelboards, load terminals for field wiring shall be so located that it is not necessary to reach across or beyond a(n) _____ ungrounded line bus in order to make connections.

   (a) insulated
   (b) uninsulated
   (c) grounded
   (d) high impedance

2. Panelboards supplied by a three-phase, 4-wire, delta-connected system shall have the phase with higher voltage-to-ground (high-leg) connected to the _____ phase.

   (a) A
   (b) B
   (c) C
   (d) any of these

## Article 408 | Switchboards, Switchgear, and Panelboards

3. A switchboard or panelboard containing a 4-wire, _____ system where the midpoint of one phase winding is grounded, shall be legibly and permanently field-marked to caution that one phase has a higher voltage-to-ground.

   (a) wye-connected
   (b) delta-connected
   (c) solidly grounded
   (d) ungrounded

4. Circuit directories can include labels that depend on transient conditions of occupancy.

   (a) True
   (b) False

5. The purpose or use of panelboard circuits and circuit _____, including spare positions, shall be legibly identified on a circuit directory located on the face or inside of the door of a panelboard, and at each switch or circuit breaker in a switchboard.

   (a) manufacturers
   (b) conductors
   (c) feeders
   (d) modifications

6. All switchboards and panelboards supplied by a feeder(s) in _____ shall be marked to indicate each device or equipment where the power supply originates.

   (a) other than one- or two-family dwellings
   (b) all dwelling units
   (c) all nondwelling units
   (d) b and c

7. Conduits and raceways, including end fittings, shall not rise more than _____ in. above the bottom of a switchboard enclosure.

   (a) 3
   (b) 4
   (c) 5
   (d) 6

8. Unused openings for circuit breakers and switches in switchboards and panelboards shall be closed using _____ or other approved means that provide protection substantially equivalent to the wall of the enclosure.

   (a) duct seal and tape
   (b) identified closures
   (c) exothermic welding
   (d) sheet metal

9. A panelboard shall be protected by an overcurrent device within the panelboard, or at any point on the _____ side of the panelboard.

   (a) load
   (b) supply
   (c) a or b
   (d) none of these

10. Plug-in-type circuit breakers that are backfed shall be _____ by an additional fastener that requires more than a pull to release.

    (a) grounded
    (b) secured in place
    (c) shunt tripped
    (d) none of these

11. When separate equipment grounding conductors are provided in panelboards, a _____ shall be secured inside the cabinet.

    (a) grounded conductor
    (b) terminal lug
    (c) terminal bar
    (d) none of these

12. Each _____ conductor shall terminate within the panelboard at an individual terminal that is not used for another conductor.

    (a) grounded
    (b) ungrounded
    (c) grounding
    (d) all of these

13. A panelboard shall be provided with physical means to prevent the installation of more _____ devices than that number for which the panelboard was designed, rated, and listed.

    (a) overcurrent
    (b) equipment
    (c) circuit breaker
    (d) all of these

# ARTICLE 410 LUMINAIRES, LAMPHOLDERS, AND LAMPS

## Introduction to Article 410—Luminaires, Lampholders, and Lamps

This article covers luminaires, lampholders, lamps, decorative lighting products, and lighting accessories for temporary seasonal and holiday use, including portable flexible lighting products, and the wiring and equipment of such products and lighting installations. Even though Article 410 is highly detailed, it's broken down into 16 parts. The first five are sequential, and apply to all luminaires, lampholders, and lamps:

- Part I. General
- Part II. Location
- Part III. Boxes and Covers
- Part IV. Supports
- Part V. Equipment Grounding Conductors

The first five parts contain mostly mechanical information, and aren't hard to follow or absorb. Part VI, Wiring, ends the sequence. The seventh, ninth, and tenth parts provide requirements for manufacturers to follow—use only equipment that conforms to these requirements. Part VIII provides requirements for installing lampholders. The rest of Article 410 addresses specific types of lighting.

### Author's Comment:

- Article 411 addresses "Lighting Systems Operating at 30 Volts or Less."

# Article 410 | Luminaires, Lampholders, and Lamps

Please use the 2014 *Code* book to answer the following questions.

1. Article 410 covers luminaires, portable luminaires, lampholders, pendants, incandescent filament lamps, arc lamps, electric-discharge lamps, and _____, and the wiring and equipment forming part of such products and lighting installations.

   (a) decorative lighting products
   (b) lighting accessories for temporary seasonal and holiday use
   (c) portable flexible lighting products
   (d) all of these

2. Closet storage space is defined as a volume bounded by the sides and back closet walls extending from the closet floor vertically to a height of _____ ft or the highest clothes-hanging rod at a horizontal distance of 2 ft from the sides and back of the closet walls.

   (a) 6
   (b) 7
   (c) 8
   (d) 9

3. A luminaire marked "Suitable for Wet Locations" _____ be permitted to be used in a damp location.

   (a) shall
   (b) shall not
   (c) a or b
   (d) none of these

4. Luminaires can be installed in a commercial cooking hood if the luminaire is identified for use within a _____ cooking hood.

   (a) nonresidential
   (b) commercial
   (c) multifamily
   (d) all of these

5. No parts of cord-connected luminaires, chain-, cable-, or cord-suspended luminaires, lighting track, pendants, or paddle fans shall be located within a zone measured 3 ft horizontally and _____ ft vertically from the top of the bathtub rim or shower stall threshold.

   (a) 4
   (b) 6
   (c) 8
   (d) 10

6. Luminaires located within the actual outside dimension of a bathtub and shower shall be marked for damp locations, or marked for wet locations where they are _____.

   (a) below 7 ft in height
   (b) below 6 ft 7 in. in height
   (c) subject to shower spray
   (d) not GFCI protected

7. Luminaires using a _____ lamp, that is subject to physical damage and installed in playing and spectator seating areas of indoor sports, mixed-use, or all-purpose facilities, shall be of the type that protects the lamp with a glass or plastic lens.

   (a) mercury vapor
   (b) metal halide
   (c) fluorescent
   (d) a or b

8. Which of the following types of luminaires can be installed in a clothes closet?

   (a) A surface or recessed incandescent luminaire with completely enclosed light source.
   (b) A surface or recessed fluorescent luminaire.
   (c) A surface-mounted or recessed LED luminaire with a completely enclosed light source.
   (d) all of these

9. Incandescent luminaires that have open lamps, and pendant-type luminaires, shall be permitted in clothes closets where proper clearance is maintained from combustible products.

   (a) True
   (b) False

10. Surface-mounted fluorescent luminaires in clothes closets shall be permitted on the wall above the door, or on the ceiling, provided there is a minimum clearance of _____ in. between the luminaire and the nearest point of a storage space.

    (a) 3
    (b) 6
    (c) 9
    (d) 12

11. In clothes closets, recessed incandescent or LED luminaires with a completely enclosed light source can be installed in the wall or the ceiling, provided there is a minimum clearance of _____ in. between the luminaire and the nearest point of a storage space.

    (a) 3
    (b) 6
    (c) 9
    (d) 12

12. Luminaires must maintain a minimum clearance from the closet storage space of _____.

    (a) 12 in. for surface-mounted incandescent or LED luminaires with a completely enclosed light source
    (b) 6 in. for surface-mounted fluorescent luminaires
    (c) 6 in. for recessed fluorescent luminaires or recessed incandescent or LED luminaires with a completely enclosed light source
    (d) all of these

13. The *NEC* allows a lighting outlet on the wall in a clothes closet when it is at least 6 in. away from storage space.

    (a) True
    (b) False

14. Surface-mounted fluorescent or LED luminaires are permitted within the closet storage space if identified for this use.

    (a) True
    (b) False

15. Coves for luminaires shall be located so that the lamps and equipment can be properly installed and _____.

    (a) maintained
    (b) protected from physical damage
    (c) tested
    (d) inspected

16. Electric-discharge and LED luminaires supported independently of the outlet box shall be connected to the branch circuit through _____.

    (a) raceways
    (b) Type MC, AC, MI, or NM cable
    (c) flexible cords
    (d) any of these

17. When electric-discharge and LED luminaires that are designed not to be supported solely by the outlet box are surface mounted over a concealed outlet box, the luminaire shall provide access to the wiring within the outlet box by means of suitable openings in the back of the luminaire.

    (a) True
    (b) False

18. The maximum weight of a luminaire permitted to be supported by the screw shell of a lampholder is _____ lb.

    (a) 2
    (b) 3
    (c) 4
    (d) 6

19. Handholds in poles supporting luminaires shall not be required for poles _____ ft or less in height above finished grade, if the pole is provided with a hinged base.

    (a) 5
    (b) 10
    (c) 15
    (d) 20

20. Poles over 20 ft in height above grade, without a hinged base, that support luminaires shall _____.
    (a) have an accessible handhole (sized 2 x 4 in.) with a cover suitable for use in wet locations
    (b) have an equipment grounding terminal that is accessible from the handhole
    (c) a and b
    (d) none of these

21. Metal raceways shall be bonded to the metal pole with a(n) _____.
    (a) grounding electrode
    (b) grounded conductor
    (c) equipment grounding conductor
    (d) any of these

22. Luminaires attached to the framing of a suspended ceiling shall be secured to the framing member(s) by mechanical means such as _____.
    (a) bolts
    (b) screws
    (c) rivets
    (d) any of these

23. _____ clips identified for use with the type of ceiling framing member(s) and luminaires shall be permitted to be used to secure luminaires to the ceiling framing members.
    (a) Marked
    (b) Labeled
    (c) Identified
    (d) listed

24. Outdoor luminaires and associated equipment can be supported by trees.
    (a) True
    (b) False

25. Luminaires and equipment must be mechanically connected to an equipment grounding conductor as specified in 250.118 and must be sized in accordance with _____.
    (a) Table 250.66
    (b) Table 250.122
    (c) Table 310.16
    (d) a and c

26. Luminaires made of insulating material that are directly wired or attached to outlets supplied by a wiring method that does not provide a ready means for grounding attachment to an equipment grounding conductor shall be made of insulating material and shall have no exposed conductive parts.
    (a) True
    (b) False

27. Replacement luminaires aren't required to be connected to an equipment grounding conductor if no equipment grounding conductor exists at the outlet box and the luminaire is _____.
    (a) more than 20 years old
    (b) mounted to the box using nonmetallic fittings and screws
    (c) mounted more than 6 ft above the floor
    (d) GFCI protected

28. Luminaires shall be wired so that the _____ of each lampholder is connected to the same luminaire or circuit conductor or terminal.
    (a) stem
    (b) arm
    (c) supplemental protection
    (d) screw shell

29. Luminaires that require adjustment or aiming after installation can be cord-connected without an attachment plug, provided the exposed cord is of the hard-usage type and is not longer than that required for maximum adjustment.
    (a) True
    (b) False

30. An electric-discharge or LED luminaire or listed assembly can be cord connected if located _____ the outlet, the cord is visible for its entire length outside the luminaire, and the cord is not subject to strain or physical damage.

    (a) within
    (b) directly below
    (c) directly above
    (d) adjacent to

31. Luminaires can be used as a raceway for circuit conductors only when listed and marked for use as a raceway.

    (a) True
    (b) False

32. Luminaires identified for _____, with an integral outlet box in accordance with 410.21 shall be permitted to be used as a conductor raceway.

    (a) through-wiring
    (b) wet locations
    (c) Class 1, Division 1 locations
    (d) b and c

33. Luminaires designed for end-to-end assembly, or luminaires connected together by _____, can contain a 2-wire branch circuit, or one multiwire branch circuit, supplying the connected luminaires. One additional 2-wire branch circuit separately supplying one or more of the connected luminaires is permitted.

    (a) rigid metal conduit
    (b) recognized wiring methods
    (c) flexible wiring methods
    (d) EMT

34. Branch-circuit conductors within _____ in. of a ballast shall have an insulation temperature rating not lower than 90°C (194°F).

    (a) 1
    (b) 3
    (c) 6
    (d) 8

35. Lampholders of the screw-shell type shall be installed for use as lampholders only.

    (a) True
    (b) False

36. Lampholders installed in wet locations shall be listed for use in _____ locations.

    (a) damp
    (b) wet
    (c) dry
    (d) any of these

37. Lampholders installed in damp locations shall be listed for use in _____ locations.

    (a) damp
    (b) wet
    (c) dry
    (d) a or b

38. Lampholders shall be constructed, installed, or equipped with shades or guards so that _____ isn't subjected to temperatures in excess of 90°C (194°F).

    (a) ferrous material
    (b) the shade or guard
    (c) combustible material
    (d) a or b

39. Luminaires installed in _____ shall comply with 410.115 through 410.122.

    (a) recessed cavities in walls or ceilings
    (b) suspended ceilings
    (c) Class I classified locations
    (d) a and b

40. Recessed incandescent luminaires shall have _____ protection and shall be identified as thermally protected.

    (a) physical
    (b) corrosion
    (c) thermal
    (d) all of these

## Article 410 | Luminaires, Lampholders, and Lamps

41. A recessed luminaire not identified for contact with insulation shall have all recessed parts spaced not less than _____ in. from combustible materials, except for points of support.

    (a) ¼
    (b) ½
    (c) 1¼
    (d) 6

42. Type IC recessed luminaires are permitted to make contact with combustible material at _____.

    (a) recessed parts
    (b) points of support
    (c) portions passing through or finishing off the opening in the building structure
    (d) all of these

43. Thermal insulation shall not be installed above a recessed luminaire or within _____ in. of the recessed luminarie's enclosure, wiring compartment, ballast, transformer, LED driver, or power supply unless it is identified as a Type IC luminaire.

    (a) ½
    (b) 3
    (c) 6
    (d) 12

44. The minimum distance that an outlet box containing tap supply conductors is permitted to be placed from a recessed luminaire is _____ ft.

    (a) 1
    (b) 2
    (c) 3
    (d) 4

45. The raceway or cable for tap conductors to recessed luminaires shall have a minimum length of _____ in.

    (a) 6
    (b) 12
    (c) 18
    (d) 24

46. Luminaires containing a metal halide lamp (other than a thick-glass PAR lamp) shall be provided with a containment barrier that encloses the lamp, or shall be provided with a physical means that only allows the use of a(n) _____.

    (a) Type O lamp
    (b) Type CB lamp
    (c) a or b
    (d) inert gas

47. In indoor locations other than dwellings and associated accessory buildings, fluorescent luminaires that utilize double-ended lamps and contain ballast(s) and can be serviced in place shall have a disconnecting means either internal or external to each luminaire.

    (a) True
    (b) False

48. For existing installed luminaires in indoor locations, other than dwellings and associated accessory structures, a disconnecting means _____ in fluorescent luminaires that utilize double-ended lamps (typical fluorescent lamps) at the time a ballast is replaced.

    (a) shall be installed
    (b) is not required to be added
    (c) shall not be installed
    (d) can be a screw terminal

49. If more than one luminaire is installed on a branch circuit that isn't of the multiwire type, a disconnecting means isn't required for every luminaire when the light switch for the space ensures that some of the luminaires in the space will still provide illumination.

    (a) True
    (b) False

50. When connected to multiwire branch circuits, the fluorescent luminaire disconnect must simultaneously break all circuit conductors of the ballast, including the grounded conductor.

    (a) True
    (b) False

51. When the fluorescent luminaire disconnecting means for fluorescent luminaires that utilize double-ended lamps (typical fluorescent lamps) is external to the luminaire, it shall be _____.

    (a) accessible to qualified persons
    (b) a single device
    (c) located in sight of the disconnecting means
    (d) all of these

52. Lighting track fittings can be equipped with general-purpose receptacles.

    (a) True
    (b) False

53. The connected load on lighting track is permitted to exceed the rating of the track under some conditions.

    (a) True
    (b) False

54. A 120V section of lighting track that is continuously loaded shall not exceed 12 ft in length, in accordance with 220.43(B).

    (a) True
    (b) False

55. Track lighting shall not be installed _____.

    (a) where likely to be subjected to physical damage
    (b) in wet or damp locations
    (c) a and b
    (d) none of these

56. Lighting track shall not be installed less than _____ ft above the finished floor except where protected from physical damage or where the track operates at less than 30V rms, open-circuit voltage.

    (a) 4
    (b) 5
    (c) 5½
    (d) 6

57. Lighting track shall not be installed within the zone measured 3 ft horizontally and _____ ft vertically from the top of the bathtub rim or shower stall threshold.

    (a) 2
    (b) 3
    (c) 4
    (d) 8

58. Lighting track shall have two supports for a single section of _____ ft or shorter in length and each individual section of not more than 4 ft attached to it shall have one additional support, unless the track is identified for supports at greater intervals.

    (a) 2
    (b) 4
    (c) 6
    (d) 8

# Notes

# ARTICLE 411 — LIGHTING SYSTEMS OPERATING AT 30V OR LESS AND LIGHTING EQUIPMENT CONNECTED TO CLASS 2 POWER SOURCES

## Introduction to Article 411—Lighting Systems Operating at 30V or Less and Lighting Equipment Connected to Class 2 Power Sources

Article 411 provides the requirements for lighting systems operating at 30V or less, which are often found in such applications as landscaping, kitchen over-the-counter lighting, commercial display lighting, and museums. These systems are limited in their voltage, but the current rating can be as high as 25A, which means they're still a potential source of fire. Installation of these systems is widespread and becoming more so.

Many of these systems now use LEDs, and 30V halogen lamps are also fairly common. All 30V lighting systems have an ungrounded secondary circuit supplied by an isolating transformer. These systems have restrictions that effect where they can be located, and they can have a maximum supply breaker size of 25A.

**Please use the 2014 *Code* book to answer the following questions.**

1. A lighting system covered by Article 411 shall have a power supply output rated not more than _____ and not more than 30V.

    (a) 15A
    (b) 20A
    (c) 25A
    (d) 30A

2. Lighting systems operating at 30V or less shall be listed or assembled with listed components.

    (a) True
    (b) False

3. Lighting systems operating at 30V or less can be concealed or extended through a building wall, floor or ceiling without regard to the wiring method used.

    (a) True
    (b) False

4. Lighting systems operating at 30V or less shall not be installed within _____ ft of pools, spas, fountains, or similar locations.

    (a) 5
    (b) 6
    (c) 10
    (d) 20

5. Exposed secondary circuits of lighting systems operating at 30V or less shall be _____.

   (a) installed in a Chapter 3 wiring method
   (b) supplied by a Class 2 power source and shall use Class 2 cable in accordance with Article 725
   (c) at least 7 ft above the finished floor unless listed for a lower installation height
   (d) any of these

# ARTICLE 422 APPLIANCES

## Introduction to Article 422—Appliances

Article 422 covers electric appliances used in any occupancy. The meat of this article is contained in Parts II and III. Parts IV and V are primarily for manufacturers, but you should examine appliances for compliance before installing them. If the appliance has a label from a recognized labeling authority (for example UL), it complies [90.7].

**Please use the 2014 *Code* book to answer the following questions.**

1. A vending machine is defined as any self-service device that dispenses products or merchandise without the necessity of replenishing the device between each vending operation and designed to require insertion of a _____.

    (a) coin or paper currency
    (b) token or card
    (c) key or payment by other means
    (d) all of these

2. Branch-circuit conductors to individual appliances shall not be sized _____ than required by the appliance markings.

    (a) larger
    (b) smaller

3. Individual circuits for nonmotor-operated appliances that are continuously loaded shall have the branch-circuit rating sized not less than _____ percent of the appliance marked ampere rating, unless otherwise listed.

    (a) 80
    (b) 100
    (c) 125
    (d) 150

4. If a protective device rating is marked on an appliance, the branch-circuit overcurrent device rating shall not exceed _____ percent of the protective device rating marked on the appliance.

    (a) 50
    (b) 80
    (c) 100
    (d) 115

## Article 422 | Appliances

5. If a branch circuit supplies a single nonmotor-operated appliance, the rating of overcurrent protection shall not exceed _____ if the overcurrent protection rating is not marked and the appliance is rated 13.30A or less.

   (a) 15A
   (b) 20A
   (c) 25A
   (d) 30A

6. If a branch circuit supplies a single nonmotor-operated appliance, the rating of overcurrent protection shall not exceed _____ percent of the appliance rated current if the overcurrent protection rating is not marked and the appliance is rated over 13.30A.

   (a) 100
   (b) 125
   (c) 150
   (d) 160

7. Central heating equipment, other than fixed electric space-heating equipment, shall be supplied by a(n) _____ branch circuit.

   (a) multiwire
   (b) individual
   (c) multipurpose
   (d) small-appliance

8. A fixed storage-type water heater having a capacity of _____ gallons or less shall be considered a continuous load for the purposes of sizing branch circuits.

   (a) 60
   (b) 75
   (c) 90
   (d) 120

9. An in-sink waste disposer can be cord-and-plug-connected, but the cord shall not be less than 18 in. or more than _____ in. in length.

   (a) 30
   (b) 36
   (c) 42
   (d) 48

10. The length of the cord for a dishwasher or trash compactor shall not be longer than _____ ft, measured from the rear of the appliance.

    (a) 2
    (b) 4
    (c) 6
    (d) 8

11. Wall-mounted ovens and counter-mounted cooking units shall be permitted to be _____.

    (a) permanently connected
    (b) cord-and-plug-connected
    (c) a or b
    (d) none of these

12. Each appliance shall have a means that _____ disconnects all ungrounded circuit conductors.

    (a) sequentially
    (b) automatically
    (c) simultaneously
    (d) all of these

13. For permanently connected appliances rated over _____, the branch-circuit switch or circuit breaker can serve as the disconnecting means where the switch or circuit breaker is within sight from the appliance, or is lockable in accordance with 110.25.

    (a) 200 VA
    (b) 300 VA
    (c) 400 VA
    (d) 500 VA

14. For permanently connected motor-operated appliances with motors rated over _____, a switch or circuit breaker located within sight from the motor operated appliance can serve as the appliance disconnect.

    (a) ⅛ hp
    (b) ¼ hp
    (c) 15A
    (d) b and c

15. If an appliance of more than ⅛ hp is provided with a unit switch that complies with 422.34(A), (B), (C), or (D), the switch or circuit breaker serving as the other disconnecting means shall be permitted to be out of sight from the appliance.

    (a) True
    (b) False

16. For cord-and-plug-connected appliances, a(n) _____ plug and receptacle is permitted to serve as the disconnecting means.

    (a) labeled
    (b) accessible
    (c) metal enclosed
    (d) none of these

17. For cord-and-plug-connected household electric ranges, an attachment plug and receptacle connection at the rear base of the range can serve as the disconnecting means, if it is _____.

    (a) less than 40A
    (b) a flush-mounted receptacle
    (c) GFCI-protected
    (d) accessible from the front by the removal of a drawer

18. Appliances that have a unit switch with a marked _____ position that disconnects all the ungrounded conductors can serve as the appliance disconnecting means.

    (a) on
    (b) off
    (c) on/off
    (d) all of these

19. Cord-and-plug-connected vending machines manufactured or remanufactured on or after January 1, 2005 shall include a ground-fault circuit interrupter identified for portable use as an integral part of the attachment plug or in the power-supply cord within 12 in. of the attachment plug. Older vending machines not incorporating integral GFCI protection shall be _____.

    (a) remanufactured
    (b) disabled
    (c) connected to a GFCI-protected outlet
    (d) connected to an AFCI-protected circuit

20. Electric drinking fountains shall be _____ protected.

    (a) GFCI
    (b) AFCI
    (c) a or b
    (d) none of these

## Notes

# ARTICLE 424 — FIXED ELECTRIC SPACE-HEATING EQUIPMENT

## Introduction to Article 424—Fixed Electric Space-Heating Equipment

Many people are surprised to see how many pages Article 424 has. This is a nine-part article on fixed electric space heaters. Why so much text for what seems to be a simple application? The answer is that Article 424 covers a variety of applications—heaters come in various configurations for various uses. Not all of these parts are for the electrician in the field—the requirements in Part IV are for manufacturers.

Fixed space heaters (wall-mounted, ceiling-mounted, or free-standing) are common in many utility buildings and other small structures, as well as in some larger structures. When used to heat floors, space-heating cables address the thermal layering problem typical of forced-air systems—so it's likely you'll encounter them. Duct heaters are very common in large office and educational buildings. These provide a distributed heating scheme. Locating the heater in the ductwork, but close to the occupied space, eliminates the waste of transporting heated air through sheet metal routed in unheated spaces, so it's likely you'll encounter those as well.

**Please use the 2014 Code book to answer the following questions.**

1. Fixed electric space-heating equipment and motors shall be considered a _____ load for branch circuit sizing.

    (a) noncontinuous
    (b) intermittent
    (c) continuous
    (d) none of these

2. If a permanently installed electric baseboard heater has factory-installed receptacle outlets, the receptacle is permitted to be connected to the heater circuits.

    (a) True
    (b) False

3. Means shall be provided to simultaneously disconnect the _____ of all fixed electric space-heating equipment from all ungrounded conductors.

    (a) heater
    (b) motor controller(s)
    (c) supplementary overcurrent device(s)
    (d) all of these

4. A unit switch with a marked _____ position that is part of a fixed space heater, and disconnects all ungrounded conductors, shall be permitted to serve as the required disconnecting means.

    (a) on
    (b) closed
    (c) off
    (d) none of these

5. Conductors located above an electric space-heated ceiling are considered to be operating in an ambient temperature of _____.

    (a) 20°C
    (b) 30°C
    (c) 50°C
    (d) 86°C

6. Electric space-heating cables shall not extend beyond the room or area in which they _____.

    (a) provide heat
    (b) originate
    (c) terminate
    (d) are connected

7. The minimum clearance between an electric space-heating cable and an outlet box used for surface luminaires shall not be less than _____ in.

    (a) 6
    (b) 8
    (c) 14
    (d) 18

8. Ground-fault circuit-interrupter protection for personnel shall be provided for cables installed in electrically heated floors of _____.

    (a) bathrooms
    (b) hydromassage bathtub locations
    (c) kitchens
    (d) all of these

9. Duct heater controller equipment shall have a disconnecting means installed within _____ the controller except as allowed by 424.19(A).

    (a) 25 ft of
    (b) sight from
    (c) the side of
    (d) none of these

# ARTICLE 430 — MOTORS, MOTOR CIRCUITS, AND CONTROLLERS

## Introduction to Article 430—Motors, Motor Circuits, and Controllers

Article 430 contains the specific rules for conductor sizing, overcurrent protection, control circuit conductors, controllers, and disconnecting means for electric motors. The installation requirements for motor control centers are covered in Part VIII, and air-conditioning and refrigeration equipment are covered in Article 440.

Article 430 is one of the longest articles in the *NEC*. It's also one of the most complex, but motors are also complex equipment. They're electrical and mechanical devices, but what makes motor applications complex is the fact that they're inductive loads with a high-current demand at start-up that's typically six, or more, times the running current. This makes overcurrent protection for motor applications necessarily different from the protection employed for other types of equipment. So don't confuse general overcurrent protection with motor protection—you must calculate and apply them differently using the rules in Article 430.

You might be uncomfortable with the allowances for overcurrent protection found in this article, such as protecting a 10 AWG conductor with a 60A overcurrent protection device, but as you learn to understand how motor protection works, you'll understand why these allowances aren't only safe, but necessary.

Please use the 2014 *Code* book to answer the following questions.

1. For general motor applications, the motor branch-circuit short-circuit and ground-fault protection device shall be sized based on the _____ values.

    (a) motor nameplate
    (b) NEMA standard
    (c) *NEC* Table
    (d) Factory Mutual

2. The motor _____ currents listed in Tables 430.247 through 430.250 shall be used to determine the ampacity of motor circuit conductors and short-circuit and ground-fault protection devices.

    (a) nameplate
    (b) full-load
    (c) power factor
    (d) service factor

3. Motor controllers and terminals of control circuit devices shall be connected with copper conductors unless identified for use with a different conductor.

   (a) True
   (b) False

4. Torque requirements for motor control circuit device terminals shall be a minimum of _____ lb-in. (unless otherwise identified) for screw-type pressure terminals used for 14 AWG and smaller copper conductors.

   (a) 7
   (b) 9
   (c) 10
   (d) 15

5. Motors shall be located so that adequate _____ is provided and so that maintenance, such as lubrication of bearings and replacing of brushes, can be readily accomplished.

   (a) space
   (b) ventilation
   (c) protection
   (d) all of these

6. In determining the highest rated motor for purposes of 430.24, the highest rated motor shall be based on the rated full-load current as selected _____.

   (a) from the motor nameplate
   (b) from Tables 430.247, 430.248, 430.249, and 430.250
   (c) from taking the horsepower times 746 watts
   (d) using the largest horsepower motor

7. Branch-circuit conductors supplying a single continuous-duty motor shall have an ampacity not less than _____ rating.

   (a) 125 percent of the motor's nameplate current
   (b) 125 percent of the motor's full-load current rating as determined by 430.6(A)(1)
   (c) 125 percent of the motor's full locked-rotor
   (d) 80 percent of the motor's full-load current

8. Feeder tap conductors supplying motor circuits, with an ampacity at least one-third that of the feeder, shall not exceed _____ ft in length.

   (a) 10
   (b) 15
   (c) 20
   (d) 25

9. Overload devices are intended to protect motors, motor control apparatus, and motor branch-circuit conductors against _____.

   (a) excessive heating due to motor overloads
   (b) excessive heating due to failure to start
   (c) short circuits and ground faults
   (d) a and b

10. A separate overload device used to protect continuous-duty motors rated more than 1 hp shall be selected to trip at no more than _____ percent of the motor nameplate full-load current rating if marked with a service factor of 1.15 or greater.

    (a) 110
    (b) 115
    (c) 120
    (d) 125

11. Unless overload protection is provided by other approved means, the minimum number of overload units required for a three-phase ac motor is _____.

    (a) one
    (b) two
    (c) three
    (d) any of these

12. The motor branch-circuit short-circuit and ground-fault protective device shall be capable of carrying the _____ current of the motor.

    (a) varying
    (b) starting
    (c) running
    (d) continuous

13. The maximum rating or setting of an inverse time breaker used as the motor branch-circuit short-circuit and ground-fault protective device for a single-phase motor is _____ percent of the full-load current given in Table 430.248.

    (a) 125
    (b) 175
    (c) 250
    (d) 300

14. Where the motor short-circuit and ground-fault protection devices determined by Table 430.52 do not correspond to the standard sizes or ratings, a higher rating that does not exceed the next higher standard ampere rating shall be permitted.

    (a) True
    (b) False

15. A motor can be provided with combined overcurrent protection using a single protective device to provide branch-circuit _____ protection where the rating of the device provides the overload protection specified in 430.32.

    (a) short-circuit
    (b) ground-fault
    (c) motor overload
    (d) all of these

16. A feeder supplying fixed motor load(s) shall have a protective device with a rating or setting _____ branch-circuit short-circuit and ground-fault protective device for any motor in the group, plus the sum of the full-load currents of the other motors of the group.

    (a) not greater than the largest rating or setting of the
    (b) 125 percent of the largest rating of any
    (c) equal to the largest rating of any
    (d) none of these

17. Overcurrent protection for motor control circuits shall not exceed _____ percent if the conductor is based on Table 310.15(B)(17) and does not extend beyond the motor control equipment enclosure.

    (a) 100
    (b) 150
    (c) 300
    (d) 400

18. Motor control circuit conductors that extend beyond the motor control equipment enclosure shall have short-circuit and ground-fault protection sized not greater than _____ percent of value specified in Table 310.15(B)(16) for 60°C conductors.

    (a) 100
    (b) 150
    (c) 300
    (d) 400

19. Motor control circuits shall be arranged so they will be disconnected from all sources of supply when the disconnecting means is in the open position.

    (a) True
    (b) False

20. The motor controller shall have horsepower ratings at the application voltage not _____ the horsepower rating of the motor.

    (a) lower than
    (b) higher than
    (c) equal to
    (d) none of these

21. A _____ rated in amperes shall be permitted as a controller for all motors.

    (a) branch-circuit inverse time circuit breaker
    (b) molded case switch
    (c) a and b
    (d) none of these

22. For stationary motors of 2 hp or less and 300V or less on ac circuits, the controller can be an ac-rated only general-use snap switch where the motor full-load current rating is not more than _____ percent of the rating of the switch.

    (a) 50
    (b) 60
    (c) 70
    (d) 80

23. A motor controller shall open all conductors to the motor where not used as a disconnecting means.

    (a) True
    (b) False

24. Each motor shall be provided with an individual controller.

    (a) True
    (b) False

25. A _____ shall be located in sight from the motor location and the driven machinery location.

    (a) controller
    (b) protection device
    (c) disconnecting means
    (d) all of these

26. The motor disconnecting means shall not be required to be in sight from the motor and the driven machinery location, provided _____.

    (a) the controller disconnecting means is lockable, in accordance with 110.25
    (b) locating the motor disconnecting means within sight of the motor is impractical
    (c) locating the motor disconnecting means within sight of the motor introduces additional or increased hazards to people or property
    (d) all of these

27. The disconnecting means for the controller and motor shall open all ungrounded supply conductors.

    (a) True
    (b) False

28. The disconnecting means for a motor controller shall be designed so that it cannot _____ automatically.

    (a) open
    (b) close
    (c) restart
    (d) shut down

29. The motor disconnecting means for a motor shall _____ whether it is in the open (off) or closed (on) position.

    (a) plainly indicate
    (b) provide current
    (c) be in the upper position
    (d) none of these

30. Where more than one motor disconnecting means is provided in the same motor branch circuit, at least one of the disconnecting means shall be readily accessible.

    (a) True
    (b) False

31. A motor disconnecting means can be a listed _____.

    (a) molded case circuit breaker
    (b) motor-circuit switch rated in horsepower
    (c) molded case switch
    (d) any of these

32. If a motor disconnecting means is a motor-circuit switch, it shall be rated in _____.

    (a) horsepower
    (b) watts
    (c) amperes
    (d) locked-rotor current

33. A branch-circuit overcurrent device can serve as the disconnecting means for a stationary motor of ⅛ hp or less.

    (a) True
    (b) False

34. A horsepower-rated _____ having a horsepower rating not less than the motor rating shall be permitted to serve as the disconnecting means.

    (a) attachment plug and receptacle
    (b) flanged surface inlet and cord connector
    (c) automatic controller
    (d) a or b

# ARTICLE 440 — AIR-CONDITIONING AND REFRIGERATION EQUIPMENT

### Introduction to Article 440—Air-Conditioning and Refrigeration Equipment

This article applies to electrically driven air-conditioning and refrigeration equipment. The rules in this article add to, or amend, the rules in Article 430 and other articles.

Each equipment manufacturer has the motor for a given air-conditioning unit built to its own specifications. Cooling and other characteristics are different from those of nonhermetic motors. For each motor, the manufacturer has worked out all of the details and supplied the correct protection, conductor sizing, and other information on the nameplate. So when wiring an air conditioner, trust the information on the nameplate and don't try to over-complicate the situation. The math for sizing the overcurrent protection and conductor minimum ampacity has already been done for you.

Please use the 2014 *Code* book to answer the following questions.

1. Article 440 applies to electric motor-driven air-conditioning and refrigerating equipment that has a hermetic refrigerant motor-compressor.

   (a) True
   (b) False

2. The _____ current for a hermetic refrigerant motor-compressor is the current resulting when the motor-compressor is operated at the rated load, rated voltage, and rated frequency of the equipment it serves.

   (a) full-load
   (b) nameplate rating
   (c) selection
   (d) rated-load

3. The rules of _____, as applicable, shall apply to air-conditioning and refrigerating equipment that does not incorporate a hermetic refrigerant motor-compressor.

   (a) Article 422
   (b) Article 424
   (c) Article 430
   (d) any of these

4. Equipment such as _____ shall be considered appliances, and the provisions of Article 422 apply in addition to Article 440.

   (a) room air conditioners
   (b) household refrigerators and freezers
   (c) drinking water coolers and beverage dispensers
   (d) all of these

## Article 440 | Air-Conditioning and Refrigeration Equipment

5. A disconnecting means that serves a hermetic refrigerant motor-compressor shall have an ampere rating of at least _____ percent of the nameplate rated-load current or branch-circuit selection current, whichever is greater.

   (a) 80
   (b) 100
   (c) 115
   (d) 125

6. An attachment plug and receptacle can serve as the disconnecting means for cord-connected _____.

   (a) room air conditioners
   (b) household refrigerators and freezers
   (c) drinking water coolers and beverage dispensers
   (d) all of these

7. The disconnecting means for air-conditioning and refrigerating equipment shall be _____ from the air-conditioning or refrigerating equipment.

   (a) readily accessible
   (b) within sight
   (c) a or b
   (d) a and b

8. Disconnecting means for air-conditioning or refrigerating equipment can be installed _____ the air-conditioning or refrigerating equipment, but not on panels that are designed to allow access to the equipment, and not over the equipment nameplate.

   (a) on
   (b) within
   (c) a or b
   (d) none of these

9. Where the air conditioner disconnecting means is not within sight from the equipment, the disconnecting means must be _____.

   (a) guarded
   (b) exposed
   (c) lockable
   (d) elevated

10. Short-circuit and ground-fault protection for an individual air-conditioner motor-compressor shall not exceed _____ percent of the motor-compressor rated-load current or branch-circuit selection current, whichever is greater.

    (a) 80
    (b) 125
    (c) 175
    (d) 250

11. Branch-circuit conductors supplying a single air-conditioner motor-compressor shall have an ampacity not less than _____ percent of either the motor-compressor rated-load current or the branch-circuit selection current, whichever is greater.

    (a) 100
    (b) 125
    (c) 150
    (d) 200

12. The total marked rating of a cord-and-plug-connected room air conditioner, connected to the same branch circuit which supplies lighting units, other appliances, or general-use receptacles, shall not exceed _____ percent of the branch-circuit rating.

    (a) 40
    (b) 50
    (c) 70
    (d) 80

13. An attachment plug and receptacle can serve as the disconnecting means for a single-phase room air conditioner rated 250 volts or less if _____.

    (a) the manual controls on the room air conditioner are readily accessible and located within 6 ft of the floor
    (b) an approved manually operable disconnecting means is installed in a readily accessible location within sight from the room air conditioner
    (c) a or b
    (d) a and b

14. When supplying a room air conditioner rated 120V, the length of a flexible supply cord shall not exceed _____ ft.

    (a) 4
    (b) 6
    (c) 8
    (d) 10

# ARTICLE 445 — GENERATORS

## Introduction to Article 445—Generators

This article contains the electrical installation, and other requirements, for generators. These requirements include such things as where generators can be installed, nameplate markings, conductor ampacity, and disconnecting means.

Generators are basically motors that operate in reverse—they produce electricity when rotated, instead of rotating when supplied with electricity. Article 430, which covers motors, is the longest article in the *NEC*. Article 445, which covers generators, is one of the shortest. At first, this might not seem to make sense. But you don't need to size and protect conductors to a generator. You do need to size and protect them to a motor.

Generators need overload protection, and it's necessary to size the conductors that come from the generator. But these considerations are much more straightforward than the equivalent considerations for motors. Before you study Article 445, take a moment to read the definition of "Separately Derived System" in Article 100.

Please use the 2014 *Code* book to answer the following questions.

1. Introduction to Article 445 contains installation and other requirements for generators.

    (a) True
    (b) False

2. Each generator shall be provided with a _____ listing the manufacturer's name, the rated frequency, power factor, number of phases (if of alternating current), and its rating in kilowatts or kilovolt-amperes.

    (a) list
    (b) faceplate
    (c) nameplate
    (d) sticker

3. Constant-voltage generators, except ac generator exciters, shall be protected from overload by _____ or other acceptable overcurrent protective means suitable for the conditions of use.

    (a) inherent design
    (b) circuit breakers
    (c) fuses
    (d) any of these

Article 445 | Generators

4. The ampacity of the conductors from the generator terminals to the first distribution device containing overcurrent protection shall not be less than _____ percent of the nameplate rating of the generator.

   (a) 75
   (b) 115
   (c) 125
   (d) 140

5. Separately derived system generators must have the _____ conductor sized not smaller than required to carry the maximum unbalanced current as determined by 220.61.

   (a) neutral
   (b) grounding
   (c) a and b
   (d) none of these

6. Generators must have a disconnecting means that is lockable in the open position, except where the _____.

   (a) driving means for the generator can be readily shut down, is rendered incapable of restarting, and is lockable in the OFF position
   (b) generator isn't arranged to operate in parallel with another generator or other source of voltage
   (c) a and b
   (d) a or b

# ARTICLE 450 — TRANSFORMERS

## Introduction to Article 450—Transformers

Article 450 opens by saying, "This article covers the installation of all transformers." Then it lists eight exceptions. So what does Article 450 really cover? Essentially, it covers power transformers and most kinds of lighting transformers.

A major concern with transformers is preventing overheating. The *Code* doesn't completely address this issue. Article 90 explains that the *NEC* isn't a design manual, and it assumes that the person using the *Code* has a certain level of expertise. Proper transformer selection is an important part of preventing it from overheating.

The *NEC* assumes you've already selected a transformer suitable to the load characteristics. For the *Code* to tell you how to do that would push it into the realm of a design manual. Article 450 then takes you to the next logical step—providing overcurrent protection and the proper connections. But this article doesn't stop there; 450.9 provides ventilation requirements, and 450.13 contains accessibility requirements.

Part I of Article 450 contains the general requirements such as guarding, marking, and accessibility, Part II contains the requirements for different types of transformers, and Part III covers transformer vaults.

**Please use the 2014 *Code* book to answer the following questions.**

1. The primary overcurrent protection for a transformer rated 1,000V, nominal, or less, with no secondary protection and having a primary current rating of over 9A must be set at not more than _____ percent.

   (a) 125
   (b) 167
   (c) 200
   (d) 300

2. Transformers with ventilating openings shall be installed so that the ventilating openings are _____.

   (a) a minimum 18 in. above the floor
   (b) not blocked by walls or obstructions
   (c) aesthetically located
   (d) vented to the exterior of the building

## Article 450 | Transformers

3. Transformers and transformer vaults shall be readily accessible to qualified personnel for inspection and maintenance, except _____.

    (a) dry-type transformers 1,000V or less, located in the open on walls, columns, or structures
    (b) dry-type transformers 1,000V, nominal, or less and not exceeding 50 kVA in hollow spaces of buildings not permanently closed in by structure
    (c) a or b
    (d) none of these

4. For transformers, other than Class 2 and Class 3, a means is required to disconnect all transformer ungrounded primary conductors. The disconnecting means must be located within sight of the transformer unless the disconnect _____.

    (a) location is field marked on the transformer
    (b) is lockable in accordance with 110.25
    (c) is nonfusible
    (d) a and b

# ARTICLE 480 STORAGE BATTERIES

## Introduction to Article 480—Storage Batteries

The stationary battery is the heart of any uninterruptible power supply. Article 480 addresses stationary batteries for commercial and industrial grade power supplies, not the small, "point of use," UPS boxes.

Stationary batteries are also used in other applications, such as emergency power systems. Regardless of the application, if it uses stationary batteries, Article 480 applies.

Lead-acid stationary batteries fall into two general categories: flooded, and valve regulated (VRLA). These differ markedly in such ways as maintainability, total cost of ownership, and scalability. The *NEC* doesn't address these differences, as they're engineering issues and not fire safety or electrical safety matters [90.1].

The *Code* doesn't address such design issues as optimum tier height, distance between tiers, determination of charging voltage, or string configuration. Nor does it address battery testing, monitoring, or maintenance. All of these involve highly specialized areas of knowledge, and are required for optimizing operational efficiency. Standards other than the *NEC* address these topics.

What the *Code* does address, in Article 480, are issues related to preventing electrocution and the ignition of the gases that all stationary batteries (even "sealed" ones) emit.

Please use the 2014 *Code* book to answer the following questions.

1. The provisions of Article _____ apply to stationary storage battery installations.
   (a) 450
   (b) 460
   (c) 470
   (d) 480

2. Nominal battery voltage, as it relates to storage batteries, is the value of a(n) _____ of a given voltage class for convenient designation.
   (a) cell or battery
   (b) container
   (c) electrolyte
   (d) intertier connector

## Article 480 | Storage Batteries

3. Nominal battery voltage is typically _____.
   (a) 2V per cell for lead-acid systems
   (b) 1.20V for per cell for alkali systems
   (c) 3.60 to 3.80V per cell for Li-ion systems
   (d) all of these

4. Wiring and equipment supplied from storage batteries must be in accordance with Chapters 1 through 4 of the NEC unless otherwise permitted by 480.5.
   (a) True
   (b) False

5. A disconnecting means is required within sight of the storage battery for all ungrounded battery system conductors operating at over _____ nominal.
   (a) 20V
   (b) 30V
   (c) 40V
   (d) 50V

6. A(n) _____ disconnecting means is required within sight of the storage battery for all ungrounded battery system conductors operating at over 50V nominal.
   (a) accessible
   (b) readily accessible
   (c) safety
   (d) all of these

7. A vented alkaline-type battery, as it relates to storage batteries, operating at not over 250V shall be installed with not more than _____ cells in the series circuit of any one tray.
   (a) 10
   (b) 12
   (c) 18
   (d) 20

8. Racks (rigid frames designed to support battery cells or trays) must be made of which of the following?
   (a) Metal, treated to be resistant to deteriorating action by the electrolyte and provided with nonconducting or continuous insulating material members directly supporting the cells.
   (b) Fiberglass.
   (c) Other suitable nonconductive materials.
   (d) any of these

9. Provisions appropriate to the battery technology shall be made for sufficient diffusion and ventilation of the gases from a storage battery to prevent the accumulation of a(n) _____ mixture.
   (a) corrosive
   (b) explosive
   (c) toxic
   (d) all of these

10. The required working space for battery systems is measured from the edge of the battery _____.
    (a) terminals
    (b) enclosure
    (c) rack or cabinet
    (d) any of these

11. Each vented cell of a battery, as it relates to storage batteries, shall be equipped with _____ that is(are) designed to prevent destruction of the cell due to ignition of gases within the cell by an external spark or flame under normal operating conditions.
    (a) pressure relief
    (b) a flame arrester
    (c) fluid level indicators
    (d) none of these

# FINAL EXAM A

# FINAL EXAM QUESTIONS FOR CHAPTERS 1–4

Please use the 2014 *Code* book to answer the following questions.

1. The *NEC* is _____.

   (a) intended to be a design manual
   (b) meant to be used as an instruction guide for untrained persons
   (c) for the practical safeguarding of persons and property
   (d) published by the Bureau of Standards.

2. A _____ is an area that includes a basin with a toilet, urinal, tub, shower, bidet, or similar plumbing fixtures.

   (a) bath area
   (b) bathroom
   (c) rest area
   (d) none of these

3. Connected to ground or to a conductive body that extends the ground connection is called "_____."

   (a) equipment grounding
   (b) bonded
   (c) grounded
   (d) all of these

4. NFPA 70E—*Standard for Electrical Safety in the Workplace*, provides information to help determine the electrical safety training requirements expected of a qualified person.

   (a) True
   (b) False

5. Many terminations and equipment are either marked with _____, or have that information included in the product's installation instructions.

   (a) an etching tool
   (b) a removable label
   (c) a tightening torque
   (d) the manufacturer's initials

6. The continuity of a grounded conductor shall not depend on a connection to a _____.

   (a) metallic enclosure
   (b) raceway
   (c) cable armor
   (d) all of these

7. An individual 20A branch circuit can supply a single dwelling unit bathroom for receptacle outlet(s) and other equipment within the same bathroom.

   (a) True
   (b) False

8. At least one 125V, 15A or 20A receptacle outlet shall be installed within 18 in. of the top of a show window for each _____ linear ft, or major fraction thereof, of show-window area measured horizontally at its maximum width.

   (a) 10
   (b) 12
   (c) 18
   (d) 24

9. Overhead feeder conductors installed over roofs shall have a vertical clearance of _____ above the roof surface, unless permitted by an exception.

   (a) 3 ft
   (b) 8 ft
   (c) 12 ft
   (d) 15 ft

10. Overhead service conductors shall have a horizontal clearance of not less than _____ ft from a pool.

    (a) 8
    (b) 10
    (c) 12
    (d) 14

11. For installations consisting of not more than two 2-wire branch circuits, the service disconnecting means shall have a rating of not less than _____.

    (a) 15A
    (b) 20A
    (c) 25A
    (d) 30A

12. An 800A fuse rated at 1,000V _____ on a 250V system.

    (a) shall not be used
    (b) shall be used
    (c) can be used
    (d) none of these

13. The grounding electrode conductor shall be connected to the grounded service conductor at the _____.

    (a) load end of the service drop
    (b) load end of the service lateral
    (c) service disconnecting means
    (d) any of these

14. A ground ring encircling the building or structure can be used as a grounding electrode when _____.

    (a) the ring is in direct contact with the earth
    (b) the ring consists of at least 20 ft of bare copper conductor
    (c) the bare copper conductor is not smaller than 2 AWG
    (d) all of these

15. The normally noncurrent-carrying metal parts of service equipment, such as _____, shall be bonded together.

    (a) service raceways or service cable armor
    (b) service equipment enclosures containing service conductors, including meter fittings, boxes, or the like, interposed in the service raceway or armor
    (c) service cable trays
    (d) all of these

16. Where used, the surge protective device shall be connected to the grounded conductor of the circuit.

    (a) True
    (b) False

17. The ampacities listed in 310.15 do not take _____ into consideration.

    (a) continuous loads
    (b) voltage drop
    (c) insulation
    (d) wet locations

18. Type AC cable installed through, or parallel to, framing members shall be protected against physical damage from penetration by screws or nails.

    (a) True
    (b) False

19. Bends in FMC shall be made so that the conduit is not damaged and the internal diameter of the conduit is _____.

    (a) larger than ⅜ in.
    (b) not effectively reduced
    (c) increased
    (d) larger than 1 in.

20. Cable trays shall be supported at intervals in accordance with the installation instructions.

    (a) True
    (b) False

21. A switchboard or panelboard containing a 4-wire, _____ system where the midpoint of one phase winding is grounded, shall be legibly and permanently field-marked to caution that one phase has a higher voltage-to-ground.

    (a) wye-connected
    (b) delta-connected
    (c) solidly grounded
    (d) ungrounded

22. Individual circuits for nonmotor-operated appliances that are continuously loaded shall have the branch-circuit rating sized not less than _____ percent of the appliance marked ampere rating, unless otherwise listed.

    (a) 80
    (b) 100
    (c) 125
    (d) 150

23. For transformers, other than Class 2 and Class 3, a means is required to disconnect all transformer ungrounded primary conductors. The disconnecting means must be located within sight of the transformer unless the disconnect _____.

    (a) location is field marked on the transformer
    (b) is lockable in accordance with 110.25
    (c) is nonfusible
    (d) a and b

24. This *Code* covers the installation of _____ for public and private premises, including buildings, structures, mobile homes, recreational vehicles, and floating buildings.

    (a) optical fiber cables
    (b) electrical equipment
    (c) raceways
    (d) all of these

25. For a circuit to be considered a multiwire branch circuit, it shall have _____.

    (a) two or more ungrounded conductors with a voltage potential between them
    (b) a grounded conductor having equal voltage potential between it and each ungrounded conductor of the circuit
    (c) a grounded conductor connected to the neutral or grounded terminal of the system
    (d) all of these

26. A conductor used to connect the system grounded conductor or the equipment to a grounding electrode or to a point on the grounding electrode system is called the "_____ conductor."

    (a) main grounding
    (b) common main
    (c) equipment grounding
    (d) grounding electrode

27. When one electrical circuit controls another circuit through a relay, the first circuit is called a "_____."

    (a) primary circuit
    (b) remote-control circuit
    (c) signal circuit
    (d) controller

28. Connection of conductors to terminal parts shall ensure a thoroughly good connection without damaging the conductors and shall be made by means of _____.

    (a) solder lugs
    (b) pressure connectors
    (c) splices to flexible leads
    (d) any of these

29. Receptacles shall have the terminal intended for connection to the grounded conductor identified by a metal or metal coating that is substantially _____ in color.

    (a) green
    (b) white
    (c) gray
    (d) b or c

30. The total rating of utilization equipment fastened in place shall not exceed _____ percent of the branch-circuit ampere rating where lighting units and cord-and-plug-connected utilization equipment are supplied.

    (a) 50
    (b) 75
    (c) 100
    (d) 125

31. In a dwelling unit, illumination for outdoor entrances that have grade-level access can be controlled by _____.

    (a) remote
    (b) central
    (c) automatic control
    (d) any of these

32. If a set of 120/240V overhead feeder conductors terminates at a through-the-roof raceway or approved support, with less than 6 ft of these conductors passing over the roof overhang, the minimum clearance above the roof for these conductors is _____.

    (a) 12 in.
    (b) 18 in.
    (c) 2 ft
    (d) 5 ft

33. Where communications cables and electric service drop conductors are supported by the same pole, communications cables must have a minimum separation of _____ in. at any point in the span, including the point of attachment to the building.

    (a) 2
    (b) 6
    (c) 12
    (d) 24

34. The service conductors shall be connected to the service disconnecting means by _____ or other approved means.

    (a) pressure connectors
    (b) clamps
    (c) solder
    (d) a or b

35. Cartridge fuses and fuse holders shall be classified according to their _____ ranges.

    (a) voltage
    (b) amperage
    (c) a or b
    (d) a and b

36. Where the main bonding jumper is installed from the grounded conductor terminal bar to the equipment grounding terminal bar in service equipment, the _____ conductor is permitted to be connected to the equipment grounding terminal bar.

    (a) grounding
    (b) grounded
    (c) grounding electrode
    (d) none of these

37. Grounding electrodes of the rod type less than _____ in. in diameter shall be listed.

    (a) ½ in.
    (b) ⅝ in.
    (c) ¾ in.
    (d) none of these

38. Bonding jumpers for service raceways shall be used around impaired connections such as _____.

    (a) oversized concentric knockouts
    (b) oversized eccentric knockouts
    (c) reducing washers
    (d) any of these

39. Wiring methods installed behind panels that allow access shall be _____ according to their applicable articles.

    (a) supported
    (b) painted
    (c) in a metal raceway
    (d) all of these

40. On a three-phase, 4-wire, wye circuit, where the major portion of the load consists of nonlinear loads, the neutral conductor shall be counted when applying 310.15(B)(3)(a) adjustment factors.

    (a) True
    (b) False

41. At Type AC cable terminations, a(n) ____ shall be provided.

    (a) fitting (or box design) that protects the conductors from abrasion
    (b) insulating bushing between the conductors and the cable armor
    (c) a and b
    (d) none of these

42. When FMC is used where flexibility is necessary to minimize the transmission of vibration from equipment or to provide flexibility for equipment that requires movement after installation, ____ shall be installed.

    (a) an equipment grounding conductor
    (b) an expansion fitting
    (c) flexible nonmetallic connectors
    (d) none of these

43. TPT and TST cords shall be permitted in lengths not exceeding ____ ft when attached directly to a portable appliance rated 50W or less.

    (a) 8
    (b) 10
    (c) 15
    (d) 20

44. When separate equipment grounding conductors are provided in panelboards, a ____ shall be secured inside the cabinet.

    (a) grounded conductor
    (b) terminal lug
    (c) terminal bar
    (d) none of these

45. Wall-mounted ovens and counter-mounted cooking units shall be permitted to be ____.

    (a) permanently connected
    (b) cord-and-plug-connected
    (c) a or b
    (d) none of these

46. A vented alkaline-type battery, as it relates to storage batteries, operating at not over 250V shall be installed with not more than ____ cells in the series circuit of any one tray.

    (a) 10
    (b) 12
    (c) 18
    (d) 20

47. The NEC does not cover electrical installations in ships, watercraft, railway rolling stock, aircraft, or automotive vehicles.

    (a) True
    (b) False

48. The NEC defines a(n) "____" as a structure that stands alone or that is cut off from adjoining structures by fire walls or fire barriers, with all openings therein protected by approved fire doors.

    (a) unit
    (b) apartment
    (c) building
    (d) utility

49. A "____" is an accommodation that combines living, sleeping, sanitary, and storage facilities within a compartment.

    (a) guest room
    (b) guest suite
    (c) dwelling unit
    (d) single-family dwelling

50. Equipment enclosed in a case or cabinet with a means of sealing or locking so that live parts cannot be made accessible without opening the enclosure is said to be "____."

    (a) guarded
    (b) protected
    (c) sealable
    (d) lockable

51. Each disconnecting means shall be legibly marked to indicate its purpose unless located and arranged so ____.

    (a) that it can be locked out and tagged
    (b) it is not readily accessible
    (c) the purpose is evident
    (d) that it operates at less than 300 volts-to-ground

52. The screw shell of a luminaire or lampholder shall be connected to the ____.

    (a) grounded conductor
    (b) ungrounded conductor
    (c) equipment grounding conductor
    (d) forming shell terminal

53. ____ in dwelling units shall supply only loads within that dwelling unit or loads associated only with that dwelling unit.

    (a) Service-entrance conductors
    (b) Ground-fault protection
    (c) Branch circuits
    (d) none of these

54. In a dwelling unit, at least one lighting outlet ____ shall be located at the point of entry to the attic, underfloor space, utility room, or basement where these spaces are used for storage or contain equipment requiring servicing.

    (a) that is unswitched
    (b) containing a switch
    (c) controlled by a wall switch
    (d) b or c

55. A building or structure shall be supplied by a maximum of ____ feeder(s) or branch circuit(s), unless specifically permitted otherwise.

    (a) one
    (b) two
    (c) three
    (d) four

56. The general requirement for each service drop, set of overhead service conductors, set of underground service conductors, or service lateral is that it shall supply ____ set(s) of service-entrance conductors.

    (a) only one
    (b) only two
    (c) up to six
    (d) an unlimited number of

57. The next higher standard rating overcurrent device above the ampacity of the ungrounded conductors being protected shall be permitted to be used, provided the ____.

    (a) conductors are not part of a branch circuit supplying more than one receptacle for cord-and-plug-connected portable loads
    (b) ampacity of the conductors doesn't correspond with the standard ampere rating of a fuse or circuit breaker
    (c) next higher standard rating selected doesn't exceed 800A
    (d) all of these

58. Circuit breakers used to switch high-intensity discharge lighting circuits shall be listed and marked as ____.

    (a) SWD
    (b) HID
    (c) a or b
    (d) a and b

59. A grounding electrode conductor, sized in accordance with 250.66, shall be used to connect the equipment grounding conductors, the service-equipment enclosures, and, where the system is grounded, the grounded service conductor to the grounding electrode(s).

    (a) True
    (b) False

60. Where the supplemental electrode is a rod, that portion of the bonding jumper that is the sole connection to the supplemental grounding electrode shall not be required to be larger than ____ AWG copper.

    (a) 8
    (b) 6
    (c) 4
    (d) 1

61. At existing buildings or structures, an intersystem bonding termination is not required if other acceptable means of bonding exits. An external accessible means for bonding communications systems together can be by the use of a(n) ____.

    (a) nonflexible metallic raceway
    (b) exposed grounding electrode conductor
    (c) connection to a grounded raceway or equipment approved by the authority having jurisdiction
    (d) any of these

62. Rigid metal conduit that is directly buried outdoors shall have at least ____ in. of cover.

    (a) 6
    (b) 12
    (c) 18
    (d) 24

63. Surface-type cabinets, cutout boxes, and meter socket enclosures in damp or wet locations shall be mounted so there is at least ____ in. airspace between the enclosure and the wall or supporting surface.

    (a) 1/16
    (b) 1/4
    (c) 1 1/4
    (d) 6

64. Type MC cable containing four or fewer conductors, sized no larger than 10 AWG, shall be secured within ____ in. of every box, cabinet, fitting, or other cable termination.

    (a) 8
    (b) 12
    (c) 18
    (d) 24

65. ____ connectors shall not be concealed when used in installations of LFMC.

    (a) Straight
    (b) Angle
    (c) Grounding-type
    (d) none of these

66. Flexible cords and cables shall be protected by ____ where passing through holes in covers, outlet boxes, or similar enclosures.

    (a) bushings
    (b) fittings
    (c) a or b
    (d) none of these

67. No parts of cord-connected luminaires, chain-, cable-, or cord-suspended luminaires, lighting track, pendants, or paddle fans shall be located within a zone measured 3 ft horizontally and ____ ft vertically from the top of the bathtub rim or shower stall threshold.

    (a) 4
    (b) 6
    (c) 8
    (d) 10

68. Cord-and-plug-connected vending machines manufactured or remanufactured on or after January 1, 2005 shall include a ground-fault circuit interrupter identified for portable use as an integral part of the attachment plug or in the power-supply cord within 12 in. of the attachment plug. Older vending machines not incorporating integral GFCI protection shall be ____.

    (a) remanufactured
    (b) disabled
    (c) connected to a GFCI-protected outlet
    (d) connected to an AFCI-protected circuit

69. Communications wiring such as telephone, antenna, and CATV wiring within a building shall not be required to comply with the installation requirements of Chapters 1 through 7, except where specifically referenced in Chapter 8.

    (a) True
    (b) False

70. A communications raceway is an enclosed channel of nonmetallic materials designed for holding communications wires and cables in ____ applications.

    (a) plenum
    (b) riser
    (c) general-purpose
    (d) all of these

# Final Exam A | Final Exam Questions for Chapters 1–4

71. Within sight means visible and not more than _____ ft distant from the equipment.

    (a) 10
    (b) 20
    (c) 25
    (d) 50

72. The overhead system service-entrance conductors are the service conductors between the terminals of _____ and a point where they are joined by a tap or splice to the service drop or overhead service conductors.

    (a) service equipment
    (b) service point
    (c) grounding electrode
    (d) equipment grounding conductor

73. The *NEC* requires tested series-rated installations of circuit breakers or fuses to be legibly marked in the field to indicate the equipment has been applied with a series combination rating.

    (a) True
    (b) False

74. The ungrounded and grounded conductors of each _____ shall be grouped by wire ties or similar means at the panelboard or other point of origination.

    (a) branch circuit
    (b) multiwire branch circuit
    (c) feeder circuit
    (d) service-entrance conductor

75. Receptacle outlets in or on floors shall not be counted as part of the required number of receptacle outlets for dwelling unit wall spaces, unless they are located within _____ in. of the wall.

    (a) 6
    (b) 12
    (c) 18
    (d) 24

76. Ground-fault protection of equipment shall not be required at a feeder disconnect if ground-fault protection of equipment is provided on the _____ side of the feeder and on the load side of any transformer supplying the feeder.

    (a) load
    (b) supply
    (c) service
    (d) none of these

77. The disconnecting means for a building supplied by a feeder shall be installed at a(n) _____ location.

    (a) accessible
    (b) readily accessible
    (c) outdoor
    (d) indoor

78. A single-family dwelling unit and its accessory structure(s) shall be permitted to have one set of service conductors run to each structure from a single service drop, set of overhead service conductors, set of underground service conductors, or service lateral.

    (a) True
    (b) False

79. If the circuit's overcurrent device exceeds _____, the conductor ampacity must have a rating not less than the rating of the overcurrent device.

    (a) 800A
    (b) 1,000A
    (c) 1,200A
    (d) 2,000A

80. A circuit breaker with a _____ voltage rating, such as 240V or 480V, can be used where the nominal voltage between any two conductors does not exceed the circuit breaker's voltage rating.

    (a) straight
    (b) slash
    (c) high
    (d) low

81. A main bonding jumper shall be a _____ or similar suitable conductor.

    (a) wire
    (b) bus
    (c) screw
    (d) any of these

82. When a ground ring is used as a grounding electrode, it shall be buried at a depth below the earth's surface of not less than _____.

    (a) 18 in.
    (b) 24 in.
    (c) 30 in.
    (d) 8 ft

83. When bonding enclosures, metal raceways, frames, and fittings, any nonconductive paint, enamel, or similar coating shall be removed at _____.

    (a) contact surfaces
    (b) threads
    (c) contact points
    (d) all of these

84. Direct-buried service conductors that are not encased in concrete and that are buried 18 in. or more below grade shall have their location identified by a warning ribbon placed in the trench at least _____ in. above the underground installation.

    (a) 6
    (b) 10
    (c) 12
    (d) 18

85. Enclosures for switches or overcurrent devices are allowed to have conductors feeding through where the wiring space at any cross section is not filled to more than _____ percent of the cross-sectional area of the space.

    (a) 20
    (b) 30
    (c) 40
    (d) 60

86. Type NM cables shall not be used in one- and two-family dwellings exceeding three floors above grade.

    (a) True
    (b) False

87. PVC conduit shall not be used _____, unless specifically permitted.

    (a) in hazardous (classified) locations
    (b) for the support of luminaires or other equipment
    (c) where subject to physical damage unless identified for such use
    (d) all of these

88. Single-throw knife switches shall be installed so that gravity will tend to close the switch.

    (a) True
    (b) False

89. The NEC allows a lighting outlet on the wall in a clothes closet when it is at least 6 in. away from storage space.

    (a) True
    (b) False

90. Electric space-heating cables shall not extend beyond the room or area in which they _____.

    (a) provide heat
    (b) originate
    (c) terminate
    (d) are connected

91. Chapters 1 through 4 of the NEC apply _____.

    (a) generally to all electrical installations
    (b) only to special occupancies and conditions
    (c) only to special equipment and material
    (d) all of these

92. A separate portion of a raceway system that provides access through a removable cover(s) to the interior of the system, defines the term _____.

    (a) junction box
    (b) accessible raceway
    (c) conduit body
    (d) cutout box

93. The highest current at rated voltage that a device is identified to interrupt under standard test conditions is the ____.

    (a) interrupting rating
    (b) manufacturer's rating
    (c) interrupting capacity
    (d) withstand rating

94. The underground system service-entrance conductors are the service conductors between the terminals of ____ and the point of connection to the service lateral or underground service conductors.

    (a) service equipment
    (b) service point
    (c) grounding electrode
    (d) equipment grounding conductor

95. Concrete, brick, or tile walls are considered ____, as applied to working space requirements.

    (a) inconsequential
    (b) in the way
    (c) grounded
    (d) none of these

96. Where more than one nominal voltage system supplies branch circuits in a building, each ____ conductor of a branch circuit shall be identified by phase and system at all termination, connection, and splice points.

    (a) grounded
    (b) ungrounded
    (c) grounding
    (d) all of these

97. Receptacles installed for countertop surfaces as required by 210.52(c) shall not be used to meet the receptacle requirements for wall space as required by 210.52(A).

    (a) True
    (b) False

98. Where a premises wiring system contains feeders supplied from more than one nominal voltage system, each ungrounded conductor of a feeder shall be identified by phase or line and system by ____, or other approved means.

    (a) color coding
    (b) marking tape
    (c) tagging
    (d) any of these

99. A building disconnecting means that supplies only limited loads of a single branch circuit shall have a rating of not less than ____.

    (a) 15A
    (b) 20A
    (c) 25A
    (d) 30A

100. Service-entrance cables which are not installed underground, where subject to physical damage, shall be protected by ____.

    (a) rigid metal conduit
    (b) IMC
    (c) Schedule 80 PVC conduit
    (d) any of these

# FINAL EXAM B

# FINAL EXAM QUESTIONS FOR CHAPTERS 1–4

Please use the 2014 *Code* book to answer the following questions.

1. Supplementary overcurrent devices used in luminaires or appliances are not required to be readily accessible.

    (a) True
    (b) False

2. For grounded systems, normally noncurrent-carrying conductive materials enclosing electrical conductors or equipment shall be connected to earth so as to limit the voltage-to-ground on these materials.

    (a) True
    (b) False

3. Where a supply-side bonding jumper of the wire type is run with the derived phase conductors from the source of a separately derived system to the first disconnecting means, it shall be sized in accordance with 250.102(C), based on ____.

    (a) the size of the primary conductors
    (b) the size of the secondary overcurrent protection
    (c) the size of the derived ungrounded conductors
    (d) one third the size of the primary grounded conductor

4. Grounding electrode conductors of the wire type shall be ____.

    (a) solid
    (b) stranded
    (c) insulated or bare
    (d) any of these

5. What is the minimum size copper equipment bonding jumper for a 40A rated circuit?

    (a) 14 AWG
    (b) 12 AWG
    (c) 10 AWG
    (d) 8 AWG

6. Cables or raceways installed using directional boring equipment shall be ____ for this purpose.

    (a) marked
    (b) listed
    (c) labeled
    (d) approved

# Final Exam B | Final Exam Questions for Chapters 1–4

7. When counting the number of conductors in a box, a conductor running through the box with an unbroken loop or coil not less than twice the minimum length required for free conductors shall be counted as _____ conductor(s).

    (a) one
    (b) two
    (c) three
    (d) four

8. Grommets or bushings for the protection of Type NM cable shall be _____ for the purpose.

    (a) marked
    (b) approved
    (c) identified
    (d) listed

9. EMT, elbows, couplings, and fittings can be installed in concrete, in direct contact with the earth, or in areas subject to severe corrosive influences if _____.

    (a) protected by corrosion protection
    (b) approved as suitable for the condition
    (c) a and b
    (d) listed for wet locations

10. The metal mounting yoke of a replacement switch isn't required to be connected to an equipment grounding conductor if the wiring at the existing switch doesn't contain an equipment grounding conductor, and _____

    (a) the switch faceplate is nonmetallic with nonmetallic screws
    (b) the replacement switch is GFCI protected
    (c) a or b
    (d) the circuit is AFCI protected

11. Metal raceways shall be bonded to the metal pole with a(n) _____.

    (a) grounding electrode
    (b) grounded conductor
    (c) equipment grounding conductor
    (d) any of these

12. Torque requirements for motor control circuit device terminals shall be a minimum of _____ lb-in. (unless otherwise identified) for screw-type pressure terminals used for 14 AWG and smaller copper conductors.

    (a) 7
    (b) 9
    (c) 10
    (d) 15

13. In the *NEC*, the words "_____" indicate a mandatory requirement.

    (a) shall
    (b) shall not
    (c) shall be permitted
    (d) a or b

14. An enclosure or piece of equipment constructed so that dust will not enter the enclosure under specified test conditions is known as "_____."

    (a) dusttight
    (b) dustproof
    (c) dust rated
    (d) all of these

15. Lighting track is a manufactured assembly designed to support and _____ luminaires that are capable of being readily repositioned on the track.

    (a) connect
    (b) protect
    (c) energize
    (d) all of these

16. A structure is that which is built or constructed.

    (a) True
    (b) False

17. The required working space for access to live parts operating at 300 volts-to-ground, where there are exposed live parts on one side and grounded parts on the other side, is _____.

    (a) 3 ft
    (b) 3½ ft
    (c) 4 ft
    (d) 4½ ft

18. All 15A and 20A, 125V receptacles installed in crawl spaces at or below grade level of dwelling units shall have GFCI protection.

    (a) True
    (b) False

19. When breaks occur in dwelling unit kitchen countertop spaces for range tops, refrigerators or sinks, each countertop surface shall be considered a separate counter space for determining receptacle placement.

    (a) True
    (b) False

20. The 3 VA per-square-foot general lighting load for dwelling units includes general-use receptacles and lighting outlets.

    (a) True
    (b) False

21. For installations consisting of not more than two 2-wire branch circuits, the building disconnecting means shall have a rating of not less than ____.

    (a) 15A
    (b) 20A
    (c) 25A
    (d) 30A

22. Individual open conductors and cables, other than service-entrance cables, shall not be installed within ____ ft of grade level or where exposed to physical damage.

    (a) 8
    (b) 10
    (c) 12
    (d) 15

23. Ground-fault protection of equipment shall be provided for solidly grounded wye electrical systems of more than 150 volts-to-ground, but not exceeding 1,000V phase-to-phase for each individual device used as a building or structure main disconnecting means rated ____ or more, unless specifically exempted.

    (a) 1,000A
    (b) 1,500A
    (c) 2,000A
    (d) 2,500A

24. For grounded systems, normally noncurrent-carrying conductive materials enclosing electrical conductors or equipment, or forming part of such equipment, shall be connected together and to the ____ to establish an effective ground-fault current path.

    (a) ground
    (b) earth
    (c) electrical supply source
    (d) none of these

25. The grounding electrode for a separately derived system shall be as near as practicable to, and preferably in the same area as, the grounding electrode conductor connection to the system.

    (a) True
    (b) False

26. Where used outside, aluminum or copper-clad aluminum grounding electrode conductors shall not be terminated within ____ of the earth.

    (a) 6 in.
    (b) 12 in.
    (c) 15 in.
    (d) 18 in.

27. An equipment bonding jumper can be installed on the outside of a raceway, providing the length of the equipment bonding jumper is not more than ____ and the equipment bonding jumper is routed with the raceway.

    (a) 12 in.
    (b) 24 in.
    (c) 36 in.
    (d) 72 in.

28. An exposed wiring system for indoor wet locations where walls are frequently washed shall be mounted so that there is at least a ____ between the mounting surface and the electrical equipment.

    (a) ¼ in. airspace
    (b) separation by insulated bushings
    (c) separation by noncombustible tubing
    (d) none of these

29. Conduit bodies that are durably and legibly marked by the manufacturer with their volume can contain splices, taps, or devices

    (a) True
    (b) False

30. Type _____ cable is an assembly primarily used for services.

    (a) NM
    (b) TC
    (c) SE
    (d) none of these

31. When a building is supplied with a fire sprinkler system, ENT can be installed above any suspended ceiling.

    (a) True
    (b) False

32. Snap switches rated _____ or less directly connected to aluminum conductors shall be listed and marked CO/ALR.

    (a) 15A
    (b) 20A
    (c) 25A
    (d) 30A

33. Luminaires that require adjustment or aiming after installation can be cord-connected without an attachment plug, provided the exposed cord is of the hard-usage type and is not longer than that required for maximum adjustment.

    (a) True
    (b) False

34. The motor branch-circuit short-circuit and ground-fault protective device shall be capable of carrying the _____ current of the motor.

    (a) varying
    (b) starting
    (c) running
    (d) continuous

35. When the *Code* uses "_____," it means the identified actions are allowed but not required, and they may be options or alternative methods.

    (a) shall
    (b) shall not
    (c) shall be permitted
    (d) a or b

36. "Continuous duty" is defined as _____.

    (a) when the load is expected to continue for five hours or more
    (b) operation at a substantially constant load for an indefinitely long time
    (c) operation at loads and for intervals of time, both of which may be subject to wide variations
    (d) operation at which the load may be subject to maximum current for six hours or more

37. Equipment or materials included in a list published by a testing laboratory acceptable to the authority having jurisdiction is said to be "_____."

    (a) book
    (b) digest
    (c) manifest
    (d) listed

38. A surge-protective device (SPD) intended for installation on the load side of the service disconnect overcurrent device, including SPDs located at the branch panel, is a _____ SPD.

    (a) Type 1
    (b) Type 2
    (c) Type 3
    (d) Type 4

39. When normally enclosed live parts are exposed for inspection or servicing, the working space, if in a passageway or general open space, shall be suitably _____.

    (a) accessible
    (b) guarded
    (c) open
    (d) enclosed

40. All 15A and 20A, 125V receptacles installed in _____ of dwelling units shall have GFCI protection.

    (a) unfinished attics
    (b) finished attics
    (c) unfinished basements and crawl spaces
    (d) finished basements

41. Kitchen and dining room countertop receptacle outlets in dwelling units shall be installed above the countertop surface, and not more than _____ in. above the countertop.

    (a) 12
    (b) 18
    (c) 20
    (d) 24

42. Branch circuits that supply lighting units that have ballasts, autotransformers, or LED drivers shall have the calculated load based on _____ of the units, not to the total wattage of the lamps.

    (a) 50 percent of the rating
    (b) 80 percent of the rating
    (c) the total ampere rating
    (d) 150 percent of the rating

43. Conductors are considered outside a building when they are installed _____.

    (a) Under not less than 2 in. of concrete beneath a building or structure
    (b) Within a building or structure in a raceway encased in not less than a 2 in. thickness of concrete or brick
    (c) Installed in a vault that meets the construction requirements of Article 450, Part III
    (d) all of these

44. Service-entrance and overhead service conductors shall be arranged so that _____ will not enter the service raceway or equipment.

    (a) dust
    (b) vapor
    (c) water
    (d) none of these

45. Overcurrent devices shall be _____.

    (a) accessible (as applied to wiring methods)
    (b) accessible (as applied to equipment)
    (c) readily accessible
    (d) inaccessible to unauthorized personnel

46. Electrically conductive materials that are likely to _____ in ungrounded systems shall be connected together and to the supply system grounded equipment in a manner that creates a low-impedance path for ground-fault current that is capable of carrying the maximum fault current likely to be imposed on it.

    (a) become energized
    (b) require service
    (c) be removed
    (d) be coated with paint or nonconductive materials

47. Tap connections to a common grounding electrode conductor for multiple separately derived systems may be made to a copper or aluminum busbar that is _____.

    (a) smaller than ¼ in. x 4 in.
    (b) not smaller than ¼ in. x 2 in.
    (c) not smaller than ½ in. x 2 in.
    (d) a and c

48. A grounding electrode conductor shall be permitted to be run to any convenient grounding electrode available in the grounding electrode system where the other electrode(s), if any, is connected by bonding jumpers in accordance with 250.53(C).

    (a) True
    (b) False

49. Lightning protection system ground terminals _____ be bonded to the building or structure grounding electrode system.

    (a) shall
    (b) shall not
    (c) shall be permitted to
    (d) none of these

50. Electrical wiring within the cavity of a fire-rated floor-ceiling or roof-ceiling assembly shall not be supported by the ceiling assembly or ceiling support wires.

    (a) True
    (b) False

51. \_\_\_\_ can be used to fasten boxes to a structural member using brackets on the outside of the enclosure.

    (a) Nails
    (b) Screws
    (c) Bolts
    (d) a and b

52. The ampacity of Type UF cable shall be that of \_\_\_\_ conductors in accordance with 310.15.

    (a) 60°C
    (b) 75°C
    (c) 90°C
    (d) 105°C

53. Bushings or adapters shall be provided at ENT terminations to protect the conductors from abrasion, unless the box, fitting, or enclosure design provides equivalent protection.

    (a) True
    (b) False

54. Where a grounding means exists in the receptacle enclosure a(n) \_\_\_\_-type receptacle shall be used.

    (a) isolated ground
    (b) grounding
    (c) GFCI
    (d) dedicated

55. Lampholders installed in damp locations shall be listed for use in \_\_\_\_ locations.

    (a) damp
    (b) wet
    (c) dry
    (d) a or b

56. The motor controller shall have horsepower ratings at the application voltage not \_\_\_\_ the horsepower rating of the motor.

    (a) lower than
    (b) higher than
    (c) equal to
    (d) none of these

57. Admitting close approach not guarded by locked doors, elevation, or other effective means, is referred to as \_\_\_\_.

    (a) accessible (as applied to equipment)
    (b) accessible (as applied to wiring methods)
    (c) accessible, readily
    (d) all of these

58. As used in the *NEC*, equipment includes \_\_\_\_.

    (a) fittings
    (b) appliances
    (c) machinery
    (d) all of these

59. "Nonautomatic" is defined as requiring \_\_\_\_ to perform a function.

    (a) protection from damage
    (b) human intervention
    (c) mechanical linkage
    (d) all of these

60. A(n) \_\_\_\_ enclosure is constructed or protected so that exposure to the weather will not interfere with successful operation.

    (a) weatherproof
    (b) weathertight
    (c) weather-resistant
    (d) all weather

61. For equipment rated 1,200A or more and over 6 ft wide that contains overcurrent devices, switching devices, or control devices, there shall be one entrance to and egress from the required working space not less than 24 in. wide and \_\_\_\_ high at each end of the working space.

    (a) 5½ ft
    (b) 6 ft
    (c) 6½ ft
    (d) any of these

62. In other than dwelling locations, GFCI protection is required in ____.

    (a) indoor wet locations
    (b) locker rooms with associated showering facilities
    (c) garages, service bays, and similar areas other than vehicle exhibition halls and showrooms
    (d) all of these

63. At least one receptacle outlet not more than ____ above a balcony, deck, or porch shall be installed at each balcony, deck, or porch that is attached to and accessible from a dwelling unit.

    (a) 3 ft
    (b) 6½ ft
    (c) 8 ft
    (d) 24 in.

64. The load for electric clothes dryers in a dwelling unit shall be ____ watts or the nameplate rating, whichever is larger, per dryer.

    (a) 1,500
    (b) 4,500
    (c) 5,000
    (d) 8,000

65. Service conductors installed in overhead masts on the outside surface of the building traveling through the eave, but not the wall, of that building are considered to be outside of the building.

    (a) True
    (b) False

66. On a three-phase, 4-wire, delta-connected service where the midpoint of one phase winding is grounded, the service conductor having the higher phase voltage-to-ground shall be durably and permanently marked by an outer finish that is ____ in color, or by other effective means, at each termination or junction point.

    (a) orange
    (b) red
    (c) blue
    (d) any of these

67. Overcurrent devices shall be readily accessible and installed so the center of the grip of the operating handle of the switch or circuit breaker, when in its highest position, is not more than ____ above the floor or working platform.

    (a) 2 ft
    (b) 4 ft 6 in.
    (c) 5 ft
    (d) 6 ft 7 in.

68. In ungrounded systems, electrical equipment, wiring, and other electrically conductive material likely to become energized shall be installed in a manner that creates a low-impedance circuit from any point on the wiring system to the electrical supply source to facilitate the operation of overcurrent devices should a(n) ____ fault from a different phase occur on the wiring system.

    (a) isolated ground
    (b) second ground
    (c) arc
    (d) high impedance

69. In an area served by a separately derived system, the ____ shall be connected to the grounded conductor of the separately derived system.

    (a) structural steel
    (b) metal piping
    (c) metal building skin
    (d) a and b

70. A service consisting of 12 AWG service-entrance conductors requires a grounding electrode conductor sized no less than ____.

    (a) 10 AWG
    (b) 8 AWG
    (c) 6 AWG
    (d) 4 AWG

71. Type MC cable provides an effective ground-fault current path and is recognized by the *NEC* as an equipment grounding conductor when ____.

    (a) it contains an insulated or uninsulated equipment grounding conductor in compliance with 250.118(1)
    (b) the combined metallic sheath and uninsulated equipment grounding/bonding conductor of interlocked metal tape–type MC cable is listed and identified as an equipment grounding conductor
    (c) only when it is hospital grade Type MC cable
    (d) a or b

72. In multiwire branch circuits, the continuity of the ____ conductor shall not be dependent upon the device connections.

    (a) ungrounded
    (b) grounded
    (c) grounding electrode
    (d) a and b

73. Boxes used at luminaire or lampholder outlets in a ceiling shall be designed so that a luminaire or lampholder can be attached and the boxes shall be required to support a luminaire weighing a minimum of ____ lb.

    (a) 20
    (b) 30
    (c) 40
    (d) 50

74. Trade size 1 IMC shall be supported at intervals not exceeding ____ ft.

    (a) 8
    (b) 10
    (c) 12
    (d) 14

75. The ampacity adjustment factors in 310.15(B)(3)(a) shall be applied to a metal wireway only where the number of current-carrying conductors in any cross section of the wireway exceeds ____.

    (a) 30
    (b) 40
    (c) 50
    (d) 60

76. Receptacles mounted to and supported by a cover shall be secured by more than one screw unless listed and identified for securing by a single screw.

    (a) True
    (b) False

77. The raceway or cable for tap conductors to recessed luminaires shall have a minimum length of ____ in.

    (a) 6
    (b) 12
    (c) 18
    (d) 24

78. The disconnecting means for a motor controller shall be designed so that it cannot ____ automatically.

    (a) open
    (b) close
    (c) restart
    (d) shut down

79. Capable of being removed or exposed without damaging the building structure or finish, or not permanently closed in by the structure or finish of the building is known as ____.

    (a) accessible (as applied to equipment)
    (b) accessible (as applied to wiring methods)
    (c) accessible, readily
    (d) all of these

80. Equipment enclosed in a case that is capable of withstanding an explosion of a specified gas or vapor that may occur within it, and of preventing the ignition of a specified gas or vapor surrounding the enclosure by sparks, flashes, or explosion of the gas or vapor within, and that operates at such an external temperature that a surrounding flammable atmosphere will not be ignited thereby defines the phrase "____."

    (a) overcurrent device
    (b) thermal apparatus
    (c) explosionproof equipment
    (d) bomb casing

81. A(n) ____ is a point on the wiring system at which current is taken to supply utilization equipment.

    (a) box
    (b) receptacle
    (c) outlet
    (d) device

82. Equipment intended to interrupt current at fault levels shall have an interrupting rating at nominal circuit voltage sufficient for the current that is available at the line terminals of the equipment.

    (a) True
    (b) False

83. The dedicated space above a panelboard extends to a dropped or suspended ceiling, which is considered a structural ceiling.

    (a) True
    (b) False

84. All 15A and 20A, 125V receptacles installed within 6 ft of the outside edge of a sink in locations other than dwelling units must be ____.

    (a) AFCI protected
    (b) GFCI protected
    (c) tamperproof
    (d) a and b

85. A laundry receptacle outlet shall not be required in each dwelling unit of a multifamily building, if laundry facilities are provided on the premises for all building occupants.

    (a) True
    (b) False

86. Using the standard load calculation method, the feeder demand factor for five household clothes dryers is ____ percent.

    (a) 50
    (b) 70
    (c) 85
    (d) 100

87. Service-drop conductors shall have ____.

    (a) sufficient ampacity to carry the load
    (b) adequate mechanical strength
    (c) a or b
    (d) a and b

88. There shall be no more than ____ disconnects installed for each service or for each set of service-entrance conductors as permitted in 230.2 and 230.40.

    (a) two
    (b) four
    (c) six
    (d) eight

89. Plug fuses of the Edison-base type shall be used ____.

    (a) where overfusing is necessary
    (b) as a replacement in existing installations
    (c) as a replacement for Type S fuses
    (d) 50A and above

90. ____ on equipment to be grounded shall be removed from contact surfaces to ensure good electrical continuity.

    (a) Paint
    (b) Lacquer
    (c) Enamel
    (d) any of these

91. High-impedance grounded neutral systems shall be permitted for three-phase ac systems of 480V to 1,000V where ____.

    (a) the conditions of maintenance ensure that only qualified persons service the installation
    (b) ground detectors are installed on the system
    (c) line-to-neutral loads are not served
    (d) all of these

92. Exothermic or irreversible compression connections, together with the mechanical means used to attach to fireproofed structural metal, shall not be required to be accessible.

    (a) True
    (b) False

93. Where conductors are run in parallel in multiple raceways or cables and include an EGC of the wire type, the equipment grounding conductor must be installed in parallel in each raceway or cable, sized in compliance with 250.122.

    (a) True
    (b) False

94. Raceways shall be _____ between outlet, junction, or splicing points prior to the installation of conductors.

    (a) installed complete
    (b) tested for ground faults
    (c) a minimum of 80 percent complete
    (d) none of these

95. Power distribution blocks shall be permitted in pull and junction boxes over 100 cubic inches when they comply with the provisions of 314.28(E)(1) through (5).

    (a) True
    (b) False

96. Galvanized steel, stainless steel, and red brass RMC shall be permitted in or under cinder fill subject to permanent moisture, when protected on all sides by a layer of noncinder concrete not less than _____ in. thick.

    (a) 2
    (b) 4
    (c) 6
    (d) 18

97. Surface metal raceways and associated fittings shall be supported _____.

    (a) in accordance with the manufacturer's installation instructions
    (b) at intervals appropriate for the building design
    (c) at intervals not exceeding 4 ft
    (d) at intervals not exceeding 8 ft

98. Nonlocking 15A and 20A, 125V and 250V receptacles installed in damp locations shall be listed as _____.

    (a) raintight
    (b) watertight
    (c) weatherproof
    (d) weather resistant

99. Lighting track fittings can be equipped with general-purpose receptacles.

    (a) True
    (b) False

100. Where the air conditioner disconnecting means is not within sight from the equipment, the disconnecting means must be _____.

    (a) guarded
    (b) exposed
    (c) lockable
    (d) elevated

# Take Your Training to the next level & Save 25%
use discount code: **B14UND1WB25**

## 2014 Master & Journeyman Comprehensive Exam Preparation Library

A complete course designed for your success. In-depth instruction for Theory and Code, with step-by-step instructions for solving electrical calculations. The DVDs are a vital component to learning, and the Practice Questions are key to reinforcing what you learn.

**Electrical Exam Preparation textbook**
**Electrical Theory textbook**
**Understanding the National Electrical Code® Volumes 1 & 2 textbooks**
**Simulated Exam**
*Code Review (10 DVDs)*
*Theory Review (3 DVDs)*
*Calculations Review (Masters - 8 DVDs; Journeyman - 5 DVDs)*

**Product Code:** 14MACODVD  List Price: $1025.00  Now only $768.75
**Product Code:** 14JRCODVD  List Price: $925.00  Now only $693.75

## Electrical Estimating DVD Package

Mike Holt's Electrical Estimating DVD Program will give you the skills and the knowledge to get more jobs and to make sure that those jobs will be profitable. This program will also give you a comprehensive understanding of the Estimating process as well as help you understand how Electrical Estimating software can improve your process.

**Electrical Estimating textbook**
*Electrical Estimating (4 DVDs)*

**Product Code:** EST2DVD  List Price: $299.00  Now only $224.25

## Electrical Theory DVD Library

Understanding electrical theory is critical for anyone who works with electricity. The topics covered in this textbook will help you understand what electricity is, how it's produced and how it's used. You'll learn everything from a brief study of matter to how to perform basic electrical calculations critical for everyday use.

**Basic Electrical Theory textbook**
*Electrical Fundamentals and Basic Electricity DVD*
*Electrical Circuits, Systems, and Protection DVD*
*Alternating Current, Motors, Generators, and Transformers DVD*

**Product Code:** ETLIBD  List Price: $295.00  Now only $221.25

## Call Now 888.NEC.CODE (632.2633)

**Mike Holt Enterprises, Inc.**

*All prices and availability are subject to change*

# Take Your Training to the next level & Save 25%

use discount code: **B14UND1WB25**

---

## 2014 Master & Journeyman Comprehensive Exam Preparation Library

A complete course designed for your success. In-depth instruction for Theory and Code, with step-by-step instructions for solving electrical calculations. The DVDs are a vital component to learning, and the Practice Questions are key to reinforcing what you learn.

**Electrical Exam Preparation textbook**
**Electrical Theory textbook**
**Understanding the National Electrical Code® Volumes 1 & 2 textbooks**
**Simulated Exam**
*Code Review (10 DVDs)*
*Theory Review (3 DVDs)*
*Calculations Review (Masters - 8 DVDs; Journeyman - 5 DVDs)*

**Product Code:** 14MACODVD — List Price: $1025.00  Now only **$768.75**
**Product Code:** 14JRCODVD — List Price: $925.00  Now only **$693.75**

---

## Electrical Estimating DVD Package

Mike Holt's Electrical Estimating DVD Program will give you the skills and the knowledge to get more jobs and to make sure that those jobs will be profitable. This program will also give you a comprehensive understanding of the Estimating process as well as help you understand how Electrical Estimating software can improve your process.

**Electrical Estimating textbook**
*Electrical Estimating (4 DVDs)*

**Product Code:** EST2DVD — List Price: $299.00  Now only **$224.25**

---

## Electrical Theory DVD Library

Understanding electrical theory is critical for anyone who works with electricity. The topics covered in this textbook will help you understand what electricity is, how it's produced and how it's used. You'll learn everything from a brief study of matter to how to perform basic electrical calculations critical for everyday use.

**Basic Electrical Theory textbook**
*Electrical Fundamentals and Basic Electricity DVD*
*Electrical Circuits, Systems, and Protection DVD*
*Alternating Current, Motors, Generators, and Transformers DVD*

**Product Code:** ETLIBD — List Price: $295.00  Now only **$221.25**

---

## Call Now  888.NEC.CODE (632.2633)

**Mike Holt Enterprises, Inc.**

*All prices and availability are subject to change*